Darrell Stewart
39 Windermere Road
BT 8 4QY

£6

5

GW00642072

THE LEFT AGAINST ZION

THE LEFT AGAINST ZION

Communism, Israel and
the Middle East

Edited by

ROBERT S. WISTRICH

VALLENTINE, MITCHELL

First published 1979 in Great Britain by
VALLENTINE, MITCHELL & CO. LTD.
Gainsborough House, Gainsborough Road,
London, E11 1RS, England

and in the United States of America by
VALLENTINE, MITCHELL & CO. LTD.
c/o Biblio Distribution Centre
81 Adams Drive, P.O. Box 327, Totowa, N.J. 07511

This collection Copyright © 1979 Vallentine, Mitchell & Co. Ltd.

British Library Cataloguing in Publication Data

The Left against Zion.
  1. Communism and Zionism — History —
  Addresses, essays, lectures
  I. Wistrich, Robert Solomon
  956.94'001   HX550.J4

ISBN 0 85303 193 2 (Case)
ISBN 0 85303 199 1 (Paper)

*All rights reserved. No part of this publication may be
reproduced, stored in a retrieval system, or transmitted in any
form or by any means, electronic, mechanical photocopying
recording or otherwise, without the prior permission of Vallentine, Mitchell & Co. Ltd. in writing.*

Photoset in Baskerville by Saildean Limited.
Printed in Great Britain by offset lithography by
A. Wheaton & Co. Ltd., Exeter

Contents

Introduction

Communist opposition to Zionism has a long history which
pre-dates both the Russian Revolution and the Balfour
Declaration of November 1917. Yet the Communist and
Marxist critique of Zionism has always been vitiated by a
curious inconsistency; it is not applied to *all* nationalist
solutions of social problems. Thus Communists in the Soviet
Union and in China regard their Marxist-Leninist ideology as
perfectly compatible with Russian or Chinese nationalism;
the same is true of the 'people's democracies' in Eastern
Europe or Asia where nationalism has been a predominant
force. Similarly, Arab and Palestinian nationalism has been
considered 'progressive' in spite of its exceedingly thin
socialist content. Only in the case of Zionism, which historically has been an inevitable reaction to the failure of
European and Islamic societies to resolve the Jewish question
on democratic lines, has a major national movement been
judged to be a priori 'reactionary'. Yet no people in modern
times became nationalist under the pressure of such desperate
adversity as the Jews.

Zionism, which succeeded in its primary aim of reviving
the Jewish nation and establishing an independent Jewish
State, has for more than sixty years been a thorn in the side of
the Communist movement. Every conceivable distortion and
ideological absurdity has been evoked to explain why only
Zionism among national liberation movements is *illegitimate*
and ultimately condemned to extinction.

In truth, the Jews are an exceptional case and the unique
conditions of their existence and survival seem guaranteed to
bring out the blindest dogmatism and rigidity in Communist
thought on the national problem. The theoreticians who
follow orthodox Marxism-Leninism still maintain today that
the Jews do not constitute a nation but only a religious group
based on a common origin and descent. Confronted with the
fact of Israel, which they grudgingly accept, they still deny
that its legitimacy derives from the Zionist movement which

vii

created it, since this is an apparent contradiction to their ideology. Instead, they link Israel organically to imperialism in order to justify their hostility to it and the otherwise inexplicable refusal of the Jewish people to disappear through assimilation. At the same time they also argue that the Jews have survived as a distinct group solely because of antisemitism, which can only be eliminated in a 'socialist' society. For most orthodox Communists this idyllic state of affairs has already been achieved in the Soviet Union; for Trotskyists and New Leftists it will come with the world revolution yet to be accomplished.

The Marxist theory of assimilation pre-dated Auschwitz and the creation of Israel—which, as several essays in this volume demonstrate— owed its birth, at least in part, to the requirements of Communist *Realpolitik.* In spite of this fact, and the even more striking inability of Communist societies to harmoniously resolve their internal Jewish problem, Marxist-Leninist theory persists in explaining antisemitism as a *capitalist* or imperialist diversion. This altogether ignores the historical roots of the phenomenon in pagan antiquity, the Christian and Islamic Middle Ages and other pre-capitalist societies. It completely fails to explain the Judeophobia of the founders of modern socialism and anarchism (Marx, Engels, Lassalle, Bakunin, Fourier, Proudhon etc.) and its use as a diversionary tactic in the Soviet Union and Eastern Europe today.

If the anti-Zionism of the Communists and of neo-Marxist theoreticians was only a matter of ideology there might be no great cause for concern. But during the past decade it has become increasingly evident that the modern crusaders against Zion are little concerned with principles or a reasoned critique of specific Israeli policies. The anti-Zionism of the 1960s and 70s has led to a monolithic consensus in which it has become difficult if not impossible to distinguish left from right. The chorus of shrill condemnation and denunciation has assumed such an irrational and arbitrary character that traditional ideological distinctions have lost their meaning. Anti-Zionism has become the great bazaar in which Soviet and Chinese Communists, Arab and Third World Marxists, Trotskyists, anarchists and Castroists along with feudal

sheiks, conservative Islamic rulers, oil companies and capitalist interests in the West (not to speak of fascist fringe-groups)
can find common ground in their hatred of the Jewish State.
Contemporary anti-Zionism is not merely the antisemitism of
the left—Israel has even become the focal-point and alibi for
reviving the hoary Nazi myth of *Das Weltjudentum* which seeks
to control and manipulate the fate of humanity.

The essays in this book have been selected to give the
general reader a better understanding of the causes and
possible consequences of this sinister trend. Mostly written
between the Six Day War of 1967 and the October War of
1973, they remain timely and important for the light they
shed on a development whose implications are only now
becoming fully apparent. They analyze the complex and
changing factors which have influenced the position of
Communist parties and New Left movements towards the
Middle East conflict; the significance of the 'anti-Zionist'
campaigns in Russia and Eastern Europe; the dissensions and
contradictions in the position of western Communist parties:
the relations of Soviet, Chinese and East German Communists to the Arab world; and the attitudes of the post-
Auschwitz New Left to Israel and the Jewish problem. All
these disparate elements must be taken into account if one is
to understand Communist and Marxist standpoints towards
Israel and the Middle East conflict. The prospects of a shift in
Soviet and Chinese policies may appear remote from an
examination of the historical record. But there is no intrinsic
reason why Eurocommunists, willing to emancipate themselves from the ideological and political conceptions of
Moscow, should not reconsider their position. A revision of
glib Marxist theories and obsolete myths concerning Zionism
and the Jewish problem, would appear indispensable if they
are to play any constructive role in resolving one of the
burning conflicts of our time.

R.S.W.
December 1978

Acknowledgments

Most of the chapters of this book are printed by permission of the Wiener Library, and first appeared in its Bulletin. Robert Wistrich's Introduction and concluding essay were written specially for this volume, while his 'Marxism and Jewish Nationalism' first appeared in the Jewish Journal of Sociology; Peter Brod's chapter on Soviet-Israeli Relations was written specially for this book.

Notes on Contributors

Dr Robert S. Wistrich is the editor of *The Wiener Library Bulletin*. He is also the author of *Revolutionary Jews from Marx to Trotsky* (Harrap, London 1976), and *The Myth of Zionist Racism* (London 1976). He has written numerous articles on communist and left-wing attitudes to the Jewish problem.

Dr Ran Marom received his doctorate from Georgetown University, Washington DC for a thesis on Soviet Russia and the Jewish Communists in Palestine 1917-1921. He is currently teaching at the Shiloah Centre for Middle Eastern Studies, Tel Aviv University.

Ya'akov Hurwitz is the editor of a left-wing Israeli monthly, *Ba'shaar*. He is a founder-member of the Kibbutz *Ein Ha'horesh* and a member of the Central Committee of Mapam.

Professor Arnold Krammer, an American specialist in Russian area studies, is the author of a pioneering book, *The Forgotten Friendship: Israel and the Soviet Bloc, 1947-53* (Urbana/Illinois, 1974).

Peter Brod was born in Prague and is studying Political Science and East European History at the University of Munich, where he is a PhD candidate. His MA thesis dealt with Soviet-Israeli relations, 1948-1956.

Professor Meron Medzini lectures in International Relations at the Hebrew University, Jerusalem.

The late Jane Degras was Assistant Editor of *The Journal of Contemporary History* and a well-known specialist in the history of the Comintern. Her works included *The Communist International 1919-1943 Documents*, Vol. I (Cass, London).

ADAM CIOLKOSZ, who now lives in London, was formerly a leading Socialist member of the Polish Parliament and one of 21 opposition leaders imprisoned by Marshal Pilsudski. He is the author of several books and pamphlets on the problems of Socialism and Communism.

DR W. OSCHLIES is an expert on East European Affairs and has published a book on the power structure and democratization of the Czech party and trade unions.

FRANÇOIS BONDY is the editor of the monthly *Schweizer Monatshefte* and of *Die Weltwoche* (Zurich). He is an internationally respected writer on people and politics in Europe, about which he regularly contributes a column to *Encounter.*

ROGER PARET, at the time of writing, was a lecturer at the Sorbonne. He is a well-known Arabist and authority on the Middle East.

DR MANFRED STEINKUEHLER was formerly West German consul in Milan and is a specialist on contemporary Italian history. He is the author of *Eurokommunismus in Wiederspruch—Analyse und Dokumentation* (Verlag Wissenschaft und Politik, Cologne, 1977).

ARNOLD FORSTER is General Counsel of the Bn'ai Brith Anti-Defamation League and co-author of *The New Anti-Semitism* (1974).

DR RUDOLF KRAEMER-BADONI is a well-known novelist, theatre- and art-critic in West Germany. He is also the author of *Anarchismus: Geschichte und Gegenwart einer Utopie* (Fritz Molden, Vienna 1970).

PROFESSOR YEHOSHOFAT HARKABI of the Department of International Relations and Middle Eastern Studies at the Hebrew University, Jerusalem is an internationally known expert on the Arab-Israeli Conflict. His books include *Palestinians and Iyrael* (Israel Universities Press, Jerusalem 1974).

The late ERNEST HEARST was formerly Editor of *The Wiener Library Bulletin* and assistant editor of *The Journal of Contemporary History.*

GERD LANGGUTH was previously Chairman of the Ring Christlich-Demokratischer Studenten in Bonn and contributes regularly to West German periodicals.

DR BRUNO FREI, author of *Israel zwischen den Fronten* (Vienna 1965) is a member of the Austrian Communist Party, and a former editor of the Tagebuch. His most recent book is *Im Schatten von Karl Marx. Moses Hess—Hundert Jahre nach seiner Tod (1977).*

Marxism and Jewish Nationalism: The Theoretical Roots of Confrontation

Robert S. Wistrich

Marxist opposition to both Zionism and other variations of Jewish nationalism is not a recent phenomenon. The subject is not merely of academic interest, although some of the earlier arguments used both for and against the validity of Jewish nationalism ceased to be relevant after the creation of the State of Israel. What concerned me here are the more constant features in the Marxist critique of Jewish nationalism, and in particular its rejection of any special pleading or moral obligation to further a distinctively Jewish existence in group form.[1] Marxists have frequently argued that the survival of the Jewish collectivity—whether in a purely religious, a national, or state form—is politically reactionary.[2] They have followed the formula of the young Marx who dismissed Judaism as a wholly negative phenomenon, as a reflection of the money-lending era of capitalism, doomed to disappear with its demise.[3] The Marxist, like the liberal, analysis of the Jewish question assumed that antisemitism was a temporary and secondary phenomenon: with its dissipation the last factor encouraging the 'illusory' national cohesion of the Jews would also fade.

Although the march of events had clearly exposed the Marxist analysis as inadequate, there has nevertheless been a remarkable continuity in attitudes on the Left towards the problem of Jewish nationalism. In several important respects

the New Left, as well as the orthodox communist camp,
continues to echo in a vulgar and grossly over-simplified form
arguments about Zionism and the Jewish people which had
already been evolved before 1914. These arguments were misleading and tendentious then (although at least plausible)
—today they are not only badly informed, but harmful and
dangerous. My aim here is not to trace the evolution, or
perhaps more accurately, the degeneration of the Marxist
critique of Jewish nationalism, but rather to reconstruct its
original purpose. I shall analyse what leading Marxist
theorists, especially in central Europe, had to say about the
Jewish problem as it presented itself to the socialist movement at the turn of the twentieth century, and in particular
their evaluation of Jewish nationalism. That was a crucial
period which witnessed the rise of a revolutionary socialist
movement confronted by rival nationalist and antisemitic
movements throughout Europe, as well as the emergence of
political Zionism. It was also decisive for the development of
European Jewry itself, confused amidst those contradictory
movements, and having to choose for or against the revolutionary movement, between a class and a national orientation
in politics. It was the era of Jewish national emergence in the
Diaspora, of mass migrations from the lands of oppression to
America and western Europe, of full emancipation, and also
of political antisemitism.

Those Jews who joined the Marxist camp in eastern
Europe and Russia fought for a socialist revolution together
with non-Jews—they sought to achieve an emancipation
modelled on conditions in western Europe. They fought not
under a Jewish banner, but with Russian slogans for a
Russian Revolution which would end all discrimination.
They were assimilationists of principle, who rejected as
inadmissible any notion of national rights for Jews. If there
was one factor that united such well-known Marxist Jews as
Leon Trotsky, Paul Axelrod, Julius Martov, Rosa Luxemburg, Leon Jogiches, Victor Adler, and Otto Bauer, it was
their complete rejection of the very principle of Jewish
national self-determination. There can be little doubt that this
hostility of Marxist Jews to the Jewish national movement
greatly influenced the attitude of other revolutionaries to the

problem. Faced with this hostility, such a 'Galut' nationalist as the historian Simon Dubnow could remark, 'How much a Jew must hate himself who recognizes the right of every nationality and language to self-determination but doubts it or restricts it for his own people whose "self-determination" began 3,000 years ago.'[4] Anyone who has closely studied the personality and background of Marxist leaders of Jewish descent cannot deny the element of truth in this judgment—but there is no room to enter here into a deeper analysis of that psychology.[5] What I shall attempt is rather to determine whether, within the framework of the classic Marxist analysis of the Jewish problem, any other conclusions were really possible at that time.

It is an indisputable fact that the historical-materialist outlook formulated by Marx and Engels did not originally take sufficient account of the significance of the national problem in nineteenth-century Europe. In his early essay on the Jewish question, Marx had already reduced nationality to the factor of economic interest, and misleadingly identified the 'illusory' nationality of the Jew with that of the merchant and money-man.[6]

In the Communist Manifesto of 1848, national antagonisms were regarded as secondary, as a factor which would disappear with the expanding freedom of trade, the growing world market, and the resolution of class contradictions within individual nation-states. This was similar to the view of Cobdenite liberalism, of bourgeois cosmopolitanism, which held that free trade was the road to international co-operation and the termination of national rivalries. The 1848 Revolution in Europe, which witnessed the resurrection of the German, Polish, Italian, and Slavic national movements, was already disproving that optimistic theory. Marx and Engels noted that development without fully understanding it. They accepted the right of the revolutionary nations, the Germans, Hungarians, Poles, and Italians to their national independence, but denied this same right to what they termed the 'historyless' peoples in southern and eastern Europe, whose historic duty it was to be absorbed by the more progressive civilizing influence of the big nations in Europe.[7] Above all, they opposed the Slav movement for independence because they feared it could only serve the reactionary interests of Czarism. This nationality doctrine is important because it anticipated the arguments used by Kausky, Lenin, and other disciples of Marx in their polemics against Zionism and the Jewish national movement.

National movements were to be judged according to their 'revolutionism' in speeding up the disintegration of the feudal-absolutist monarchies in central and eastern Europe. Thus the Polish struggle for independence was supported because it fulfilled an important role in the revolutionary strategy of weakening Czarist Russia, but the South-Slav movement was rejected as the Pan-Slavist tool of Russian ambitions in the Balkans. It is significant that the future President of an independent Czechoslovakia, Thomas Masaryk, underlined in his *Philosphical and Sociological Foundations of Marxism* what he saw as the specific hostility of Marxism to the Slav and Jewish aspirations to independence.[8] Masaryk observed that Marx had ignored the cultural-historical side of the Jewish problem, that he had misunderstood the national and religious traditions of the Jewish communities in Russia and Austro-Polish Galicia, and that he had overestimated the prospects of assimilation of the Jewish masses in eastern Europe. He was one of the first to point to the antisemitism of Marx, who identified the Jews with the worst aspects of capitalism and one-sidedly explored their so-called 'practical' essence.[9] His conclusion was that Marxist historical materialism made the same mistake it ascribed to the Jews—it was too practical, too objectivist, and narrowly materialistic.

Masaryk was writing at a time when the untenability of Marxist propositions about the national question was becoming increasingly visible even to the most orthodox of Marx's disciples. Socialist ideology was forced to come to terms with the fact that the 'bloodless cosmopolitanism' of the Communist Manifesto was no answer to the national antagonisms between France and Germany, and above all to the national conflicts threatening to tear apart the Hapsburg monarchy in central Europe.[10] It is not surprising, therefore, that the reorientation of Marxist theory on the national problem should have first emerged in the theories of the Austro-

Marxists, most of whom were in fact 'assimilated' Jews. The most important theorists of this group were Otto Bauer and the Gentile Karl Renner. Their main purpose was to resolve the fierce internecine conflicts in the Austrian monarchy by depoliticizing national antagonisms.[11] Their solution was to offer the maximum autonomy possible in the cultural sphere to the various nationalities in conflict with the state, to grant each nationality the right to legislate on its own affairs, run its own schools, and use its own language—and to preserve a federal parliament which would decide on all political and economic issues common to the nationalities within the Hapsburg Empire. This theory departed from one of the cardinal axioms of Marxism, the identification of nationality with the territorial principle—which was inapplicable to a multinational state of mixed populations, each asserting its 'national' rights against its neighbour. In place of the territorial principle of nationality, Renner proposed the personality-principle—the right of each individual to determine to which nation he belonged and to enjoy the full right of cultural self-expression accorded to that nationality. Significantly, Otto Bauer (who was Jewish) explicitly denied this right to the Jews and devoted a whole chapter of his *Social Democracy and the Nationalities Question* to proving that cultural-national autonomy was inapplicable to the Jews.[12] Since his arguments, while original, were nonetheless in the mainstream of Marxist tradition, I shall refer to them in some detail.

Bauer's basic presupposition was that western and central European Jewry was undergoing a process of de-nationalization. As an extra-territorial nation without a common territory, a common language or culture, the Jews were particularly susceptible to those processes of modern capitalism which were breaking down the barriers between nations and bringing about their assimilation and inter-penetration.[13] Because they were a pariah-nation, the Jews were forced gradually to adopt the culture, habits, and customs of the surrounding nations in whose midst they lived.

In feudal society, the Jews were able to preserve a certain semblance of independence, because their economic function as a monied class, their role as intermediaries between landowners, and peasants, necessitated their preservation. But the evolution of industrial society was tending to level the differences between Jews and Christians, and to eliminate the specific economic functions which had hitherto preserved the traditional Jewish identity. Capitalist production made the Jews and Christians interdependent, and it was transforming the Christians into Jews—according to Marx's famous formula.[14] As Jews from the non-assimilated backward areas of Galicia and Bukovina began to be irresistably drawn into capitalist branches of production, they would lose the distinctive characteristics giving rise to the illusion that there was a Jewish nation. This process of capitalist penetration of backward areas was irreversible and would inevitably undermine the socio-economic structure of the Jews as a people-class.[15]

Unlike the other nationalities in the Hapsburg Empire, the Jews did not appear to have the territorial, linguistic, and cultural prerequisites for resisting that trend. As a scattered nation, they would inevitably gravitate to those areas which offered the best prospects of earning a living—in this way, they would become integrated in all branches of modern capitalist production.[16] This process of economic differentiation, of social mobility, and freedom from the grinding Jewish poverty of the ghettos could eliminate what remained of specific Jewish characteristics. Assimilation of the Jewish minority was, in Otto Bauer's view, eminently desirable as a proof of the extent to which modern capitalism had succeeded in wiping out medieval particularism—the real secret of Jewish survival as a separate entity. In this Marxist conception, the Jews would disappear as a collective entity and their particular qualities as individuals would merge with those of European peoples among whom they lived. Karl Renner (whose theory of personal autonomy separated the right of cultural-national autonomy more sharply from its political and economic aspects) did not, unlike Otto Bauer, specifically deny that right to the Jews, and his ideas were taken up by Bundists and Jewish bourgeois nationalists in Russia, as a justification of their demand for Jewish 'national' rights.[17]

What attracted Jewish nationalists like Dubnow to Renner's theory of personal autonomy was that it implied a decentralized federal system with guaranteed minority rights for non-territorial groups, like the Jews, to preserve their culture and identity.[18] Renner, an Austrial social democrat aware of the need to make concessions to national minorities, did not apparently regard the fate of the Jews as being entirely determined by the evolution of modern capitalism. In general, the Austro-Marxists, while in favour of the rapid assimilation of the Jews under capitalism, envisaged (unlike Marx) a flowering of national differences under socialism.[19] Otto Bauer argued that socialism was an international movement which would take on a distinctive 'national' form in each country, consonant with the cultural traditions of that nation. In every case except that of the Jewish national movement, he argued that differentiation would increase under socialism, as the working-class came to absorb the national culture. On the problem of Zionism and the Russian pogroms, however, he remained silent. The only Austrian socialist to favour a national solution to the Jewish question before 1914 was Engelbert Pernerstorfer, who stated that he saw no other alternative to the survival of the Jewish entity in Europe.[20] Pernerstorfer was the most 'nationalist' of the Austrian socialists.[21]

In order to understand the classic Marxist attitude to the Zionist movement, we must turn to the German social democrats, who were the leading socialist party in Europe before the First World War. While accepting Marx's premise that the Jews could be emancipated only in a socialist society, some of them realized that the situation of the Jewish masses in eastern Europe in no way corresponded to Marx's image of the Jews as a predatory capitalist bourgeoisie.[22] Karl Kautsky, who was of mixed Czech-German origin, and was (unlike Marx) a philosemite, saw in the Jewish proletariat a class with a future, although he dismissed Judaism as a relic of the medieval past and a parasitic ghetto phenomenon in the pores of feudal society.[23]

The Jewish proletariat led by the Bund had in his view an important role to play in the revolutionary class struggle of the future, which its declining economic conditions were irresistably forcing it to join. Marx had condemned the Jews as an excrescence of capitalism, but Kautsky at least recognized that they were undergoing a class differentiation which made them revolutionary. But this revolutionary role remained for Kautsky of a purely class-character—like other Marxists, he did not ascribe any 'national' characteristics to the Jews.[24] In his view, the existence of a non-territorial nation was a logical impossibility—which could not be reconciled with Marxist theory. The Jewish proletariat was therefore a revolutionary class without a nation. Because the Jews were not a 'normal' nation, but an anomaly, Kautsky could not find a way to accepting their claims for a non-territorial autonomy. Nevertheless, the rise of Zionism and the growing separatism of the Bund posed a problem. Kautsky's answer came in response to a request from the Polish Social Democrats Adolf Warski and Rosa Luxemburg to comment on the Kishinev pogrom in 1903.[25] In that important article, Kautsky analysed Russian antisemitism as a primitive reaction to the isolation of the Jews in the Pale, where they constituted a mass of petty-bourgeois 'Luftmenschen' and impoverished artisans. Because of this segregation, the Jews were regarded by the Russian masses as 'strangers', and as obvious scapegoats by the Russian autocracy. The Zionist movement, by emphasizing this segregation, would, in Kautsky's opinion, only strengthen antisemitism. It was playing into the hands of Czarism, aided and abetted by the financial support of Jewish capitalists in the West. Only the most rapid assimilation and participation in the Russian revolutionary movement could help the Jews, since the socialist idea was the sole counterweight to the antisemitism of the Czarist government and the Russian muzhiks. The solidarity of Jew and Gentile in the socialist movement was therefore in the interests of the Jewish masses, and corresponded for Kautsky to the best traditions of the Jewish race. The claim of the Zionist movement to transcend class interests was, on the other hand, an illusion, as was any attempt to preserve Jewish segregation in the ghetto.

Kautsky's choice for the Jews between isolation and revolutionary assimilation was the basic alternative that European Marxism had to offer. Since Jewish group survival was doomed anyway, Marxists argued, the Jews had nothing to lose by joining the revolutionary movement. But the Jewish masses had first to be re-educated, to shed their

Judaism, which had been rendered obsolete by the development of capitalism. With the vanishing of religion, Jewish
peculiarities would disappear as the remnants of a moribund
ghetto-culture. Kautsky also emphasized that Jewish nationalism was pernicious in that it would preserve the hereditary
traits of a 'caste' of urban financiers, merchants and intellectuals—who were the real targets of antisemitism. Jewish
solidarity was a poor substitute for proletarian solidarity and,
in his view, it had no future. As he wrote in his *Rasse und
Judentum*, there were no more vacant areas in the world where
the Jewish national ideal could be realized, and Palestine, for
practical reasons alone, was not a serious prospect.[26] The land
was too infertile, the Jews were hopelessly outnumbered by
the indigenous Arab population, and the prospects of a viable
industrial base were far too remote. Indeed after the First
World War, Kautsky's prognosis of Jewish prospects in
Palestine was even more pessimistic; he was convinced that
the Palestinian experiment would end tragically as soon as
Anglo-French domination of the Middle East collapsed. In
any case, on the theoretical level, he regarded Zionism and
other varieties of Jewish nationalism as reactionary, 'a spoke
in the wheel of progress', and based on an untenable doctrine
of historical rights.[28]

Kautsky's critique was repeated by German, Austrian, and
Russian communists after the First World War, even though
he was treated in other respects by Lenin and his followers as
a 'renegade' from socialism.[28] The Communists held tena-
ciously to the view expressed in *Die Neue Zeit* as early as 1897
that Zionism was an ephemeral phenomenon—the last beautiful pose of a 'moribund nation' before it left the stage of
history.[29] Otto Heller, an Austrian Jewish communist, repeated Kautsky's thesis in an orthodox Leninist form in 1931,
predicting that the assimilation of the Jewish bourgeoisie in
the West and of the Jewish lower middle-class and proletariat
in eastern Europe was an historically inevitable process.[30]
Zionism was the last and most wretched manifestation of
Jewish nationalism, the end of the road, the symbol of the
'downfall of Judaism' in capitalist society. The pre-1914
Marxists, led by Kautsky and followed by Jewish socialists
and Bundists in Russia and eastern Europe, had said much

the same thing, with perhaps more justification. Their main concern was the class struggle of the Jewish proletariat—and Jewish nationalism was perceived as a dangerous competitor in their fight for support of the Jewish masses. Zionism, it was alleged, was counter-revolutionary because it preached to Jews that they could not rely upon the solidarity of their Gentile comrades, and because it argued that antisemitism was 'eternal' and inevitable, and that the Jews should work for their own goals and interests.

What the Zionists proposed in Palestine was held to be a mirage, the shallow dream of a Jewish state where Jewish capitalists would continue to exploit the workers. This kind of argument was especially put forward by Jewish Marxists from eastern Europe, who were the most hostile of all to the idea that the Jews constituted a nation. They demanded 'democratic' rights for the Jews, not separate 'national' interests, which were portrayed as a reactionary return to the ghetto. The duty of Jewish social democrats was to raise the cultural level of the Jewish masses by introducing Western ideas of socialism and democracy.[31] This had to be done first in Yiddish and later in the language of the country; ultimately the Jewish workers should speak the same language as their Christian comrades. The goal of Jewish social democracy was not anti-national; it was revolutionary brotherhood and solidarity.

The negative attitude of Marxist Jews to nationalist 'deviations' like Zionism has had many sources. One driving force was the internationalist conviction epitomized in the later writings of Abram Léon and Isaac Deutscher, that the nation-state was an anachronism, an obsolescent relic of the capitalist era.[32] Its psychological motivation was perhaps a guilt-complex about devoting oneself to Jews when there were other more pressing problems in the world. It stemmed also from revulsion against the 'nationalist' persecution of the Jews as 'outsiders'. Whatever the underlying causes of this hostility, Jews often formed the 'internationalist' wing of the socialist movements in Europe, and this commitment seemed infinitely more important to them than the Jewish problem, which was an issue they sought to evade. Zionism especially touched a sensitive nerve which has often brought out a latent self-hatred in Jewish socialist intellectuals.[33] The latter rejected any form of Jewish particularism, insisting that nothing should distinguish Jews from other nationalities, and condemning Judaism as an archaism doomed to dissolution and absorption by international socialism.

The neutrality, the impartiality, and the apparent objectivity of the Marxist historical method provided at times, a perfect cover for the subtle repressed antisemitism that expressed itself either in silence on Jewish issues or in condemning any Jewish national aspirations. Marx, Trotsky, Rosa Luxemburg, Radek, Parvus, and Otto Bauer were all classic examples of this peculiar neurosis. Anything self-consciously 'Jewish' was intolerable in their eyes—as was the notion that the proletarian revolution could be contained within any arbitrary ethnic, geographical, or political boundaries.[34] It is equally no surprise to find that it was the 'Jewish' Bolsheviks and Mensheviks (including Martov, one of the fathers of 'Bundism') who led the polemics against the Bund in Russian social democracy and denounced with special vehemence their right to speak for the Jewish proletariat. The vision of the new society projected before 1914 by European Marxists, whether Jews or Gentiles, rejected any Jewish ethnic particularism—even of a socialist type.

It was the Gentile socialists in the labour movement, particularly those of a 'revisionist' turn of mind, who proved more sympathetic on the whole to the appeal of Zionism. The doctrine that each nation should be master in its own house gradually came to dominate socialist thought around the turn of the century. The failure of the Second International and the First World War gave this trend an irresistible impulse. Zionism could now for the first time find a hearing within the international socialist movement. Reformist social democrats like the Belgians Vandervelde and Huysmans, the Frenchman Longuet, and the Austrian Pernerstorfer, and even democratic socialists of Jewish origin like Eduard Bernstein and Léon Blum, became friendly to Poale-Zion and Zionist colonization in Palestine during the 1914-18 war.

The principle of self-determination for Jews, even the idea of a Jewish State, became increasingly acceptable to reformist socialism after 1917. The Jewish national idea was now seen as democratic, and in harmony with the main tendencies of modern development. The result was the formation of a socialist Committee for a Workers' Palestine in the 1920s, patronized among others by the British socialists Lansbury and Ramsay MacDonald, and the Dutchman Van Kol, as well as by the above-named sympathizers of Zionism.

Only the international communist movement, dominated by the Russian Bolsheviks, remained fixed in the mould of rigid pre-1914 formulas, first evolved by Kautsky and Otto Bauer. The Bolsheviks, inspired by Lenin and the Western Marxist viewpoint, were convinced that assimilation was the only answer to the Jewish problem.[35] Zionism was an ideology that promoted a fictitious Jewish solidarity and ran counter to progressive ideas, since it opposed the absorption of the Jews by the peoples among whom they lived. It was purely a reaction to antisemitism—but far from curing the evil, it would merely strengthen it. Zionism and antisemitism were, for the Bolsheviks as for Kautsky, two sides of the same coin—ideologies produced by declining classes in a moribund society.

Lenin, for example, was quite unequivocal in his condemnation of Jewish national culture, even when proclaimed in its most moderate form by the Jewish Bund, as 'a slogan of the rabbis and the bourgeoisie'.[36] Jewish nationalism in his opinion was a product of 'backward and semi-barbarous countries' like Galicia and Russia, which kept the Jews segregated from the rest of the population as a caste. Any manifestation of Jewish nationalism could not be progressive but was, by definition, motivated by a desire to perpetuate this 'caste position of the Jews' in eastern Europe.[37] In his polemics against the Bund, Lenin ridiculed with particular vehemence the Bundist and Zionist bogey of 'assimilation'—claiming that 'only those who with reverential awe contemplate the "backside" of Jewry shout against assimilation'.[38] He cited in contrast the melting-pot of New York and the conditions prevailing in America generally as proof that modern civilization was grinding up national distinctions. 'The best Jews, famous in history, who gave the world foremost leaders of democracy and socialism' were his models of progress, and they 'never shouted against assimilation'.[39]

Thus, although Lenin (like Marx) supported the national liberation movements of oppressed nationalities when it suited his revolutionary strategy, that support categorically did not apply to Jewish nationalism. The latter was seen as a backsliding movement which could serve no useful purpose in the break-up of the Czarist state; moreover, even its proletarian form as expressed in the demand for cultural-national autonomy by the Bund, it was for Lenin an example of the virus of bourgeois nationalism which might contaminate the labour movements of other oppressed nationalities in the Russian state. Stalin, writing in 1913,[40] followed Lenin's critique of the Bund and of Jewish nationalism in general —emphasizing that because the Jews lacked a common territory or culture, they were not, in any sense of the word, a nation. At least, they were not a real or living nation, but the scattered remnants of an obscure religious community, lacking the economic, territorial, and psychological prerequisites for nationhood. There was, in Stalin's view, nothing in common between Russian, American, Georgian, or west European Jews, except obsolete relics of the past.

The Marxist conception of the national problem in general, and of the Jewish question in particular, offered no framework in which it was possible to take account of Jewish national aspirations before 1914. The premise of Jewish peoplehood was denied, and with it the legitimacy of Jewish national rights, the creativity of the Jews as a group, their will to autonomy, and the validity of their traditions and culture. The negative attitude of Marx, Lenin, and their disciples to the Jewish problem before 1914 has continued to influence and shape communist doctrine right up the the present day. Not even the rise of Nazism and the appalling catastrophe of European Jewry could shake the communist belief in the infallibility of Marxist-Leninist theses on the Jewish question. But the evident failure of communist régimes in Russia and eastern Europe to resolve this problem demonstrated how over-simplified the ideal of an internationalist answer to the Jewish predicament really was. Despite its shortcomings, the Jewish national movement has proved more practical and tenacious than any of its Marxist critics ever believed it could be. The theoretical confrontation between

Marxism and Jewish nationalism has not ended, but in the light of recent history and especially of Soviet practice, the classic communist case against Zionism appears distinctly unconvincing.

NOTES

1. For a neo-Marxist critique of this idealist tradition in Jewish historiography, see Maxime Rodinson's introduction to Abraham Léon, *La Conception matérialiste de la question juive*, Paris 1968, pp. v ff.
2. ibid.
3. See István Mészáros, *Marx's Theory of Alienation*, London, 1970, pp. 29-30.
4. Simon Dubnow, 'On the Tasks of the Folks-Party', *Nationalism and History*, Philadelphia, 1961, p. 230.
5. This subject has been analysed in my doctorial dissertation, *Socialism and the Jewish Question in Germany and Austria 1880-1914*, University of London, 1974. For a detailed account, see Robert S. Wistrich, *Revolutionary Jews from Marx to Trotsky*, London, 1976.
6. *Karl Marx/Friedrich Engels Werke*, Berlin, 1964, vol. 1, p. 375.
7. See the detailed critique of this Hegelian-Marxist aberration in Roman Rosdolsky, 'Friedrich Engels und das Problem der "Geschichtslosen Völker"', *Archiv für Sozialgeschichte*, 1964, vol. IV, pp. 87-283.
8. T.G. Masaryk, *Die Philosophischen und Sociologischen Grundlagen des Marximus*, Vienna, 1899, p. 454.
9. ibid.
10. See Annie Kriegel, *Le Pain et les roses, jalons pour une histoire des socialismes*, Paris, 1968, pp. 79-94.
11. Robert A. Kann, *The Multi-national Empire*, New York, 1950.
12. Otto Bauer, *Die Nationalitätenfrage und die Sozialdemokratie*, Vienna, 1907, pp. 366-81.
13. idid., p. 370.
14. ibid., p. 368.
15. ibid., p. 376.
16. ibid., pp. 378-79.
17. See Dubnow, *Nationalism and History*, op. cit., p. 368, for a favourable reference to Karl Renner.
18. ibid., p. 368.
19. See Yves Bourdet, *Otto Bauer et la révolution*, Paris, 1968.
20. Engelbert Pernerstorfer, 'Zur Judenfrage', *Der Jude*, Berlin, 1916, p. 308.
21. See Robert S. Wistrich, *Socialism and the Jewish Question ...*, op. cit., Chapter 22, on Pernerstorfer.
22. See Robert S. Wistrich, 'Karl Marx, German Socialists and the

Jewish Question 1880-1914', *Soviet Jewish Affairs*, vol. III, no. 1, 1973, pp. 92-97.
23. Jacob Lestschinsky, *Marx i Kautskii o evreiskom voprose*, Moscow, 1907, pp. 25-29.
24. ibid.
25. Karl Kautsky, 'Das Massaker von Kischineff', *Die Neue Zeit*, 1902-03, pp. 303-09.
26. Karl Kautsky, *Rasse und Judentum*, Berlin, 1914, p. 79.
27. ibid., p. 67.
28. See Otto Heller, *Der Untergang des Judentums*, Vienna and Berlin, 1931, pp. 21-22.
29. Johann Pollack, 'Der Politische Zionismus', *Die Neue Zeit*, 1897-98, pp. 598-600.
30. Heller, *Der Untergang des Judentums*, op. cit., pp. 21-22.
31. Max Zetterbaum, 'Probleme der jüdisch-proletarischen Bewegung', *Die Neue Zeit*, 1900-01, pp. 368-73.
32. Isaac Deutscher, *The Non-Jewish Jew and other Essays*, Oxford, 1968, p. 26.
33. See Chapters 8 and 22 of my Ph.D. thesis, op. cit. Also *Revolutionary Jews from Marx to Trotsky* op. cit.
34. Deutscher, op. cit., p. 26.
35. Marc Jarblum, 'Soixante ans du problème juif dans la théorie et la pratique du bolchévisme', *La Revue Socialiste*, October 1964, no. 176. See also V.I. Lenin, 'Critical Remarks on the National Question', *Prosvescheniye*, October/December 1913.
36. V.I. Lenin, 'National Culture', *Questions of National Policy and Proletarian Internationalism*, Moscow, n.d., p. 31.
37. ibid.
38. ibid., p. 35: 'backside' of Jewry is the version given in the Moscow Foreign Publishing Translation of Lenin's article.
39. ibid.
40. J.V. Stalin, 'Marxism and the National Question', in B. Franklin, ed., *The Essential Stalin, Major Theoretical Writings 1905-52*, London, 1973, pp. 62-65.

This paper was first published in *The Jewish Journal of Sociology* and is reprinted by permission of the Editor.

The Bolsheviks and the Balfour Declaration

Ran Marom

David Lloyd George, Great Britain's Prime Minister at the time of the Balfour Declaration, testified in his memoirs that one reason for its adoption lay in the

> state of Russia herself. . . . Russian Jews had become the chief agents of German pacifist propaganda in Russia; by 1917 the Russian Jews had done much in preparing for that general disintegration of Russian society, later recognized as the revolution. It was believed that if Great Britain declared for the fulfillment of Zionist aspirations in Palestine under her own pledge, one effect would be to bring Russian Jewry to the cause of the Entente.[1]

In the view of the British government, the Germans too were 'engaged actively in courting favour with that [Zionist] Movement'.[2] It reasoned that 'a friendly Russia would mean not only more food and raw material for Germany . . . but fewer German . . . troops on the Eastern front, and therefore, more available for the West'.[3]

According to Lloyd George, Balfour had emphasized the importance of a declaration which would appear 'to be favourable to Zionism. If we could make a declaration favourable to such an ideal, we should be able to carry on extremely useful propaganda . . . in Russia'.[4] Another report published in 1918 made this point clearer: 'The total effect of

16

this propaganda in Russia has been considerable, though perhaps hardly as much as had been hoped.... It is even possible that had the declaration come sooner the course of the revolution might have been affected'.[5] As for Palestine, Balfour himself privately stated it was clear that 'it was inadequate to form a home for either the Jewish or any other people'.[6] In this context one should mention that the British government was also convinced that the activities of the Bolshevik party might be influenced through its Jewish leaders and hence prevent a future German-Russian pact.[7] This view was referred to indirectly by Trotsky himself. He claimed that the Bolsheviks knew about the Anglo-French manoeuvres designed to support 'chauvinist' activities in Russia. In this view, the British hoped that such activities would be useful in disrupting the Russo-German peace contracts.[8] But as Lloyd George later admitted, the British assumption had been wrong as a political assessment. The anti-nationalist position taken by the Bolshevik Jewish leaders who denied the Jewish national tradition was expressed by Leon Trotsky and Adolph Joffe. Immediately after the announcement of the Balfour Declaration, the Chief Rabbi of Petrograd in a conversation with Trotsky quoted the latter as saying: 'I am not a Jew; I am an Internationalist'.[9] Joffe too had opposed the Zionist idea of a national home in Palestine, according to disclosures made by his widow to Joseph Barzilai, who had been a top leader of the Palestine Communist Party in the 1920s.[10]

At the time the Bolsheviks came to power following their coup d'état of 7 November 1917, they faced a difficult situation in which to implement their general theories. With regard to Palestine, they faced two major closely linked problems. The one dealt with the future attitude of the Bolsheviks to the conquest of Palestine by the British and their proposal for a 'Jewish National Home' in Palestine, in the context of previous ideological formulations on the colonial question. The other dealt with the impact of the Balfour Declaration upon Russian Jewry and the status of this national minority in the context of Marxist-Leninist theory on the Jewish question. As such, the Bolshevik response to the idea of a Jewish national home in Palestine should be seen in the

framework of the correlation between the ideological stand of
Lenin, the developments within the newly established and
struggling Bolshevik régime and its foreign policy, i.e., in the
context of the situation in Russia itself.

The Balfour Declaration had coincided with the beginning
of the British conquest of Palestine, following the disruption
of this part of the Ottoman Empire. For the newly established
Bolshevik régime, this meant direct contact between Great
Britain and its colonies not so far from the Russian border.[11]

In view of the long-standing Marxist-Leninist ideological
opposition to Great Britain as the bastion of capitalism and
imperialism, the Bolsheviks also saw the Balfour Declaration
and the British conquest of Palestine as hostile to their own
newly-established régime. Trotsky had already hinted that
the Bolsheviks opposed the British presence in Palestine
because of the threat to the Soviet Republic, despite the fact
that Palestine was not 'so close' to Soviet territory.[12] Moreover, the Bolsheviks considered the British presence in
Palestine as a pretext used by the Entente which 'helped all
counter-revolutionary armies in their fight against Russia'.[13]
The Bolsheviks showed their opposition to the Balfour
Declaration and the British conquest of Palestine by significantly dissociating themselves from any agreement that
involved Russia, England, and Palestine. Beginning with 23
November 1917, they published the full texts of secret
documents from the Sykes-Picot Treaty pertaining to Palestine, embodying the Allies' agreement for the future partition
of Asiatic Turkey and the subordination of Palestine to
British control.[14] By disclosing the provisions of the secret
treaty which provided England with Mesopotamia and
Palestine, and France with the Mediterranean coast of Syria
and other territories as far as the Russian border, the
Bolsheviks distanced themselves from the 'world politics of
England' which 'comes to a plan aimed at . . . the isolation
and replacement of the Soviet Union in the Middle East'.[15]
Moreover, although 'Tsarist Russia did not exist any more,
the hostile attitude of England toward Russia in the Middle
East not only persisted but also received a new colour'.[16] In
the Bolshevik view, the occupation of Palestine was part of
the British play for the division of the Ottoman Empire and

its dismemberment which would subsequently be followed by the 'destruction of Revolutionary Russia'.

Another attempt at emphasizing this attitude was made in the framework of the negotiations held with the Germans at Brest-Litovsk when the Bolshevik delegation demanded that any 'general peace' be based upon the following principles: (a) The union by violence of territories conquered during the war will not be tolerated. The troops in occupied territories shall evacuate them within a brief time; (b) The entire restoration of the political independence of peoples who have been deprived of their independence during the course of the present war; (c) The groups of different nationalities which did not enjoy political independence before the war shall have guaranteed to them the right of deciding freely the question of whether they shall belong to one state or another, or shall enjoy national independence by means of a referendum. At the referendum entire liberty to vote shall be given to all inhabitants of the respective teritories, including refugee immigrants.[17]

Trotsky, the President of the Russian Delegation, claimed that the Bolshevik government could not recognize a state which was formed by a 'superior authority of such or such powerful empire'. It could recognize only one that is created by the people, since 'control should consist in an inquiry put to the whole population convoked to exercise the right of free self-determination'.[18] Palestine was included in this category: 'When Great Britain takes African colonies, Baghdad and Jerusalem, then that is certainly not a defensive war. . . . That is a struggle for the partition of the globe'.[19]

The Bolsheviks treated the 'allotment of Palestine as a Jewish shelter', as an act performed by the English Imperialists, which aimed at masking and justifying the 'abolition of the Ottoman Empire'.[20] Moreover, the Bolshevik position was based upon a suspicion of the relations between Great Britain and the Zionist leaders, which derived mainly from ideological formulations about British imperialism and the bourgeois character of Zionism:

The aim of the Palestinian idea in the present international conditions, because of its very content, makes out of the

Zionist bourgeoisie and the Zionist party one of the branches of the imperialist counter-revolution. The Zionist party had linked its fate to the Entente, which gave the Zionists certain promises at the time the division of Turkey was considered. This causes the Zionists to support the Entente. . . . Only the victory of Denikin, the Entente's Ally, will give the Zionist organization the possibility to achieve its expectations.[21]

In May 1920 the Bolsheviks still continued to regard the Balfour Declaration as an alleged British-Zionist anti-Bolshevik campaign. On 16 May 1920 *Izvestia V.Ts.K.* issued for example the text of a proclamation which claimed:

> The Zionist organization is assigned officially to the Paris Peace Conference, and its representatives sit together with Lloyd George, with Millerand and others. The Entente promised to deliver them the land of the Hebrews, Palestine, in exchange for their support of the Entente armies. . . . *The members of their party there directed vigorous propaganda against Soviet Russia.*[22]

The announcement continued by detailing the establishment of a British-Zionist bloc of Russian elements against the Bolshevik government:

> The Zionist mobilized soldiers for their armies [i.e., for the Entente] from among Russian Jews and transferred them to outside the Russian borders in different ways. There were Jewish soldiers in the British army and they fought against Soviet Russia on the Archangelsk front and Odessa.[23]

This was a reference to Litvinov's appeal to the British government at the beginning of 1918, in which the Bolsheviks had announced that they would not recognize the military convention between Kerensky's government and the British government. The above convention provided Britain with the right to recruit Russian citizens into the British army. Litvinov protested the inclusion of Russians 'in the work battalions for the promotion of auxiliary labour in the army . . . [and] dispatched to Egypt for enrolment in the Jewish Palestinian Legion'.[24]

The attitude of the Bolsheviks toward the Balfour Declaration was also influenced by their awareness of its implications for Russian Jewry at a time the Bolsheviks were pre-occupied with the post coup d'état situation.

Weekly news dispatches from Russia described the impact of the Declaration upon Russian Jewry and especially on Jewish support for the British government. This support was expressed by the Central Zionist Committee in Russia in form of an address to the British Ambassador in Petrograd on 13 November 1917,[25] demonstrations in Petrograd and Odessa,[26] pro-British articles in the Jewish newspapers, and continuous appeals to the Jews of Russia to oppose the Bolshevik régime.[27] Moreover, British officials had participated at different street demonstrations. In Odessa, at the same pro-British demonstration held on 3 December 1917 in support of the Balfour Declaration, the British Consul declared his government's opposition to the Bolshevik policy on war.[28]

The Bolsheviks interpreted the sympathy for Zionism in Russia and the strong support for the Declaration to be a result of the deteriorating socio-political and economic situation of the Russian Jewish masses in a time of war, pogroms, and strong antisemitic feelings. Moreover, they were convinced that in view of the mounting difficulties in Russia, Zionism and emigration would increase among the Jewish masses and would direct their attention from the revolutionary cause.[29] In Lenin's view, 'the Jewish aspiration to preserve its national uniqueness' was 'a conservative aspiration, a remnant of the Middle Ages'; it was a 'result of antisemitic persecutions and the existence of the Jewish ghetto'.[30] Lenin however had to deal after 1917 with a large population which could not be assimilated yet asked for equal rights. In face of such a state of affairs and in view of Lenin's ideological position on Zionism, the Bolsheviks had emphasized the need of attracting the Jewish population in order to prevent its emigration.[31]

Their strategy was based upon the concept of dividing the Jewish population into clear-cut social classes and finding who were their potential allies and rivals. In this context, Lenin believed that the secularized Jewish intelligentsia, up to 1917, opposed the nationalist trend of Zionism while the proletariat aspired to move out of the ghetto in order to assimilate itself within the surrounding environment. Therefore, since the revolution 'opened the gates to civil progress for the Jewish population' and 'Russia was opened to all Jews', they should become partners in the ruling the country, and actively participate in the creation of Russia's future.[32] Why should the Jews reconstruct the walls of the ghetto by nursing a special Jewish culture or aspire for a Jewish state with the help of British imperialism in a distant and desolate country? Lenin in fact hoped to neutralize the Zionist movement by attracting the Jewish intelligentsia through the offer of high positions in the government, thus fulfilling its expectations for civil rights after the Bolshevik Revolution.[33] On the other hand, he believed that the Jewish masses would be dissuaded from supporting Zionism and emigrating to Palestine by the suppression of antisemitic pogroms in Russia.[34] According to Dimanshtein, one of the problems of the Bolshevik leaders had been the increasing attraction of Jewish youth toward Zionism and Palestine, as a result of these pogroms.[35] Another document expressed more specifically the inter-relationship in Bolshevik eyes between the situation in Rusia and emigration to Palestine:

> If Zionism, a movement that includes almost all the Jewish intelligentsia, will be realized, it will immediately take from us large numbers of workers, such as engineers, doctors, pharmacists, architects and other specialists, whom we badly need in order to build up our national economy and whom we are obliged to honour because of our inferiority. . . . But if we are interested in achieving our communist principles, we cannot disregard this practical concept.[36]

Since the end of 1917, the Bolsheviks had faced the problem of running a system with no professional bureaucrats and specialists. Without support from the Tsarist bureaucracy, they had to turn to the Jewish intelligentsia which saw in the Bolshevik Revolution an opportunity to achieve full civil rights.[37] Many Jewish figures suddenly appeared in the Bolshevik administration, in the highest echelons of the bureaucracy and especially in education, justice, banks, commerce, foreign affairs, and the secret police. The Bolsheviks believed that the Jewish intelligentisa was co-operating with their régime out of 'chauvinistic interests, without adhering to the Communist programme, or surrendering any of their nationalist views'.[38] But they also knew, as Agurskii suggested, that this influx of Jewish intelligentsia in governmental functions had created a situation in which it could not perform any Zionist activity in 'the special Jewish field'.[39] Moreover, the need for qualified personnel to fill vacant posts in the bureaucracy, Bolshevik knowledge of the nationalist-oriented ideological adherence of the Jews and the impact of the Balfour Declaration had created a situation in which the Bolsheviks had to make some concessions to Russian Jews in comparison with other national movements. Hence, in the first few years of the Soviet régime, Zionist activities, unlike those of other bourgeois parties and institutions, were allowed to continue more or less undisturbed. For tactical reasons, at a time when the Soviet régime was still militarily and economically weak, the sensibilities of the Jewish national movement inside Russia had to be taken into account.

The anti-Zionist campaigns were not launched before 1920, because the Bolsheviks were still preoccupied with internal and external problems. However, they believed that Russian Zionist aspirations should be combated among the Russian Jewish masses through the newly established party and state branches such as *Evsektsia, Komfarband* (Communist League), and *Evkom* (Jewish Commissariat) manned by people of Jewish origin but with no Jewish religious background. These institutions were aimed at winning the Jewish masses for the communist cause through appeals in their own language.

There was no direct connection between the Balfour Declaration and the establishment of the different Jewish sections in the party and government. Nevertheless it would appear from Dimanshtein's own writings that these institutions were aimed at carrying out the nationality policy of the Soviet government among the Jewish masses, in order to divert them from supporting the Zionist movement in Russia.[40] The Bolsheviks felt the need for such a policy because after the revolution the Jews 'aspired to redemption, democratic rights and national self-determination, which in the minds of the (Jewish) masses was linked with the yearning for political independence in Palestine'.[41]

They understood the impact of the Jewish masses' lack of adjustment to the revolution and of the activities of the Zionist parties among the Jews. This was reflected in Dimanshteins's own speech at the time of his appointment on 18 January 1918 as the Commissar for Jewish Affairs, when he claimed that his aim would be to combat Zionism because the Balfour Declaration had aroused Jewish aspirations for the homeland in Palestine and, at the same time, encouraged sympathy toward England.[42]

It was further confirmed by Agurskii who claimed that 'the first problem the Jewish Commissariat faced was the spreading of the idea of the October Revolution among the Jewish masses and their liberation from the influence of the social-chauvinists . . . of the *Bund* and other small bourgeois groups'. He included the Zionists in the same category, since their activities among the Jewish masses were aimed toward Palestine.[43]

In the Soviet view, the home of the Jewish masses was not in Palestine but in Russia. 'They should build the basis of a future order in a place where there will be no masters and rabbis, exploiters and exploited, where there will be no inequality, but where liberty and happiness will rule'.[44] Only in this way would the Jewish masses be able to achieve their 'liberation from the capitalist yoke which is the international bourgeoisie and the Jewish bourgeoisie'.[45] The definition of Zionism adopted by the Bolsheviks was in line with these assumptions:

> Zionism is the part of the Jewish bourgeoisie which sees as its task the right to protect the establishment of a national home for the Jews in Palestine. This movement is support-ed by the Jewish capitalists and clerical religious elements. The Zionists walk arm in arm with the rabbis (Jewish clergymen). Reactionary ideas had some success among the Zionists after the Tsarist pogroms in Russia. The Zionists aspire to increase capital in Palestine, where they will create a separate state, and hence they hope to solve the

Jewish question. The utopian and reactionary Zionist idea is fully assessed by the Jewish labourers who do resist the Zionist agitation and do not migrate to Palestine.[46]

Lenin, in another document, further explained that 'among the Jews there are kulaks, exploiters, capitalists, just as there are among the Russians and every other nation. . . . The rich Jews just like the rich Russians and the rich of all countries are united in treading upon, oppressing and dividing the workers'.[47]

The Bolsheviks tried not only to limit the further expansion of the Zionist movement in Russia but also to prevent the Jewish masses from emigrating to Palestine in exchange for the prospect of civil equality in Russia itself. Moreover, they tried to connect their anti-Zionist campaign with a proposal in 1918 for agricultural settlement of Jewish people in Russia instead of Palestine:

> The aim of the Jewish Commissariat is the construction of a Jewish national life on proletarian socialist principles. The Jewish masses have the right and possibility to control all Jewish public institutions, to give a socialist orientation to our national schools, to present the Jews with the possibility of starting agricultural work on socialized land, . . . and to use all methods in order that the needy will receive the necessary governmental aid to struggle against antisemitism, pogroms, etc.[48]

The first conference of the Jewish Section of the Bolshevik Party and Jewish Commissars held in October 1918 had made decisions on what was then considered as one of the 'significant questions on the agenda'—the attempt to draw the Jewish labourers to agriculture.[49] The efforts to inaugurate a programme of agricultural settlement of the Jewish labourers in Russia was made out of the need to solve the socio-economic situation of the Jewish population which in the Bolshevik view had pushed it to support Zionism. On 19 June 1919, the second conference discussed Dimanshtein's proposal for 'special attention to be given to the enlisting of the Jewish masses in the work on nationalized and socialized land'.[50] Moreover, the Commissariat for Jewish Affairs issued on 20 December 1919 an appeal to the Jewish masses in which it claimed:

> In the Russian Socialist Federative Republic, the Jewish working clases have their socialist mother country, which they defend. . . . The Jewish question in Soviet Russia does not exist anymore. The Jewish labourers . . . have all civic and national rights. . . . They do not need any other countries. We demand no civic rights for them in the Palestinian domain.[51]

The Bolsheviks also intended to enlarge their activites among the Jewish masses. In order to attract them to the Bolshevik side and to prevent them from emigrating to Palestine, without the use of force, the Bolsheviks had to crack down on the activities of the socialist parties in the 'Jewish street', including the Bund and the United Jewish Socialist Party.

> Owing to the specific conditions in which the Jewish masses find themselves, the struggle of the proletariat against the bourgeoisie has become serious. The Jewish socialist parties were not pure proletarian parties. Their rank and file include a large number of petit-bourgeois and intelligentsia elements which are alien to proletarian ideology.[52]

Moreover, 'the petty-bourgeois character of socialist parties such as Poale Tsyion', which supported a 'Jewish National Home' in Palestine, had reinforced in the minds of Jewish Communists, the need to halt the spread of a 'synagogal nationalism' among the Jewish masses.[53]

The rise of the Zionist labour movement in Russia and Palestine and its alliance with Social Democratic elements in Europe also clearly disturbed the Bolsheviks. They were aware of the fact 'that within the labour movement . . . there were forces that adhered to the tradition of the Second International . . . and the establishment of a socialist fatherland . . . in Palestine'.[54] In view of Lenin's split with Western socialists during World War I, such a 'coalition' with organizations outside Soviet Russia, who were inimical to Bolshevism was considered ideologically dangerous to the Bolsheviks themselves. In the Bolshevik view, all socialist

Jewish parties adopted one and the same attitude toward Bolshevism and Palestine:

> During the struggle which finally put the Bolsheviki in power the *Bund* made every effort to defeat them, and to prevent a dictatorship of the proletariat. It tried to unite Jewish workingmen and small property holders on a bourgeois democratic platform, demanding a national constitutional assembly and Jewish national autonomy. . . . During the Bolshevist revolution of October the *Bund* advocated a coalition of all Socialist groups. . . . The United Jewish Socialist Labour Party and the Zionists adopted the same attitude.[55]

The Bolsheviks assumed that 'their nationalistic aspirations held them together . . . because the Entente promised Palestine to the Jews'.[56] These were the forces 'of bourgeois restoration in the Jewish environment. Clericals, Zionists, Mensheviks, Bundists, all these political varieties belong to the same social structure'.[57]

In the context of the internal affairs of Russia, the Bolsheviks had emphasized the need for combating these political parties especially because of what they called the 'alliance' made between Jewish socialists of the Ukraine and the Central Rada:

> Jewish Socialists at the time supported the nationalist movement. They fought shoulder to shoulder with the Nationalists against the Bolshevist element of the community and the peasants.[58]

As such, Zionists and Jewish socialists were accused of attempting to undermine the newly established Bolshevik regime and of embarking on an anti-Soviet campaign through the encouragement of other nationalities to secede from Russia. The Bolsheviks feared that both the Zionists and the Jewish socialist parties through their support of nationalist trends might create an impact upon other nationalities in Russia. For example, the Bolsheviks gave prominence to the declaration issued by an Ukrainian minister in which he

expressed his joy at the British [Balfour] Declaration. As

Minister of a liberated state he promised to support the
Zionist claims at the Peace Conference and he characterized the Declaration as a great national-political event. . . .
The spokesmen of the Russian and Polish Socialists greeted
the Declaration as a great act.[59]

It was important to the Bolsheviks that the Jews should not
take an anti-Soviet stand at a time when they were fighting to
keep their power and to prevent the secession of nationalities
from Russia.

The Bolsheviks also developed the theory that the Balfour
Declaration and subsequently Zionism were aimed at undermining the military capacity of the Red Army. As Rafes
testified:

> The Zionists have become an arch enemy of the Jewish
> Communists in consequence of the Entente victory and
> active Palestine propaganda. . . . The later propaganda has
> interfered with the enrolment of Jewish working men in
> the Red Army and has been generally detrimental to the
> Soviet programme.[60]

According to one of the Zionist activists in the Russian Army,
the Declaration and the idea of a national home in Palestine
did indeed have an influence upon the Jewish soldiers. Many
of them who fought during World War I in the Russian Army
deserted and asked to be drafted for Palestine.[61] The Bolsheviks regarded this phenomenon as hampering their revolutionary efforts:

> The propaganda for Palestine in its essence is nothing but
> an answer to burning questions. . . . In our present time,
> when the communists regime and party are strengthening
> all their forces in order to mobilize the workers and
> peasants against the forces of Denikin and the Poles, at a
> time when we succeeded in removing thousands of Jews
> from the influence of the proprietorship ideology, in
> tracking them into the lines of the Red Army—at this time
> the Zionist propaganda causes real damage and delays the
> activity of the Jewish masses for the front, as it always
> delayed the association of the Jewish masses with the
> revolutionary movement.[62]

The Bolsheviks were especially aware of the beginning of a trend among the Jewish soldiers to organize themselves into national units within the Red Army. They held meetings and congresses within their organizations. For example, at the 'First Convention of the Jewish Soldiers of the Fifth Army', held in November 1917, one of the decisions taken, stated 'that the radical solution of the Jewish national question may be only in the concentration of the forces of the nation in a certain territory', and therefore 'the convention demands from world democracy to promise to the Jews the right of immigration and settlement in Palestine'.[63]

Although the Bolsheviks knew about such activities, they did not interfere during late 1917. They even gave permission for such conventions to be held.[64] However, at the end of 1918, the policy was changed. In order to divert the attention of the Jewish masses from nationalist activities within the army, the Commissariat for Jewish Affairs decided in November 1918 to organize them in the provincial areas into local military units under communist supervision.[65] Moreover, under the pretext that 'the Red Army was still young and weak', and in view of the need to form new detachments which could secure and consolidate the liberation of parts of Russia from foreign occupation, the Bolsheviks had issued appeals to the Jewish masses to volunteer and enrol in the Red Army and give their lives for 'world revolution and socialism', since this was the only way to liberation. But such appeals were issued selectively according to their propagandistic aim and to the importance the Bolsheviks attached to different regions. From Agurskii it appears that the main Bolshevik efforts were concentrated in Petrograd, Moscow, Minsk, and the Ukraine, i.e., along the western and southern front.[66] This process intensified after the defeat of the German Revolution in 1918, probably because no relief could be given to Russia through other revolutions in the West and the Bolsheviks had to rely on the mobilization of their own human internal resources.

By organizing such units, the Bolsheviks tried to achieve a multi-purpose aim: to control a population influenced ideologically by other Jewish parties to which they—the Bolsheviks—had a limited access; to create a pro-Bolshevik attitude among the Jews through demagogical means; to prevent mass emigration to Palestine; to organize units with little military training which could harass the 'counter-revolutionary' forces. The emphasis was put upon the second point because of the attitude of the Bolshevik leaders during the year 1919 toward the Jews who had volunteered and joined the Red Army, the *Cheka* and other institutions.

Concerned with the problem of 'chauvinistic' tendencies among Jewish soldiers, Trotsky wrote to Lenin and the subject was placed on the agenda of the secret meeting of the Political Bureau of the Central Committee of the Russian Communist Party held 18 April 1919. The third item the meeting heard was 'Comrade Trotsky's statement that Latvians and Jews constituted a vast percentage of those employed in Cheka frontal zone units, executive committees in frontal zones and the rear, and in Soviet establishments at the centre'. The minutes state that 'strong chauvinist agitation on this subject was being carried on among the Red Army men and finding a certain response there'. The meeting decided that 'Comrade Trotsky . . . be recommended to draw up a report to this effect and pass this report, as a C.C. directive, to the commissions reponsible for the allocation of personnel between the central and local organizations and the front'.[67] Moreover, following the second conference of the Jewish Communist Section of the Russia Communist Party (June 1919), the Central Bureau decided to increase its activities among the Jewish soldiers and demanded the dissolution of Jewish national units within the army because of the attitude of Bolshevism toward 'national separatism which the Zionist Socialists endeavoured to preserve among the Jewish Red Army soldiers'.[68] The Bolsheviks further explained that the existence of Jewish national units provoked antisemitic agitation within the Red Army and the 'counter-revolutionary forces', which subsequently could have detrimental consequences upon the Jewish community in Russia.

One may conclude from all these facts that the British declaration of support for a Jewish national home in Palestine and the existence of a large Zionist movement in Russia ultimately made the Jews an object of suspicion in the eyes of the Bolshelvik leaders, especially because of their potential sympathies with foreign *foci* and impact upon other nationalities in Russia. This would tend to support the claim that the Bolsheviks were aware of British plans for using Russian Jews in anti-Bolshevik activities. The selective elimination of Russian Jews from the southern section of the eastern front in 1919 and the appointment of loyal Bolshevik Jewish elements to fight 'subversive forces' in Russia were subsequent preventive steps taken by the Bolsheviks during the years of foreign intervention and civil war. An apolitical middle road could no longer exist between Communism and its adversaries. As a leading Bolshevik put it to Eliezer Cherikover, member of the Central Committee of the Zionist Organization in Russia: 'You are obliged to fight with us . . . against our enemies. We do not oppose the idea of Palestine. The Zionists can be tolerated as long as they do not engage in the counter revolutionary activities'.[69] The meaning of this statement in the Bolshevik context was to be revealed by the gradual intensification of attacks on Zionism in Russia during the next decade.

NOTES

1. David Lloyd George, *Memoirs of the Peace Conference* (New Haven, Conn. 1939), Vol. 2, p. 726.
2. *ibid.*, p. 725.
3. *ibid.*
4. *ibid.* p. 735.
5. 'Notes on Zionism', Great Britain, War Office, 106/189 X/K 1571. Obtained from the Public Record Office. London. Hereafter WO will be used as the abbreviation for War Office. The Soviets revealed that in 1917 the above reason was known to them. See S. Dimanshtein, 'Belye Sionisty na Skamie Podsudimnykh' [The White Zionists in the Dock], *Zhizn Natsionalnostei*, No. 10 (67) (4 April 1920), p. 2.
6. Balfour's statement at the War Cabinet meeting, end of October 1917, in Lloyd George, p. 735.
7. Meeting of the War Cabinet Eastern Committee, December 1918, in *ibid.* p. 743. See also Report of Foreign Office to War Cabinet, 1918, in *ibid.* p. 725.
8. L.D. Trotskii, *Ot Oktiabr'skoi Revoliutsii do Brestogo Mira* [From the October Revolution to the Brest Peace], 3rd. ed. (Izdatelstvo Proletarii, 1924), p. 156.

9.   *Jewish Chronicle* (London), 28 December 1917, p. 7.
10. See J. Barzilai, 'A. Joffe: The Jews at the Beginning of Soviet Diplomacy', *Heawar* (May 1970), Vol. XVII, p. 215-216.
11. V. B. Lutskii, *Palenstinskaia Problema, Stenographia Publichnoi Lektsii Prochitanoi 9 Avgusta 1946 goda v Tsentral'nom Parke Kultury i Otdykha Gorikogo v Moskve* [The Problem of Palestine. Stenogramme of a Public Lecture Read on 9 August 1946 in the Central Park of Culture and Recreation 'Gorki' in Moscow] (Moscow: Izdatelstvo Pravda, 1946), p. 8.
12. 'Word to the Russian Workers and Peasants on Our Friends and Enemies, and How to Preserve and Strengthen the Soviet Republic. Speech by Leon Trotsky to the Workers' Audience in Moscow, 14 April 1918', in Leon Trotsky, *Leon Trotsky Speaks*, ed. Sarah Lovell (New York: Pathfinder Press, Inc., 1972), p. 100.
13. 'Komissariat po Evreiskim Delam, Tsentralnyi Biuro Evreiskogo Kommunisticheskogo Sektsii Kommunisticheskogo Partii; o Makhinatsiakh Sionistkoi Partii, 20 Dekabria 1919'[The Commissariat for Jewish Affairs, Central Bureau of the Jewish/Communist Section of the Communist Party: On the Machination of the/ Zionist Party, 20 December], in Samuel Agurskii, *Evreiskii Rabochii v Kommunisticheskom Dvizhenii, 1917-1921* [The Jewish Workers in the Communist Movement, 1917-1921] Minsk, 1926), p. 213.
14. K. Rakovskii and M. Rafail, *Blizhnivostochnyi Vopros* [Near Eastern Question] (Ekaterinoslav, 1923), p. 74.
15. Rakovskii and Rafail, p. 243. This book is important because of its Leninist concept of World War I and its view of the developments in the Middle East.
16. *ibid.* pp. 57-58, 69.
17. 'Russian Account of the Session of 22 December 1917', in US Department of State, *Proceedings of the Brest-Litovsk Peace Conference: The Peace Negotiations Between Russia and the Central Powers, 21 November 1917-3 March 1918* (Washington D.C.: Government Printing Office, 1918), pp. 38-39. Cited hereafter as *Brest Litovsk Proceedings.*
18. 'Russian Account of Session of 11 January 1918', *Brest-Litovsk Proceedings*, p. 74.
19. 'Russian Account of the Session of 10 February 1918', *ibid.* P. 171.
20. Rakovskii and Rafail, p. 107.
21. 'Tazkir Me-et Ha-vaad Ha-rashi shel Ha-brit Ha-yehudit "Komfarband" Be-Ukrainah el Hakomisarion Le-inianei Pnim shel Ukrainah, 4 Iuli 1919' [Memorandum from the Central Committee of the Jewish Communist League 'Komfarband' of Ukraine to the Commissariat for Internal Affairs of Ukraine, 4 July 1919], in Arieh Leib Tsentsiper, *Esser Sh'not R'difot* [Ten Years of Persecution], (Tel Aviv 1930), Appendix A, p. 262. Cited hereafter as 'Tazkir'.
22. 'Hodaat Ve.Ts.Ka. al, Ma-asarah shel Ha-veidah Ha-tzionit Ha-kol-Rusit Be-shnat 1920' [The Proclamation of V.Ts.K. on the Arrest of the All-Russian Zionist Conference in 1920], *Izvestia V.Ts,K.*, No. 105 (16 May 1920), in *ibid.* Appendix B, pp. 264-265. V.Ts.K. was

the All Russian Central Executive Committee of the Soviets. Italics as in original.

23.   *Ibid.* p. 266.
24.   See 'Doklad na V S'ezde Sovetov, 4 VII 1918' [Address to the Fifth Session of the Soviets, 4 July 1918], *Izvestia*, No. 138, 5 July 1918 in Georgii Vasilievich Chicherin, *Statii i Rechii po Voprosam Mezhdunarodnoi Politkii* [Articles and Speeches on the Question of International Politics] (Mosocw, 1961), pp. 54-55.
25.   See text in *Jewish Chronicle*, 28 December 1917, p. 14.
26.   According to one report about 100,000 people took part in the demonstration in Odessa, See, Joseph Ariel. 'The Good Tidings of the Balfour Declaration in Odessa', *Heawar* (May 1968), Vol. XV, p. 120.
27.   *Jewish Chronicle*, 25 January 1918.
28.   See Ariel, *ibid.* p. 120.
29.   Joseph Barzilai, 'My Talks with Dimanshtein', *Heawar* (May 1968), Vol. XV, pp. 216-239.
30.   *Ibid.* p. 230.
31.   N. Lenin, *O Evreiskom Voprose v Rossii* [On the Jewish Question in Russia], with an introduction by S. Dimanshtein (Moscow, 1924), p. 17.
32.   Barzilai, 'My Talks with Dimanshtein', p. 231.
33.   Lenin, *O Evreiskom Voprose v Rossii*, p. 17; *Jewish Chronicle*, 28 December 1917 and 25 January 1918.
34.   'Decree of the Council of People's Commissars on the Uprooting of the Anti-Semitic Movement, 9 August 1918', In V.I. Lenin, *On the Jewish Question* (New York: International Publishers, 1934), p. 23.
35.   Barzilai, 'My Talks with Dimanshtein', pp. 236-237.
36.   'Khozer Sodi me-et Ve.Ts.Ka. al Ha-milkhamah Be-tnuah Ha-tsionit, Iuli 1920' (Secret Circular from V.Ts.K. on the Fight Against the Zionist Movement, July 1920], in Tsentsiper, Appendix D, p. 270.
37.   Lenin, *O Evreiskom Voprose v Rossii*, p. 17.
38.   Moshe Rafes, 'Jewish Bolsheviki in Russia', *L'Internationale Communiste* (April 1920) in *The Living Age* (Boston), No. 3984 (13 November 1920), p. 399.
39.   'Vozzvanie Glavnogo Komiteta "Evreiskoi Kommunisticheskoi Partii" ko Vsem Svoim Organizatsiam, ko Vsem Sektsiam R.K.P.(B.) i ko Vsem Evreiskim Rabochim Sovetskoi Sotsialisticheskoi Respubliki' [Appeal from the Central Committee of the 'Jewish Communist party' to All Its Organizations, to All Sections of R.C.P.(B), and to All Jewish Workers of the Soviet Socialist Republic], in Agurskii, p. 205. Cited hereafter as 'Vozzvanie Glavnogo Komiteta'.
40.   Lenin, *O Evreiskom Voprose v Rossii*, p. 14.
41.   Barzilai, 'Adolph Joffe: The Jews at the Beginning of the Soviet Diplomacy', p. 209.
42.   *Jewish Chronicle*, 1 March 1918, p. 12.
43.   See Agurskii, pp. 40, 42, 45-6.

44. *Ibid.* p. 50.
45. *Ibid.* p. 51.
46. Lenin, *O Evreiskom Voprose v Rossii,* p. 98.
47. 'The Pogroms Against the Jews', in Lenin, *On the Jewish Question,* p. 6. This was part of a gramophone record made during the Civil War, in 1919.
48 'K Evreiskim Rabochim Massam' [To the Jewish Working masses], *Di Varhait,* Nos. 8-9 (June 1918), in Agurskii, p. 55.
49. *Ibid.* p. 77.
50. *Ibid.* p. 132.
51. 'Komissariat po Evreiskim Delam, Tsentralnyi Biuro Evreisikogo Kommunisticheskogo Sektsii Russkogo Kommunisticheskogo Partii: O Makhinatsiakh Sionistkoi Partii, 20 Dekabria 1919', *ibid.* p. 213.
52. Agurskii, p. 81.
53. 'Deklaratsia Evreiskoi Kommunistcheskoi Partii Belorussii, 27 Ianvaria 1919' (Declaration of the Jewish communist Party of Belorussia, 27 January 1919), in *ibid.* p. 202.
54. M. Rafes, 'Evreii i Oktiabr'skaia Revoliutsia' [The Jews and the October Revolution], *Zhizn Natsionalnostei,* No. 1 (January 1923), p. 235.
55. Rafes, 'Jewish Bolsheviki in Russia', p. 399.
56. *Ibid.* p. 402.
57. Rafes, 'Evreii i Oktiabr'skaia Revoliutsia', p. 237.
58. Rafes, 'Jewish Bolsheviki in Russia', p. 401.
59. *Jewish Chronicle,* 25 January 1919, p. 13. This was confirmed by Rafes, 'Jewish Bolsheviki in Russia', pp. 399-400.
60. Rafes, 'Jewish Bolsheviki in Russia', p. 403.
61. H.S. Kapilovich, 'In the Rear and at the Front', *Heawar,* (May 1968) Vol. XV, 86 These are his memoirs.
62. 'Tazkir', p. 262.
63. 'Decision Adopted at the First Convention of the Jewish Soldiers of the Fifth Army, October 1917', in Z. Gordin, 'Self-Organization of Jewish Soldiers in 1917', *Heawar* (May 1968). Vol. XV, 93. Gordin was at the time a military doctor and active in the organization of Jewish soldiers at the Dvinsk Front.
64. Gordin. p. 89.
65. For confirmation of this idea see 'Evreiskii Rabochii v Krasnoi Armii' [The Jewish Workers in the Red Army], see Agurskii, p. 145.
66. *Ibid.* pp. 86-88, 144-147.
67. 'Extracts from the Secret Minutes of the Meeting of the Political Bureau of the C.C. R.C.P. (B.), Held on 18 April 1919', in Lev Trotsky, *The Trotsky Papers, 1917-1922,* ed. Jan M. Meijer, 2 vols. (The Hague, 1964), Vol 1. pp. 361-363.
68. Agurskii, p. 148.
69. Tsentsiper, *op. cit.,* p. 51.

The Kibbutz—Its Socialist and National Roots

Ya'akov Hurwitz

The kibbutz belongs to the family of communes, those settlements which from ancient times and throughout the Middle Ages to the present day (the communes of the Hutter Brethren have existed for over 400 years) have searched for lasting and satisfactory modes of communal living. Kibbutzim are based on the principle of absolute equality with regard to production, consumption and the supply of services. While every kibbutz member works according to his ability, the community assumes responsibility for his well-being whatever his circumstances, sick or healthy, old or young, married or single.

The origin and growth of the kibbutz can be traced to the motives which throughout the ages have led to the establishment of collective settlements. When pioneers in a strange remote and inhospitable land have to overcome human ill-will and the inclemencies of nature, the sheer need for co-operation will triumph over man's deeply ingrained yearnings for independence and self-assertion. Indeed, among the first settlers in Palestine, the communal way of life seemed to offer the only hope of survival; this is why, at the end of the nineteenth century, strong tendencies towards communal living took root, as in the *Biluim* movement. Degania, founded in 1910 and set in the awe-inspiring, but malaria-ridden, wilderness of the Jordan valley, was the first *kvutza* in Israel.

35

However, environmental necessities do not fully explain the emergence of the kibbutz movement. There was also the impact of ideology—or to be more precise, of several ideologies. The three major ideological trends along which kibbutzim developed, represented by the *Hever Hakvutzot* (now known as the *Ihud Hakvutzot Ve'hakibbutzim* (comprising 95 kibbutzim, 17,200 members and 31,000 inhabitants), the *Hakibbutz Hameuhad* (58 kibbutzim, 14,400 members, 26,000 inhabitants) and *Hakibbutz Ha'artzi Hashomer Hatzair* (74 kibbutzim, 17,000 members, 32,000 inhabitants), were influenced by the passionate soul-searching so characteristic of much twentieth-century socialist thinking. The first people to contemplate a *kvutza* in Palestine envisaged it as a small, intimate group, whose members would belong to a closely-knit spiritual family. Convinced of their inability to change the world they hoped eventually to change man.

This mood of despondency was particularly noticeable among East European Socialists after the abortive Russian revolution of 1905, when many who had taken part were imprisoned or sent to Siberia, while the remainder despaired of ever seeing the revolution triumph. Among them was a group of intellectuals who founded an agricultural commune called *Krinitzah* (Fountain) and who described their aims in a book entitled *The Sons of Krinitza*. This was translated into Hebrew and became a source of inspiration to young Jews dreaming of a better world. Many of them were suffering the burden of a dual despair; the failure of the 1905 revolution, and the emergence of antisemitism among the Russian socialist intellectuals. Tolstoy's view that man could be redeemed by physical labour and a return to the land strongly informed the spirit of the times and is reflected in the philosophy of A.D. Gordon who in his turn exerted considerable influence on the founders of the *kvutza* in Palestine. Later, Gordon and his disciples met Martin Buber* and Gustav Landauer.† They too believed that a communal existence could only truly flower within small groups where man could

---

* M. Buber, *Path in Utopia*, London, 1949.
† G. Landauer, *Der Werdende Mensch: Aufsätze über Leben und Schriften,* Potsdam, 1921.

once more come into his own. Although many of the early *kvutza* members, including Gordon, regarded themselves as nationalists, their nationalism was deeply coloured by socialist thinking. They abhorred the exploitation of man by man; they believed in a life based on individual toil, mutual aid and goodwill towards all men, in the principle of land nationalization and in striving for peace and understanding with their Arab neighbours.

The Russian Revolution which, coming after the slaughter of World War I, was a source of inspiration to youth throughout Europe also stimulated Jewish youth, even those who had already made up their minds to emigrate and to build a homeland for the Jewish people in Palestine. Thousands, many of whom had fought in the Red Army, tried to reach Palestine. Once there, they strove to re-enact the October Revolution among the Jewish people of Palestine. However what they found there was a small and poverty-stricken Jewish community, mostly old people who had come to the Holy Land solely to die and be buried there. A handful of pioneers laboured in *Moshavot* orange groves and a few isolated communes had been established. There was no 'established order' to be overthrown, only a wilderness to be tamed. Everything had to be built from scratch and this, it was felt, could best be achived on communist foundations. In 1920, the *Gedud Ha'avoda* was founded with its declared aim of 'building up Palestine by a general commune of Palestine workers'. In the early twenties the country had about 2,000 workers, one-third of whom belonged to the *Gedud Ha'avoda*. In the *Gedud*, moreover, a large group was committed to the principles expounded in *Fields, Factories and Workshops*, by the well-known anarchist, Prince Kropotkin.

In 1923, the most representative body of Palestine workers, *The Zionist-Socialist Union (Ahdut Ha'avoda)* passed the following resolution: 'The conference notes that the chief basis and instrument of our economic acitvity in Palestine—whether concerned with agriculture, industry or public works—is the kibbutz, where ideology and practice have been merged and which is ready to embark on a collective life under the auspices of *Hevrat Ha'ovdim.'* In 1927, the *Gedud Ha'avoda* and the *Kevutza Hagedola* united to form what became known as the *Hakibbutz Hameuhad* movement.

The third major development, also dating back to 1927, was *Hakibbutz Ha'artzi Hashomer Hatzair*, consisting of four kibbutzim whose members had mainly come from the first Jewish youth movement (founded in 1913). Like others of its kind throughout Europe, this movement, having first accepted the vaguely romantic, anti-establishment feelings of pre-1914 youth, succumbed to the post-World War I disillusionment of those who had seen the hopes and dreams of an entire generation drown in blood.

After a cataclysm in which Jews had had to endure expulsion, murder, pogroms, and had been driven from sanctuary to sanctuary, the *Hashomer Hatzair* believed that their salvation could only be achieved by redeeming the whole man through new ways of living which tended to stress man's collective dependence rather than his personal independence. They were undoubtedly influenced by Ferdinand Toennies, who maintained in his *Community and Association* that in society the individual—every individual—must remain alienated. Only in a community will he be set free, live without barriers among his fellows and resolve the conflict between the individual and the group. The *Hashomer Hatzair* kibbutzim combined the philosophy of the small, intimate group with the social vision of *Gedud Ha'avoda* and the large *kvutza*.

The ideological platform of *Hakibbutz Ha'artzi* rests on three planks: Zionism, socialism and kibbutz collectivism; these are understood as interconnected principles within an organic whole. The section on Zionism, to give an example, postulates that 'national and human experience will be fully complemented by the establishment of a socialist society in Palestine. . . .' It also refers to 'the socialist revolution and the withering away of classes'. Similarly, the section dealing with socialism refers to the establishment of a Jewish National Home and the strengthening of the *General Federation of Jewish Workers* (the *Histadrut*), while the passages devoted to 'the kibbutz principle' lay stress on the 'complete integration of the individual into the community', and on 'deepening personal-moral relations'. Kibbutzim are therefore held to be 'the germ-cells of the new society'. Common to all kibbutz philosophies is the idea of 'self realization', according to which no national or social ideal is valid unless it is personally implemented. Theory and practice must be merged in the individual.

Jewish communities in Palestine were isolated and each kibbutz was, in a sense a training ground for self-defence, thus providing cadres for the later Jewish defence forces. In this way, *Hashomer* (League of Watchmen) became the forerunner of the *Palmach* and the *Hagana*. A Jewish homeland implied the existence of a body of Jewish agricultural and industrial workers. Because Jews had been cut off from the soil and from the acquisition of basic industrial skills through the centuries of the diaspora, kibbutz members regarded the return to the soil and to manual labour as their first and most important task. Belief in the redemptive value of 'physical work', through which Jews could realize their national aspirations and regain their individual self-respect, inevitably made it a matter of principle that all work required by the kibbutz was to be done by members of the community.

The hope of *Gedud Ha'avoda* that Eretz-Israel would become a commune of workers was not fulfilled. Instead a private enterprise economy developed and flourished: citrus groves were planted, towns built, and industries expanded rapidly. The *Histadrut*, founded in the same year as the *Gedud Ha'avoda*, organized within its ranks not only the settlers of *Herrat Ha'ovdim* but also wage-earners. Controversies arose over the link between the kibbutz and the party. The two major labour parties, *Hapoel Hatzair* (founded in 1919) established their patronage: the first over the *Hever Hakvutzot*, and the second over the *Gedud Ha'avoda* and later over *Hakibbutz Hameuhad*. Although in the kibbutzim themselves each individual was free to choose his party allegiance, it nevertheless proved impossible to prevent the parties from exerting influence on the kibbutzim. In the *Gedud Ha'avoda* leftist trends arose; the anti-Zionist and communist views of some members provoked a split, after which a small section of the dissident Left emigrated to the Soviet Union. Although the shock of this controversy served as a warning of how easily political feuds could wreck the life of the kibbutz, it left unanswered the important question whether the kibbutz was entitled, or indeed able, to cut itself off from political life? How else could the kibbutz make its contribution to society—particularly a society which, as in Israel, was still in a stage of development?

Since ways of integrating politics into the fabric of kibbutz life had to be found, the concept of 'collective ideology' emerged and gained general acceptance. Its purpose was to give each member the opportunity to engage in politics, while preventing the imposition of ideas and doctrines. Just as the kibbutz rejects any permanent leadership in any field, and calls for continual rotation of all administrative posts, the principle of ideological collectivism aims at the full democratization of political life. Hence, delegates to the movement's political councils regularly stand for election and, among the cadre of political workers, a system of regular rotation of posts must be maintained. Just as there is no narrow specialization in kibbutz tasks, whether productive, social, cultural or educational, neither is there room for political specialization.

The kibbutz as a whole subscribes to the political approach of the *Hashomer Hatzair* movement, but a member holding different views may reject the *Hashomer Hatzair* policy and vote for any other party represented in *Histadrut*; for example, a *Ha'artzi* kibbutz in which the percentage of those rejecting the hitherto accepted political alignment exceeds an agreed minimum of 15 per cent., ceases to belong to the movement. This is why the first *Hashomer* kibbutz, 'Bet Alfa', was not included in the movement's 1940 list: at that time not more than a third of its members accepted its political line, and it was not until 1948 that *Hashomer Hatzair's* first kibbutz returned to the fold. Only *Hakibbutz Ha'artzi* adopted the principle of 'ideological collectivism': the other two movements were reluctant to introduce it, fearing that politics might interfere with kibbutz life. They developed the concept of 'ideological unity' which in practice, however, differed very little from *Ha'artzi's* approach.

Although all the kibbutzim were equally devoted to Zionist ideals, their approach to socialism became more controversial with the expansion of a capitalist economy. The new industries required a growing labour force which soon insisted on

its trade union and class rights. Socialist utopias, so convinc-
ing when the *Histadrut* was founded, had to give way to a
socialist realism based on the actual conditions of life in
Palestine. The emergence of *Mapai* signified the strengthening
of reformist trends in Israeli socialism even though it
remained quite different from the European type of reformist
parties. The *Histadrut's* pioneering settlement movement, the
Hevrat Ha'ovdim and its subsidiary institutions, continued to
call for a revolutionary approach. Hence, Berl Katznelson's
assertion that *Mapai* had created a new form of 'revolutionary
constructivism' was no empty phrase. It implied that the
efforts of the workers' settlement and co-operative movements
of the *Histadrut* and of the mutual aid institutions to develop
the country along socialist lines do indeed constitute a
revolutionary act and a rejection of the existing capitalist
system. In its trade union policy, *Mapai* adopted a reformist
attitude, persuaded by one of its leaders that in so doing it
would advance 'from class to people'; a slogan which in the
eyes of some smacks of Israeli facism.

The *Israeli Communist Party* opposed *Mapai* and rejected
Zionism and its efforts to build up the country. It insisted
that the *Histadrut* should give up its commercial enterprises
and concentrate on its trade union functions in close co-
operation with the Arab workers, that it should support Arab
national movements, sever all contacts with world Jewry and
Zionism and regard the struggle against imperialism as its
main task. In the party's view, the triumph of international
socialism under the guidance of the *CPSU* was the sole
solution to the region's social, ethnic and national problems.

Even within *Mapai*, not everyone had lost his revolutionary
zeal and accepted the party's reformist attitude. Some former
members of the *Ahdut Ha'avoda*, emphasizing the reality of the
class struggle in Israel and the need for international solidarity, expressed support for the October Revolution and the
building of socialism in the USSR. *Ha'artzi* formulated a
programme which attempted a dialectical solution to the
apparent contradictions between Zionism and socialism,
between the need to build up the homeland and the
exigencies of the class struggle. The latter was perceived as
having two phases; the first devoted to the laying of Zionist

foundations, and the second to the inevitable social revolution which would be brought about after the Jewish people had been gathered in from the lands of dispersion. No sharp division between the two phases was envisaged; socialist developments were to take place during the first phase, while during the second the ingathering of the Jews would continue. Nor was the problem of the Palestinian Arabs overlooked; according to the *Hashomer Hatzair* theorists 'only an international federation of workers could achieve revolution in Palestine'. In their kibbutz this theory of phases allowed both a Zionist and a socialist awareness to grow up and be practised side by side.

Hakibbutz Ha'artzi has never regarded itself as a political party. It was prepared to join any political force willing to support its Zionist, socialist and kibbutz-oriented programme. Negotiations for a merger with *Mapai* had begun even before the kibbutz federation was founded, but came to nothing because of disagreements on such basic issues as the class struggle, scientific socialism, joint organization, the bi-national solution of the Palestine problem, etc. Subsequent attempts at unification ended in failure. At both *Histadrut* and Knesset elections, the *Kibbutz Ha'artzi* movement put up its own candidates who polled more than double the votes which the members of its kibbutzim could have mustered.

In 1936, workers supporting *Hashomer Hatzair* formed *The Socialist League* which was to assist the *Hakibbutz Ha'artzi* in the towns and villages. After the 1944 *Mapai* split, when the *Ahdut Ha'avoda-Poale Zion* faction broke away, the *Hashomer Hatzair* party was founded in 1946. In 1948, it merged with *Ahdut Ha'avoda* to form the 'United Workers Party', *Mapam*. In 1954, the party split once more over the Arab question and its relations with the Soviet Union and the socialist camp. Controversies within the *Ahdut Ha'avoda's* kibbutz federation finally led to a split (1951) and the break-up of some kibbutzim, causing members to leave the homes in which they had invested so much of their energies and to move to politically more congenial kibbutzim. This was a socio-ideological development of major importance, showing that the principle of collective ideology—far from being an arbitrary imposition, as some of the leading ideologists of the

Palestinian Labour movement suggested (Arlosoroff, B. Katznelson, Eliahu Golomb, Y. Laufbahn)—really responded to kibbutz needs essential for their continuity and stability.

The *Ihud Hakvutzot Ve'hakibbutzim* suffered a severe shock when its veteran leader David Ben-Gurion, after the split in *Mapai*, formed the rival *Rafi (Israel Workers' List)* party. With the example of the *Hakibbutz Hameuhad* split before them, *Ihud* members made every possible effort to safeguard the delicate fabric of kibbutz life. Many of them preferred to evade the issue altogether and a process of depoliticization set in, which, with the general decline of political interest, has become quite a fashion among the younger kibbutz members.

This process has not left the *Hashomer Hatzair* kibbutzim unaffected, even though the principle of ideological collectivism forms an integral part of their philosophy. The movement had suffered greatly from the disillusionment of members who had pinned their hopes on the socialist achievements of the Soviet Union. Without identifying itself completely with the USSR, *Hashomer Hatzair* combined enthusiasm for the October Revolution with an unequivocal rejection of such organizations as the Comintern or the Cominform by which the Soviet Union imposes her will on fraternal parties. *Hashomer Hatzair's* wholehearted support for the USSR between 1941 and 1952 covered the years of her heroic resistance to Nazi Germany and her early appreciation of the need for, and support of, a Jewish state. At that critical time, Soviet goodwill amounted to more than lip-service, expressing itself tangibly in military aid and diplomatic backing. The Prague trials, exposing the cynicism and duplicity of Soviet leadership at home and among satellites, killed all warm pro Soviet feelings among kibbutz members. The generation which grew up during the period of Soviet adulation suffered a profound shock when confronted with a Russia enthusiastically supporting reactionary and dictatorial Arab regimes bent on destroying Israel. Whereas the veteran *Hashomer Hatzair* generation had always, even during the honeymoon period immediately before and after the attainment of statehood, had reservations about Soviet socialism, and was never quite convinced that the Soviet reality approximated the socialist ideal, many of the young kibbutzniks faced with the subsequent Soviet nightmare tended to despair of socialism as such.

Political attitudes in the kibbutz movement are influenced by several mutually contradictory factors. Among these the problem of national security is indubitably the most important, particularly now that Israel has endured a state of war for many years and still faces the ultimate struggle for survival. For a number of reasons the kibbutzim are particularly affected by this war. Being strung out along the country's frontiers, they form the first line of defence. Moreover, owing to their upbringing the kibbutz youth have contributed a vital, almost an elite, element to the Israeli forces, many pilots, paratroopers, naval commandos and armoured corps men being kibbutzniks. The fact that they had to face Soviet aircraft, guns, missiles and warships was not lost on these young socialist kibbutzniks. Although their movement represents only 4 per cent. of the population, 25 per cent. of those killed in action came from its ranks. The decisive role they played in war may well be the result of their collective way of life and their ingrained devotion to the larger community. The fact that in the kibbutz pursuit of career advancement and material gain never was a motivating force, has informed the outlook and ethos of all Israeli defence forces. The *Palmach, Haganah's* pioneering force, was born in and developed by the kibbutz movement; and after the attainment of statehood, its traditions of service and daring were taken over by the Israeli Army. Most of Israel's top commanders belonged to the *Palmach,* which is now being replaced by *Nahal.* This corps combines military service with the establishment of protective border settlements as well as with educational work in the youth movement and the training of pioneers ready to set up new kibbutzim.

Israel has a mixed economy with a continually expanding free enterprise sector, whose principles of competition, profit-making, management control and economic incentives have become major social influences. On the other hand, the *Histadrut,* with over one million affiliated members, runs flourishing agricultural and industrial enterprises, as well as producer and consumer co-operatives and a remarkable system of mutual aid institutions of which it is justly proud.

It, too, represents a powerful social and economic force inspired by the socialist ideal of working people building up their reclaimed homeland. However, the pressures of the private enterprise mentality have also affected the *Histadrut*. Because of its sheer size and ramifications, it is increasingly dominated by a bureaucracy which threatens to overwhelm the spontaneous and idealistic forces responsible for its foundation and growth. The *Histadrut* must therefore try to restore its participatory and democratic character, giving rank-and-file members a say in the running of their own federation. It must also confront the hostile class forces bent on breaking it up and eager to separate its commercial from its trade union activities: forces in short, which are only too anxious to deprive the Israeli worker of the assets, investments and enterprises he has accumulated over the years.

The kibbutz both challenges almost every capitalist precept, and represents a working model of socialism. However, exposed to the blandishments of a capitalistic economy, the kibbutz, unless firm in its socialist resolve and aware of its own mission, is always in danger of ideological erosion. A proper appreciation of its part in the scheme of things would benefit not only the kibbutz itself, but also the *Histadrut*, suffering from diminishing confidence, self-questioning and, paradoxically enough, Israel's very progressiveness. Ber Borochov, a universally respected scholar of socialist Zionism, said that the State of Israel would either become socialist or not exist at all. A truly reactionary Israeli society would endanger more than Israel's socialist settlements and her independent labour movement: it would threaten the self-denying pioneering spirit on which the state and its defence forces were built. The sense of mission generated by the kibbutzim ensures its survival as a creative ideological force ready to re-examine its approach to socialism.

The fact that a group of people have consistently acted in accordance with their pledges has strongly impressed contemporary youth, all too ready to criticize the 'hypocrisy' of their elders, whether parents, teachers, priests or government. In this sense, the kibbutz is the prototype of a new kind of socialism fit for a generation disillusioned by the sad failure of the so-called socialist countries to achieve any meaningful degree of socialism. This has been attained and turned into a living reality only in the kibbutzim, where all members are truly equal and all participate in decision making. By depriving members of any personal power or authority, the kibbutz has realized another socialist ideal: the abolition of dominance by one individual over another. Kibbutz life is based on absolute equality; there are neither managers nor managed, only members who for a year or two assume public functions until replaced. Office holders in the kibbutz have no economic or social privileges. Manual labour is, on principle, to be performed by all members, whether employed in productive work or in service. The kibbutz gives equal honour to intellectual work, provided it benefits the community. In other words, it seeks to fulfil the socialist ideal of bridging the gap between mental and physical labour. It rejects narrow specialization and insists on proficiency in both types of work. Members are expected to qualify for several trades or professions and to be prepared to switch from one task to another in accordance with communal needs. Kibbutz teachers and other white-collar workers are obliged, after three or four years in their profession, to put in a year of manual labour.

Kibbutz education is based on socialist principles, and children are taught early on to help in the fields and workshops and with domestic tasks; indeed throughout the twelve years of their schooling their curriculum combines practical work with academic pursuits. Similarly, collective non-specialist teaching is one of the major success stories of the kibbutzim. The most highly esteemed members are assigned educational tasks, whether as teachers or guides or housemothers. Although children are housed in quarters specially designed for them, collective life does not cut them off from their parents, and family ties are close and warm. Educational achievements are quite remarkable; generally speaking, the kibbutz youth is above average in health, working ability and academic attainments. While independent research workers are impressed by its discipline, highly developed community sense, and the absence of delinquent or otherwise deviant social behaviour, its outstanding record in the army, to which it contributed a disproportionately large number of officers, has won general admiration.

Complete economic, social, cultural and political equality allows kibbutz members to develop their full personal potential, unhampered by any material pressures. This makes them self-reliant, fully conversant with the economic, administrative and educational problems of the kibbutz as well as with the more general artistic, cultural and political issues. Their life is thus in tune with the material endeavours and moral ideals of the community.

On the psychological plane, relations between members of the kibbutz are marked by directness and absence of those inhibiting factors which in a capitalist society all too often mar relationships. Because kibbutzim, advanced economic units though they are, have remained immune from the process of alienation both between individuals and between the producer and his work, the producer here really owns the product of his labour. Women, too, are assured of equal rights. Relieved of her domestic duties, the kibbutz woman can, like the men, work in the fields, offices, service workshops, schools or industry.

Seventy per cent. of kibbutz production is agricultural, the remainder being industrial. Kibbutzim represent 32 per cent. of the rural population, and their productivity and the ability to compete with the private sector is constantly increasing. Kibbutz living standards are certainly equal to, and levels of education and culture are higher than, those attained by the majority of the working population.

From the Middle Ages onward, the communes which endured longest were those motivated by religious faith. Most kibbutzim, however, are secular in outlook, believing in socialism and its promise of creating a 'new man' in a new and better social environment.

The kibbutzim's remarkable economic successes conclusively disprove the assumption that economic advancement depends on the material incentives of free competition. They prove, in fact, that economic advances as spectacular as those in the private sector can be obtained by relying on the community spirit and sense of purpose of the collective. The strength and influence of the kibbutz movement far exceeds its share of the population. While the kibbutzim account for 4 per cent. of the total population and 5.5 per cent. of all employed, they provide 10 per cent. of the productively employed (i.e. in agriculture, industry, building and public works). They cultivate 42 per cent. of all available land, on which they produce 50 per cent. of the total agricultural output; they account for 20 per cent. of the *Histadrut's* and 5 per cent. of the country's industrial production. Their main revenue still comes from farming but by branching out into light and service industries, the kibbutzim have created additional employment for about five times their own membership. The kibbutz contribution to the national larder is outstanding; its share of the country's agricultural output is:

Commodity	Percentage	Commodity	Percentage
Pond bred fish	95	Cereals	69
Bananas	90	Fertile eggs	65
Cotton	76	Apples & pears	60
Olives	71	Cows' milk	40
Ewes' milk	71	Potatoes	35

This hope spurs them on to persevere on a path, which, far from easy, nevertheless offers spiritual compensation and a many-sided and richly stimulating life. In 1969, out of Israel's 230 kibbutzim, comprising a membership of 51,400 and a total population of 93,000, only 13, with 1,800 members, were affiliated to religious movements.

Although as has been seen, conditions in Palestine favoured the growth of the kibbutz movement, this was by no means the only reason for its success: what was perhaps of even greater importance was the presence in the country of a group of people inspired by the ideal of transforming man and creating a new society. The kibbutzim were the result, both of external circumstances and the existence of a human group uniquely responsive to them. To those who pioneered the kibbutz, socialism meant creating conditions in which man could liberate himself through work and service and live in a community of like-minded equals. Experience has taught our generation that nationalization of the means of production without a corresponding reform in social relations does not necessarily promote socialism. It merely creates a managerial society ruled by bureaucrats. The Soviet Union and the People's Democracies following her lead did not create a new breed of men truly free and in charge of their destiny. Workers in those countries have no control over their material and social environment. Everything is decreed from above, and nationalization has hardly affected their position, neither has it liberated them from exploitation and alienation. The economic and social success of the kibbutz, on the other hand, proves that it is possible to build socialism in a community within which competition, the profit motive and the rule of man over his fellows are unknown.

Politically, the kibbutz movements remain divided by their party allegiances. It is quite possible, however, that as time goes on there will be some ideological and political rapprochement. This depends on whether the younger generation, having proved its mettle in the country's defence and economy, will divert some of its proved talents and originality to the resolution of factional divisions.

Soviet-Israeli Relations 1948-56:
from Courtship to Crisis

Peter Brod

Unlike the majority of other modern states, the Soviet Union and Israel share an important feature: their whole political structure and its development cannot be properly understood without reference to a highly complex ideology with claims to scientific validity. Marxism-Leninism and Zionism both explain and legitimize the historical necessity of the movements they have created and show their adherents an ideal, an ultimate state of society, towards which history is or should be moving. Moreover, the two ideologies were in constant contact even in pre-state times, i.e. well before the establishment of Bolshevik rule in Russia and of the Jewish state in Palestine. In considering the Soviet-Israeli relationship, it is therefore necessary to examine, at least briefly, the genesis of communist views on Zionism.

The prevailing attitude towards the Jewish question among 19th century socialists oscillated between support for Jewish civil emancipation and echoes of the rising antisemitic mood of European politics, especially in Germany and France. The situation was further complicated by the ambivalent attitude of many Jewish socialists towards their own background. The classic example was that of Karl Marx in his 'On the Jewish Question' (1844), in which he declared himself in favour of Jewish legal emancipation and then proceeded to denounce Judaism for its alleged spirit of profit-making, using it as a synonym for capitalist society. Later socialist theoreticians like Karl Kautsky and Otto Bauer ignored the young Marx's abstract equation of Judaism and capitalism, but continued to view the survival of Jews in modern society as a burdensome legacy from the Middle Ages. They argued that with the disappearance of the feudal order, the peculiar economic functions that obliged Jews to remain a separate entity would also wither away. Once they could enter all walks of life as equal citizens, the Jews would gradually lose their obsolete identity. The process of assimilation actually under way in western and central parts of Europe in the second half of the 19th century seemed to confirm these views. This led socialist writers to believe that both the new racial antisemitism and political Zionism were reactionary phenomena, each in their own way trying to turn back the wheel of history. Both were considered ephemeral phenomena and in the coming socialist society it was assumed that the Jewish question would cease to exist.[1]

In their writings on the Jewish problem, Lenin and Stalin followed in the footsteps of the German social democrats and the Austro marxists, while making allowances for the specific situation of Jews in the Russian empire. They rejected Zionism as well as the theory of the Jewish socialist 'Bund' which saw in the Yiddish-speaking Ostjuden a non-territorial nationality entitled to cultural-national autonomy in a future socialist Russia. Though the Soviet state in a sense tacitly accepted the tenets of Bundist ideology by giving to Russian Jewry the status of a 'nationality', Bolshevik theory never ceased its struggle against Jewish nationalism. Through its influence in the Communist International, the Lenin-Stalin negation of Zionism became a guideline for the world communist movement. After 1917, the Zionist alliance with Great Britain, the declared enemy of the new Soviet state and major imperial power of the day, merely reinforced earlier communist opposition to Zionism.[2]

In Russia itself, the Zionists were to share the fate of other non-communist groupings. Permitted to operate for a few years after the October Revolution, they became around 1920 the target of increasingly repressive measures. By 1924 Zionism was 'a dying movement'.[3] Only the left-wing of

Poale Zion, which tried to combine Zionism with loyalty to Leninism and whose organization abroad unsuccessfully applied for membership in the Third International, was allowed to lead a shadow existence until 1928. The anti-Zionist drive in Soviet Russia was spearheaded by the Yevsektsia, (the Jewish Section of the Bolshevik party) whose members were to a large extent former Bundists. The revolutionary zeal of these Jewish communists and the historic feud between Bundists and Zionists in pre-revolutionary Russia undoubtedly influenced the aggressiveness of Soviet anti-Zionism.[4]

Nevertheless, Jewish national feelings persisted, even within the ranks of the Communist party. The Soviet authorities hoped to counter this by establishing, in 1934, a Jewish Autonomous Region (better known as Birobidzhan) on the Chinese border. As it turned out, the region failed to attract large-scale Jewish colonization and certainly did not supersede surviving Zionist sympathies among Soviet Jews. Real and imaginary vestiges of 'Jewish bourgeois nationalism' became therefore, one of the targets of the Great Purge in the late 1930s and early 1940s.[5]

For a number of reasons, relatively little attention had been paid in Soviet foreign policy during the inter-war period to developments in the Middle East. The Soviet Union was at that time still weak and needed to consolidate its international position. Its interests focused on other areas such as Central Europe and the Far East where it hoped to find allies in the struggle against 'imperialism'. Great Britain and France still seemed to be firmly entrenched in the Middle East and prospects for revolutionary change in the region looked dim. 'There will be revolutionary developments in the Hawaiian Islands before anything will move in the Arab East', was the scathing assessment made by Stalin in the late 1920s according to Josef Berger Barzilai, once head of the Near Eastern Department in the Comintern.[6]

The only way open to Soviet policy to directly influence events in Palestine went through the Comintern and its local arm, the Palestine Communist Party (PCP). But the party was an ineffective instrument because it had to follow highly contradictory policies. Founded by disillusioned Jewish settlers, the PCP tried to appeal to Palestine Jewry by using anti-Zionist slogans and after 1929 it was required by the Comintern to show understanding for the anti-Jewish riots provoked by Arab unrest in Palestine. This, in addition to factional strife reduced it to insignificance, costing the party most of its Jewish membership and transforming it into a largely Arab organization.[7]

Throughout the years, a modicum of interest in Zionist aims and in the Palestinian problem was maintained by high-ranking Soviet personalities, mainly diplomats. Kurt Blumenfeld, a German Zionist leader, was able to talk to Chicherin during the latter's stay in Berlin.[8] And in March 1929 Stalin reportedly called in Josef Barzilai, then Secretary of the PCP Central Committee, for a five hour conversation about the Palestinian problem.[9] In 1934, the Soviet Union entered the League of Nations and confirmed her refusal to acknowledge the legitimacy of the British mandate over Palestine. Subsequently, her delegates met several times with the Jewish Agency representative in Geneva, Nahum Goldmann. These encounters gave Goldmann the impression that some day the Soviet Union might approve of the idea of a Jewish state.[10]

The number of contacts between Zionists and Soviet officials increased rapidly after the German attack on the Soviet Union. Already in July 1941, at a meeting between the Soviet ambassador to Washington, Konstantin Umanskii and a delegation representing large American Jewish organizations, the subject of Palestine came up. Umanskii said that its future would be settled in a conference after the war with Soviet participation. There followed a number of talks between Soviet and Zionist represenatives in Turkey, in London and in New York in late 1941 and early 1942. The Soviets would usually refuse to discuss such topics as the fate of imprisoned Zionists in Russia but they did show a lively interest in Palestinian developments. In the summer of 1942, two Soviet diplomats for the first time toured the Palestinian Jewish settlements in connection with a campaign in the Yishuv to aid the USSR. Both they and Deputy Foreign Minister Ivan Maiskii, who visited Palestine briefly in October 1943, seemed to have been very impressed by the

Yishuv's achievements. Although all this was very far from constituting a complete change in the Soviet outlook on Zionism, by 1944 it was clear from various hints that the Soviet government looked for an international solution to the Palestine conflict and was willing to consider Zionist arguments in the process.[11] Hence it is not surprising that the Zionist leadership put such faith in the exaggerated reports about the Roosevelt-Stalin conversation at Yalta in 1945 which seemed to indicate final Soviet consent to the establishment of a Jewish state.[12]

Though it took the Soviet Union another two years to openly support the partition of Palestine, thereby facilitating the goals of the Zionist movement, the immediate post-war period must be seen as a prelude to that important step. What mainly contributed to the change in Soviet policy was the short-lived British attempt, once more, to go it alone in Palestine. The policies of the Attlee government implied that the Soviet Union was to be excluded from the solution of a major international problem in an area in which it had recently become interested. It was no secret that this was one of the reasons for the setting-up of the Anglo-American Committee of Inquiry on Palestine.[13] Secondly, the conflict between Great Britain and the Zionist movement which resulted from continuing British adherence to the immigration restrictions of the 1939 White Paper changed, at least temporarily, the political character of Zionism. In Marxist-Leninist terms it had become transformed from an agent of British imperialism into an instrument of the struggle against British power.

Such reasoning was not immediately reflected in Soviet publications which around 1946 still gave prominence to the traditional anti-Zionist view of the Palestine conflict, though they also voiced some criticism of the Arab League.[14] There was, however, one major indication of a reassessment in Soviet policy, namely the tacit toleration of *Brichah* (Flight), the illegal, large-scale Haganah operation which brought thousands of Jewish survivors from Eastern Europe to the West and eventually to Palestine. The Czech and Polish governments which did most to facilitate the movement of Jewish displaced persons to the West, were by 1946 under strong

Soviet influence and could not have acted without Moscow's approval. There were several benefits to the Soviets from this behaviour, besides the reduction of ethnic tensions in the area now under Russian domination and the creation of difficulties for the authorities in the western occupation zones of Germany and Austria (where most of the Jewish migrants spent some time). There was now an increasing pressure on Great Britain to contribute to the solution of the DP problem by changing her closed-door policy in Palestine. The interest that world public opinion took in the fate of the Jewish inmates in DP camps in Germany, Cyprus and elsewhere helped to bring the issue of Palestine back to the international forum where, in Soviet eyes, it had belonged in the first place.[15]

With hindsight, Soviet war-time contacts with Zionist leaders and the toleration of the Brichah appear as logical steps in the reassessment of Soviet policy on Palestine. But for the general public the change only became visible when, in April 1947, Britain finally decided to transfer the question of Palestine to the United Nations. In the First Special Session of the General Assembly, which was completely devoted to Palestine, the Soviet Union, represented by Chief Delegate Andrei Gromyko, took an active part. On May 2, Gromyko expressed support for the Jewish Agency's application to testify before the Session and on May 14, 1947 he addressed the Assembly in a long speech that made history. This first post-war official Soviet declaration on Palestine differed markedly in several points from known Russian positions. Thus Gromyko did not denounce the mandatory system as such; he criticized it for its failure to achieve its aims. Without making any reference to Zionism, the Soviet delegate linked the displaced persons issue to the problem of Palestine. But he was in fact putting forward the essence of Zionism when he said:

> The fact that no western European State has been able to ensure the defence of the elementary rights of the Jewish people, and to safeguard it against the violence of the fascist executioners, explains the aspirations of the Jews to establish their own State. It would be unjust not to take this into consideration and to deny the right of the Jewish

people to realize this aspiration. It would be unjustifiable to deny this right to Jewish people, particularly in view of all it has undergone during the Second World War.[16]

The Soviet Union, Gromyko continued, saw only two solutions to the Palestine problem: to safeguard the legitimate rights of both Jews and Arabs in the country, Palestine would either have to become a binational state or else be partitioned. Gromyko indicated the Soviet preference for the first possibility but since circumstances in Palestine hardly allowed such a solution, his speech could already be interpreted as favouring partition.[17] In the autumn, when the results of the work of the United Nations Special Commission on Palestine were being discussed in the General Assembly and its committees, the Soviet delegates took sides with the commission's majority recommendations which advocated partition. On 26 November 1947, Gromyko in his final contribution to the General Assembly debate repeated the arguments of his May speech, this time with the emphasis on partition as the only practicable solution. Three days later, the resolution providing for the partition of Palestine into a Jewish and an Arab state, was adopted by a majority of member states which included the United States, the Soviet Union and her East European allies.

In the following months, the clashes in Palestine between Jews and Arabs reached civil-war dimensions. With the United States trying to replace partition by a trusteeship scheme, the Soviet Union remained the only major power in the UN to consistently advocate the realization of the partition resolution. On 18 May, 1948, four days after Israel's Declaration of Independence, the Soviet Union extended diplomatic recognition to the new state. In contrast to the immediate US *de facto* recognition, the Soviet act was the first *de jure* recognition of the Jewish state. These significant acts of public support for the establishment of Israel were paralleled by a no less important help in the form of military aid. The chief agent for military co-operation between the Eastern block and the emerging Israeli army was Czechoslovakia but, just as in the case of Brichah, her government acted with Soviet approval.

This co-operation began in late 1947 when the Haganah, faced with an Anglo-American embargo and a steady supply of British weapons to the Arabs, sent several officers to shop around for arms in Europe. A contact with Prague was quickly established and several deals were concluded under which, between January 1948 and February 1949, Czechoslovakia delivered 24,500 Mauser rifles, 84 fighter planes, 10,000 bombs and other military hardware. After the communist coup in Czechoslovakia (in February 1948) co-operation between the Jewish military mission in Prague and the Czechoslovak authorities became even smoother. A direct connection was established between the Zatec airfield in Bohemia and airfields in Jewish-held areas of Palestine. At the same time, in camps scattered over Bohemia some 120 Haganah troops were being trained by experienced Czechoslovak officers to become fighter pilots and paratroopers. Finally, in December 1948, the so-called 'Czech brigade', a force of about a thousand Jewish volunteers from Czechoslovakia, was dispatched to the Arab-Israeli front to take part in the final battles of the Israeli War of Independence. All this was done in clear contravention of repeated Security Council appeals to all UN members to prevent any measures likely to intensify the military conflict in Palestine. The military co-operation between Czechoslovakia and Israel also drew strong protests from the United States and Great Britain, when details became known to western diplomats in the Czech capital in the summer of 1948. These protests, together with the victorious advance of the Israeli army and the first cooling-off of Soviet-Israeli relations in late 1948, contributed to the gradual thinning out of Czechoslovak deliveries; by February 1949, military aid had ceased.[18]

Throughout the crucial months preceding and following Israel's declaration of independence, Soviet policy greatly aided the Jewish cause in Palestine. Already during the preparation of the partition resolution, Zionist envoys in New York were met with considerable sympathy by Soviet diplomats.[19] Both in the UN and in the Soviet press, the Arab attack on Israel was branded as an act of aggression and this did much to strengthen Israel's international position. In July 1948, for example, the Ukrainian delegate Manuilskii, in his capacity as chairman of the Security Council, designated Abba Eban as the representative of the State of Israel. Eban had been sitting in on Security Council sessions as the representative of the Jewish Agency and his elevation by Manuilskii met with objections from several delegations. Nevertheless, Soviet delegates consistently continued to support Israel's application for UN membership until it was accepted in May 1949.[20]

After Czechoslovakia, the Soviet Union was the second state to enter into diplomatic relations with Israel. The arrival of Israel's first ambassador Golda Meyerson (later Meir) in Moscow on 2 September 1948 marked the high point of what has been termed the Soviet-Israeli 'honeymoon' but it also sparked off a series of events which showed that a happy, lasting 'marriage' would not follow. To understand this transition, a brief reconsideration of Soviet motives is necessary.

Soviet behaviour on the Palestine questions in 1947/48 was so much at variance with communist anti-Zionism that even a very experienced observer has suggested that 'it is at least possible that this course of action was recommended by some Foreign Ministry advisers and approved by Stalin in a fit of absentmindedness'.[21] But if one considers Soviet global and regional interests, the decision to support the establishment of Israel fits as a perfectly rational option in Stalin's strategy. In the immediate post-war years, the Soviet Union was trying to weaken Western positions south of her borders and in several instances (Turkey, Iran, Greece) had failed to achieve her aims. Palestine was the next opportunity and this time Soviet pressure did not have to be applied to established national governments but could be put behind a movement that had fought for its national independence against a colonial power. Soviet policy, though primarily directed against British positions, had at the same time to take account of increased American interest in the Middle East. Without a Soviet commitment, the new Jewish state would almost automatically orientate its foreign policy towards the United States, in view of its pro-Zionist tradition and large Jewish electorate. This was not a prospect that the Soviets could be expected to welcome. The possibility that the Stalinist leadership also entertained some illusions about the likely development of Israel in the direction of a 'people's democracy' cannot be exluded; after all, a significant portion of the Yishuv had a more or less marxist tradition. Finally, alienating the independent Arab countries did not seem to make any difference to Soviet prospects in the Middle East. The existing Arab leadership was viewed by the Soviets as pro-western and with some antipathy because of its pro-Axis past. Even several years later, Soviet propaganda denounced Colonel Nasser as another agent of American imperialism. On the whole, then, the balance of gains and losses clearly favoured Soviet support for the emerging Jewish state regardless of its Zionist character.[22]

What upset the positive balance-sheet was the realization by the Soviet leadership that Israel's existence would not remain without effect on Soviet Jews. On the occasion of their first visits to Moscow's main synagogue and to the Jewish Theatre, Mrs Meyerson and her entourage had received an enthusiastic reception from the audience. The Israeli diplomats' visits to the main synagogue during the Jewish High Holidays in October resulted in spontaneous street demonstrations of sympathy; it was estimated that on New Year's Eve a crowd of some 30,000 people instead of the normal 2,000 blocked the neighbourhood of the synagogue. Inside, prayers were said for the Israeli soldiers who fell in the War of Independence. After thirty years of anti-Zionist indoctrination, even some members of the establishment, such as Polina Molotov, the Foreign Minister's Jewish wife, could not conceal their admiration for Israel.[23]

Another sore point was touched when Mrs Meyerson, in her first talks at the Foreign Ministry, raised the issue of Jewish emigration from the Soviet Union to Israel. Stalin's regime released its first warning in an article by Ilya Ehrenburg. Writing in *Pravda* on 21 September 1948, the prominent Jewish author underlined the Soviet Union's positive stand towards Israel and at the same time criticized Zionism in familiar terms. The Jewish question could only be solved in a socialist society and therefore Soviet Jews were not looking to the Middle East but rather to the better future into which they along with the toilers of Israel and the whole of mankind were being led by the Soviet Union.

These promises of a better future could not have been more brutally denied than by the anti-Jewish purge which started only a few weeks after Ehrenburg's article. Determined to stamp out any potential centres of Jewish national feeling, the Soviet authorities between November 1948 and November 1949 closed down all remaining Jewish cultural institutions. They dissolved the Jewish Anti-Fascist Committee which had been created during the war to represent Soviet Jewry abroad, stopped all Jewish publications and arrested dozens of Jews, among them the best Yiddish writers. In addition, the campaign against 'cosmopolitanism' that had been waged against Western influence since 1946 was now transformed into a thinly-veiled attack on Jewish intellectuals.[24]

At the inter-state level, Soviet-Israeli relations did not seem to suffer directly from this change in domestic policy. When Israeli public opinion, in late 1948, expressed dismay at internal developments in Russia, the Soviet press still chose to attack some Israeli press organs rather than the government for pursuing an 'anti-Soviet campaign'.[25] The Israeli government similarly followed a policy line designed not to give the Soviet Union any reason for changing the climate of bilateral relations. According to its declaration of March 1949, Israel would follow a policy of friendship with all peace-loving nations, particularly with the United States and the Soviet Union. This led, at least in the first seven months of Israel's UN membership, to a very cautious attitude on international issues of Soviet concern. In the UN, Israel either voted with the Soviet block or abstained until December 1949.

Israel was in some repects a precursor, at least in intention, of the policy of neutralism which, in the 1950s, came to be adopted by most of the newly independent African and Asian nations. At the height of the Cold War confrontation however, such an attempt at following a third course was doomed to be premature. Neither of the two big powers was inclined to accept vague promises of friendship instead of outright alliances. Under Stalin, Soviet ideology even lacked coherent guidelines on how to deal with the emerging post-colonial nations whose leadership belonged to the western-oriented 'national bourgeoisie'. These general conditions soon combined with the old communist distrust of

Zionism and with a new spectre of internal unrest and disloyalty among Russian Jews to produce a Soviet backlash against Israel. In the course of 1949 events giving rise to Soviet criticism multiplied. The General Secretary of the Israeli Communist Party, Shmuel Mikunis, was approvingly quoted in the Soviet press[26] when he described the first general election in Israel as neither free nor democratic. Increasingly, Soviet press coverage of Israel restricted itself to the activities of the 'progressive forces', the efforts of the 'reactionary ruling circle' to suppress them and to the deteriorating living standards of the working class. American investments in Israel, an American loan in March and a first dissenting vote in the UN in December were all seen as clear signs of Israel's drift towards Washington.[27] Already in June 1949, reviewing the situation in the Middle East, the leading Soviet orientalist Vladimir Lutskii concluded that 'the UN resolution concerning the creation in Palestine of an independent, democratic Jewish state has in essence not been realized'.[28]

By the beginning of 1950, when a visit to Israel by the former American secretary of finance Henry Morgenthau confirmed Soviet views concerning the reactionary nature of the Zionist political elite, the state of Soviet-Israeli relations was marked by contradictions. On the one hand, diplomatic ties were still maintained in a correct fashion and in the UN Israel could count on some Soviet support for her views about the Middle East conflict. Against this, there were the anti-Jewish measures within Russia, open and aggressive criticism of Israel in the Soviet press, a halt to Jewish emigration from the satellite countries and first 'anti-Zionist' purges and show trials in Hungary and Bulgaria.[29]

This ambiguous situation remained in force until late 1952. Israel tried to walk the tight-rope by replying evasively to such Western initiatives as the Tripartite Declaration on the Middle East in May 1950 and the NATO-inspired plan of an Allied Middle East Command in the autumn of 1951. She continued to assure the Soviet Union of her interest in maintaining friendly relations. But since these assurances did not contain specific pledges that Israel would not join a Western-inspired pact (pledges, which would have harmed Israel's standing with the Western powers), the Soviet Union was not satisfied. Reacting to Israel's acceptance of the UN resolution on the Korean War in June 1950, the Soviet press accused Israel of having 'sided openly with the American aggressors'.[30]

Formally speaking, however, diplomatic relations between the two countries continued to be polite and at times, talks between their diplomats ended on a warm note. In the UN, Soviet delegates did nothing to harm Israeli interests; they seldom participated in Arab-Israeli disputes and in most cases abstained from voting. Throughout the years 1950-1953 their attitude towards the Arab-Israeli conflict was one of 'strict' or 'passive' neutrality.[31] The reason lay in the respective political distance between the parties to the conflict and the Soviet Union: while the Soviet-Israeli relationship worsened, no progress had been made in Soviet-Arab relations. In the years 1952-1954, Soviet attitudes towards Egypt, Israel's most important adversary, oscillated between cautious reserve and open enmity according to the new Egyptian regime's line vis-a-vis Britain.[32]

Though the Soviet-Israeli relationship had considerably deteriorated in the four years following Golda Meyerson's arrival in Moscow, it was not so tense as to lead observers to expect a major crisis. Indeed, some hopeful signs were registered in the autumn of 1952. Prime Minister Ben Gurion's cable of congratulation to Stalin on the 35th anniversary of the October Revolution was placed very prominently in the Soviet press and in the UN, Soviet delegate Gromyko found praise for Israeli efforts to bring about a compromise on the question of Korea.[33] When the crisis between the Communist block countries and Israel finally erupted in November 1952, its origins had less to do with international issues than with domestic developments in the Soviet Union and in her satellites.

For reasons too complex to be discussed here, Stalin in the late 1940s had decided that a major purge of the leadership of communist parties in Eastern Europe had to be carried out. In a way, this was a repetition of the Moscow show trials of the 1930s which were designed to finally eliminate all potential opponents to Stalin's rule. After the first trials in Hungary and Bulgaria in 1949, whose main direction was anti-Titoist, there was a short lull. Then, on 20 November 1952, the campaign was resumed; fourteen leading party and state functionaries, including the former General Secretary of the Czechoslovak CP Rudolf Slansky (who had been arrested a year earlier), were put on trial and charged with a Trotskyite-Titoist-Zionist-bourgeois conspiracy aimed at overthrowing the socialist order in Czechoslovakia and selling out the country to Western imperialism. Of the fourteen accused persons, eleven were of Jewish origin, as was duly stressed by the state prosecutor. All defendants admitted the charges and eleven of them were sentenced to death and executed.

In the 1960s, when the Slansky trials were reviewed by party organs in Czechoslovakia, it was revealed that their antisemitic tone had been the result of orders transmitted to Czechoslovak security organs by Soviet 'advisers'. This was not purely a tactical measure to make the trials popular by diverting discontent with living conditions against a Jewish scapegoat; it was also a sign of the paranoia and the intensified antisemitism of Stalin's last years. The atmosphere of anti-Jewish suspicion reached a climax when it was announced in the Soviet press on 13 January 1953 that a group of prominent (and mostly Jewish) physicians had for years been scheming against the lives of leading Soviet personalities and of the great leader himself. As their main employer, the Soviet press named the 'Joint', the American-Jewish welfare organization, whose alleged espionage acti-vites in co-operation with US and Israeli secret services had already served as an important part in the scenario of the Slansky trial.[34]

In neither of these two cases could the Israeli government let the charges pass without comment. On behalf of his govern-ment and of the Jewish people, Foreign Minister Moshe Sharett condemned the Slansky trial while it was still under way on 24 November 1952. In an address to the Knesset on 19 January 1953 he also called the Doctors' Plot 'a fabrication whose purpose it is to frighten the Jewish community of the Soviet Union and ... in the States allied to it, and ... to prepare the population of those countries for possible reprisals against the Jews'.[35] In this emotionally charged sitation Czechoslovakia and Poland suspended their diplomatic relations with Israel. Then, in Tel Aviv, a small bomb planted by unknown perpetrators caused some damage to the building of the Soviet Legation when it exploded on 9 February. In spite of swift and sincere Israeli apologies, this incident was seized upon by the Soviet Union as a welcome opportunity to break off diplomatic relations. On 12 February 1953, a painful divorce ended the two years of 'honeymooning' and four years of a crisis-riddled 'marriage'.

A new beginning was briefly made possible by Stalin's death on 5 March 1953, which provoked some profound changes in Soviet domestic and foreign policies. Their most important expression in our context was the almost immediate halt of the antisemitic witch-hunt and the renewal of Soviet-Israeli diplomatic ties.

As early as 4 April 1953 the new Ministry of Internal Affairs announced that the accusations against the Kremlin doctors had been based on fake evidence. At the same time, Soviet diplomats in Sofia signalled their government's interest in a resumption of relations with Israel. By the end of the year the legations in Moscow and Tel-Aviv again took up their business. It was noted with satisfaction in Israel that the ceremonial handing-over of the Soviet envoy's credentials took place in Jerusalem. The Soviet Union had therefore become the first major power to recognize *de facto* the city's function as Israel's capital. There were other encouraging signs, too, such as an increase in Soviet-Israeli trade. Between 1954 and 1956, in fact, supplies from the USSR covered 30 to 40 per cent of Israeli's oil needs.[36] But the normalization of mutual relations did not result in a lasting improvement because soon new elements in Soviet policy clashed with what might have been a genuine interest in coming to terms with the Jewish state.

For Israel, one of the most important developments in 1954/55 was a gradual improvement in Soviet-Egyptian relations. In the first instance this was due to the fact that Egypt's opposition to the setting up of the Baghdad Pact in 1955 coincided with continued Soviet objections to this Western scheme. Secondly, Nasser's Egypt along with Tito's Yugoslavia and Nehru's India, had become one of the cornerstones of the newly emerging neutralist block whose first summit in Bandung on April 1955 was warmly welcomed by the

Soviet Union. The new Soviet leadership recognized the anti-Western potential of the policy of non-alignment and by courting Nasser, Tito and Nehru it hoped to gain influence within the Third World.

It is true that the two major Soviet statements on the Middle East at the time (in April 1955 and a year later) did not contain any attacks on Israel and even indicated that the Soviet government would pursue an even-handed policy on the Arab-Israeli conflict.[37] But Soviet deeds showed that it was prepared to go a long way to please Egypt. The Soviet veto in the Security Council in March 1954, which prevented Egypt from being condemned for repeated interference with ship movements through the Suez canal destined for Israel, was proof that it would not consider such cases on their own merits but rather in respect of its relationship with Egypt. Israeli interests were most clearly hurt with the conclusion of the Czechslovak-Egyptian arms deal in September 1955. Just as in 1948, Czechoslovakia was utilized as a pawn in the Soviet game since the bulk of the weaponry which Egypt received under the agreement originated in the Soviet Union.[38] By 1955, the Soviet-Israeli relationship had lost its inner dynamic and evolved into a mere function of Soviet-Arab and in particular of Soviet-Egyptian relations.[39] The Czech arms deal, concluded at the time of increasing tension on the Israeli-Egyptian border, was considered by Israelis as a serious threat to their existence, though this may not have been the Soviet intention.[40] The deal was one of the reasons which prompted Israel to join Britain and France in planning the Suez campaign even if her aims on several points differed from those of her temporary allies.

Israel's attack in the Sinai on 29 October 1956 and her co-operation in the Anglo-French Suez operation gave the Soviet Union a golden opportunity to divert world opinion from its own armed intervention in Hungary. At the same time, it could show Egypt and the rest of the world, verbally at least, that only the socialist countries were dedicated allies of ex-colonial states in their struggle against imperialism and neo-colonialism. The exceptionally aggressive tone of Russian statements marked the final deterioration of Soviet-Israeli relations. In a note to the Israeli government on 5 November 1956, Soviet Prime Minister Bulganin wrote:

> Carrying out the will of other people, acting according to instructions from abroad, the Government of Israel is toying with the fate of peace, with the fate of its own people, in a criminal and irresponsible manner. It is sowing such hatred for the State of Israel among the peoples of the East as cannot but affect the future of Israel and which will place in jeopardy the very existence of Israel as a state.[41]

In spite of the fact that this time diplomatic relations were not broken off and existed until the June 1967 war, the Soviet-Israeli relationship never recovered from the blows it received in the wake of the Soviet-Arab rapprochement during the mid-1950s. In the two decades since then, the Soviet Union has more or less consistently supported the Arab side in the Middle East conflict. But such developments as the continued Soviet stress on the right of Israel to exist, the emigration of a large number of Soviet Jews and the deterioration of Soviet-Arab relations in the 1970s might one day facilitate a Soviet reassessment of relations with Israel which would certainly make progress towards peace in the region easier. Because of the unique mixture of global, regional, domestic and ideological aspects of Soviet policy towards Israel, such a reconsideration, however, is not likely to be very near.

NOTES

1. See, Edmund Silberner, *Sozialisten zur Judenfrage* (Berlin, 1962) and Robert Wistrich, *Revolutionary Jews from Marx to Trotsky* (London, 1976). For recent brief summaries, see Bruno Frei, 'Marxist Interpretations of the Jewish Question', *Wiener Library Bulletin*, 1975, new series nos. 35/36, pp. 2-8, and Robert Wistrich's chapter, 'Marxism and Jewish Nationalism: The Theoretical Roots of Confrontation', in this book.
2. See Hyman Lumer (ed.), *Lenin on the Jewish Question* (New York, 1974). For a Soviet exposition of Lenin's views, see A.K. Azizian, *Leninskaia natsional'naia politika v razvitii i deistvii* (Moscow, 1972). For

the 'Bund', see Ezra Mendelsohn, *Class Struggle in the Pale* (Cambridge, 1970) and Henry Tobias, *The Jewish Bund in Russia from its Origins to 1905* (Stanford, 1972). *Cf.* also Ran Marom, 'The Bolsheviks and the Balfour Declaration 1917-1920', in this book.

3. Guido G. Goldman, *Zionism under Soviet Rule: 1917-1928* (New York, 1960) p. 80.

4. On the Poale Zion, see Mario Offenberg, *Kommunismus in Palästina, Nation und Klasse in der antikolonialen Revolution* (Meisenheim am Glan, 1975) pp. 64-143 (with a strong anti-Zionist bias). For a detailed study of the Yevesektsia, See Zvi. Y. Gitelman, *Jewish Nationality and Soviet Politics. The Jewish Sections of the CPSU, 1917-1930* (Princeton, 1972).

5. For the story of Birobidzhan, see Chimen Abramsky, 'The Biro-Bidzhan Project, 1927-1959', in Lionel Kochan (ed.), *The Jews in Soviet Russia since 1917* (London, 1970) pp. 62-75; *cf. ibid.* p.72, Gitelman, *op. cit.* pp. 513-523, and Benjamin West (ed.), *Struggles of a Generation. The Jews under Soviet Rule* (Tel Aviv, 1959) pp. 15, 69-136, 176-187, 200-209.

6. Oded Eran/Jerome E. Singer, 'Soviet Policy towards the Arab World 1955-71', *Survey*/London/, Vol. 17 (Autumn 1971), pp. 10-29, here pp. 10-11,fn. 2.

7. For the history of the PCP, see Walter Laqueur, *Communism and Nationalism in the Middle East* (London, 2nd ed. 1957) pp. 73-110, Ivar Spector, *The Soviet Union and the Muslim World 1917-1958* (Seattle, 1959) pp. 156-168, Jacob Ben-Tov, *Communism and Zionism in Palestine: The Comintern and the Political Unrest in the 1920's* (Cambridge/Mass., 1974), Shmuel Dothan, 'The Jewish Section of the Palestine Communist Party, 1937-1939', in Daniel Carpi/Gedalia Yogev (eds.), *Zionism. Studies in the History of the Zionist Movement and of the Jewish Community in Palestine*, Vol. 1 (Tel Aviv, 1975) pp. 243-262, and the brief but pretentious ('first full study') book by Dunia Habib Nahas, *The Israeli Communist Party* (London, 1976).

8. Kurt Blumenfeld, *Erlebte Judenfrage. Ein Vierteljahrhundert deutscher Zionismus* (Stuttgart, 1962) pp. 134-138.

9. Joseph Berger/Barzilai/, *Nothing but the Truth* (New York, 1971) p. 7.

10. Cf. Ivar Spector, 'The Soviet Union and the Palestine Conflict', in Ibrahim Abu-Lughod (ed.), *The Transformation of Palestine. Essays on the origin and development of the Arab-Israeli conflict* (Evanston/Ill., 1971) pp. 413-442, here p. 416, and *Memories. The Autobiography of Nahum Goldmann* (London, 1970).

11. Cf. Walter Laqueur, *The Soviet Union and the Middle East* (London, 1959) pp. 113-135, David Ben Gurion, 'Three New Friends for Zionism—Bolshevik Diplomat Hails the Kibbutz', *Jewish Observer and Middle East Review*, 13 March 1964, pp. 22, 24 (Ben Gurion erroneously gives 1942 as the date of Maiskii's visit), Yehoshua A. Gilboa, *The Black Years of Soviet Jewry* (Boston, 1971) pp. 56-71, Yaacov Ro'i, 'Soviet Policy in the Middle East: The Case of Palestine in World War II', *Cahiers du Monde russe et soviétique*, Vol.

XV (1974), pp. 373-408, Lucjan Dobroszycki, 'Restoring Jewish Life in Post-War Poland', *Soviet Jewish Affairs*, Vol. 3 (1973) no. 2, pp. 58-72, here p. 70, and 'The Soviet Union and the Jews during World War II. Documents from the Zionist Archives, Jerusalem, and British Colonial Office Documents. The Visit of Two Soviet Representatives in Palestine, 1942', *ibid.*, Vol. 4 (1974) no. 1, pp. 73-89.

12. On this, see Joseph Heller, 'Roosevelt, Stalin and the Palestine Problem at Yalta', *Wiener Library Bulletin*, 1977, new series nos. 41/42, pp. 25-35.

13. See Bartley C. Crum, *Behind the Silken Curtain. A personal account of Anglo-American diplomacy in Palestine and the Middle East* (New York, 1947).

14. See, *e.g.*, Vladmir B. Lutskii, *Palestinskaia problema* (Moscow, 1946), English summary on A.R.C: Bolton, *Soviet Middle East Studies: An Analysis and Bibliography* (Oxford, 1959), Part VI, pp. 4-5, and K. Serezhin, 'The Problems of the Arab East', *New Times*/Moscow/, 1 February 1946, reprinted in Yaacov Ro'i, *From Encroachement to Involvement. A Documentary Study of Soviet Policy in the Middle East,*, 1945-1973 (Jersusalem, 1974) pp. 23-27.

15. On the Brichah, see Yehuda Bauer, *Flight and Rescue: Brichah* (New York, 1970) and Ehud Avriel, *Open the Gates! A personal story of 'illegal' immigration to Israel* (London, 1975). There are reports of direct Soviet technical involvement in the Brichah such as the provision of trains; see Lester Velie, *Countdown in the Holy Land* (New York, 1969) pp. 20-23.

16. Essential excerpts from Gromyko's speech are reprinted in Ro'i, *From Encroachement . . . , op. cit.* pp. 38-41 (quotation p. 39).

17. For Zionist reactions to the speech, see Arnold Krammer, *The Forgotten Friendship: Israel and the Soviet Bloc, 1947-53* (Urbana/Ill., 1974) p. 17.

18. A detailed analysis of the Czechoslovak-Israel military co-operation forms the core of Krammer's book (*op. cit.* pp. 54-122). *Cf.* also Ezer Weizman. *On Eagles Wings* (London, 1977).

19. See David Horowitz, *State in the Making* (New York, 1953) pp. 270-274.

20. For Soviet press coverage, see Benjamin Pinkus (comp. & ed.), *Jews and the Jewish People 1948-1953. Collected Materials from the Soviet Press. Vol. 3: The State of Israel.* Parts 1 & 2 (Jerusalem, 1973). The Soviet press and Soviet actions in the UN are analyzed in great detail in Mary Newcomb Allen's unpublished Ph.D. thesis 'The Policy of the U.S.S.R. towards the State of Israel: 1948-1958' (University of London, 1961). Apart from the studies by Krammer and Ro'i cited above, the basic published works are: Avigdor Dagan, *Moscow and Jerusalem. Twenty Years of Relations between Israel and the Soviet Union* (London, 1970); Surendra Bhutani, *Israeli-Soviet Cold War* (Delhi, 1975); Rais A. Khan, 'Israel and the Soviet Union: A Review of Postwar Relations', *Orbis*/Philadelphia/, Vol. IX (1966) no. 4,

pp. 999-1012; David Morison, 'Russia, Israel and the Arabs', *Mizan*, Vol. IX (1967) no. 3, pp. 91-107; Karmi Schweitzer, 'Soviet Policy towards Israel 1946-1952/1953-1956' *ibid.*, Vol. XI (1969) nos. 1 & 3, pp. 18-30/174-181; Spector, 'The Soviet Union and the Palestine Conflict', *op. cit.;* Yehoshua A. Gilboa, 'Soviet Politics On Palestine: Tradition and Change', *International Problems*/Tel Aviv/, Vol. X (1971) no. 3-4 (20), pp. 11-19; Aryeh Y. Yodfat, 'The Soviet Union and Israel', *ibid.*, Vol. XIII (1974) no. 1-3 (25)/special issue/, pp. 347-361; Nadav Safran, 'The Soviet Union and Israel', 1947-1969', in Ivo J. Lederer/Wayne S. Vucinich (eds.), *The Soviet Union and the Middle East. The Post-World War II Era* (Stanford, 1974). Soviet publications generally avoid any detailed discussion of the Soviet-Israeli relationship and recent works tend to completely distort the historical record and contemporary Soviet positions; see, *e.g.*, G.S. Nikitina, 'Palestina posle vtoroi mirovoi voiny. Obrazovanie gosudarstva Izrail' i ego vneshniaia politika v 1948-1951 gg.', in B.M. Potskhveria/E.A. Orlov (eds'), *Mezhdunarodnye otnosheniia na Blizhnem i Srednem Vostoke posle vtoroi mirovoi voiny. /40-50-e gody/*(Moscow, 1974) pp. 168-199, who (on p. 188) maintains that one of the reasons for Israel's victory in the War of Independence was her financial means which enabled 'mass purchases of weapons *above all from the USA* ' (my emphasis).

21. Laqueur, *The Soviet Union ... op. cit.* p. 147; this is accepted by Morison, *op. cit.* p. 91. For clear refutations of this view, see Dagan, *op. cit.* p. 21, and Safran, *op. cit.* p. 162.

22. Some authors see the anti-British impulse as a sufficient reason for Soviet behaviour; see *e.g.*, Abraham S. Becker/Arnold L. Horelick, *Soviet Policy in the Middle East*/Rand Memorandum R-504-FF/ (Santa Monica/Calif., 1970) pp. 17-18. For Soviet views of the American role in the Middle East, see Izrail' A. Genin, *Palestinskiaia problema* (Moscow, 1948) pp. 9-14, and Lidiia N. Vatolina, 'Palestinskaia problema'. *Mirovoe khoziaistvo i mirovai politika*, no. 12/1947, pp. 63-77.—It has also been suggested that the Soviet Union might have been motivated by a desire to 'Balkanize' the Middle East or by humanitarian considerations; see George Lenczowski, 'Soviet Policy in the Middle East. A Summary of Developments Since 1945', *Journal of International Affairs*/New York/, Vol. VIII (1954) no. 1, pp. 52-61, here p. 59, Laqueur, *The Soviet Union ..., op. cit.* p. 146, and Wolf Kogan, 'Soviet-Israel Relations', unpublished Certificate Essay, Russian Institute, Columbia University (New York, 1950) p. 37.

23. Yehoshua A. Gilboa, 'The 1948 Zionist Wave in Moscow', *Soviet Jewish Affairs*, Vol. 1 (1971) no. 2, pp. 35-39. For the Polina Molotov episode, see Marie Syrkin, *Golda Meir. Israel's Leader* (New York, rev. ed. 1969) pp. 229-232. Golda Meir relates the story in her memoirs, too, but she obviously confuses Polina Molotov and Ivy Litvinov.

24. See Gilboa, *The Black Years ...*, *op. cit.*

25. See 'Imitative Efforts', *New Times* (Moscow), no. 51/1948, p. 16.

26. *Izvestiia*, 26 January 1949, quoted in Krammer, *op. cit.* p. 142 *Cf.* also

Yaacov Ro'i, 'A Foiled Friendship', *Soviet Jewish Affairs*, Vol. 5 (1975) no. 2, pp. 112-114, here p. 114.

27. See, *e.g.*, O. Prudkov, 'Tel'-avivskii posledovatel' Achesona', *Literaturnaia gazeta*, 25 March 1950.

28. For an English translation of Lutskii's lecture, see Ro'i, *From Encroachement ... op. cit.* pp. 73-79, quotation p. 78.

29. *Cf.* Dagan, *op. cit.* p. 48, and Krammer, *op.c it.* pp. 134, 151-159.

30. 'Podpevala amerikanskikh agressorov', *Novoe vremia*, no. 28/1950, pp. 20-21. *Cf.* Dagan, *op. cit.* pp. 57-62, Krammer, *op. cit.* pp. 181-183, Ro'i, 'Soviet-Israeli Relations ... ', op. cit. p. 137, and Walter Eytan, *The First Ten Years. A Diplomatic History of Israel* (New York, 1958) pp. 142-144.

31. See Oles Smolansky, 'Soviet Policy in the Arab East, 1945-1957', *Journal of International Affairs*/New York/, Vol. XIII (1959) no. 2, pp. 126-140, here p. 127, Ro'i, *From Encroachement ...*, *op. cit.* p. 115, and Dagan *op. cit.* p. 55.

32. *Cf.* Laqueur, *The Soviet Union ...*, *op. cit.* pp. 151-155, 194-197.

33. See *Pravda*, 8 November 1952, and Dagan, *op. cit.* pp. 62-64.

34. For details of the on-going anti-Jewish campaign in the Soviet Union, see Gilboa, *The Black Years ...*, *op. cit.* pp. 187-256, 283-310.

35. Quoted in Dagan, *op. cit.* p. 67.

36. For the significance of the Jerusalem gesture, see "Russia—Friend or Foe?', *The Israel Economist*, Vol. IX (December 1953) pp. 243-244. For trade figures, see Robert Loring Allen, *Middle Eastern Economic Relations with the Soviet Union, Eastern Europe and Mainland China* (Charlottesville/Va., 1958) pp. 18, 80, Sewer Plockier, 'Israeli Trade with the Socialist Block', *New Outlook*, September 1968, pp. 16-22, 'Trading with Communist Europe (I)', *The Israel Economist*, Vol. XI (May 1955), pp. 82-88, and Harold J. Berman, 'Force Majeure and the Denial of an Export License under Soviet Law: A Comment on Jordan Investments Ltd. v. soiuznefteksport', *Harvard Law Review*, Vol. 73 (1960) no. 6, pp. 1128-1146, here p. 1129.

37. For the English version of the two declarations, see Ro'i *From Encroachement ...*, *op. cit.* pp. 136-140, 163-165.

38. For a detailed account of the arms deal, see Uri Ra'anan, *The USSR Arms the Third World. Case Studies in Soviet Foreign Policy* (Cambridge/Mass., 1969) pp. 13-172.

39. This is also reflected in the literature on Soviet-Israeli relations; detailed scholarly analysis of post-1954 developments can only be found in the studies by Mary Allen, Dagan and Bhutani.

40. *Cf.* Dagan, *op. cit.* pp. 94-96, 127, 207.

41. Full text in Ro'i, *From Encroachement ...*, *op. cit.* pp. 190-191.

Prisoners in Prague:
Israelis in the Slansky Trial

Arnold Krammer

The years 1947 and 1948 saw a temporary rapprochement between Israel and the Soviet bloc, during which time Czechoslovakia became the chief source of military aid for the desperate Israelis. The motives on both sides were transparent. The USSR saw in the potential independence of Israel a long-sought opportunity to undermine the British position in the Middle East, and proceeded to supply the Haganah (the Jewish underground army), albeit haltingly and at great cost, with surplus war material.

However, when, by the middle of 1949, it became evident that Israel would not be politically influenced by earlier Soviet aid, the Kremlin began to support the Arabs. As diplomatic relations deteriorated, and a new wave of anti-semitic purges was initiated within the Eastern bloc, the Soviet-Zionist honeymoon came to an end, and with it an epoch in the emergence of Israel when only the Eastern bloc supplied the newly born state with the means of survival, while the West observed a crippling arms embargo.

Given the code name *Rechesh* (Purchase), Haganah buyers arrived quietly in Prague in December of 1947, armed only with an introduction from David Ben-Gurion, scribbled on a sheet of notepaper, reading:

30-9-47

To all our Comrades in Europe:
Please give the Bearer all the help he may need in carrying
out his mission which, at this time and under the conditions likely to develop, is of primary importance and at
the heart of everything we are striving for.
With greetings from Zion,
David Ben-Gurion.[1]

Thus a group of several dozen authorized buyers arrived
secretly in Prague—for the Haganah was compelled to
operate from the underground—to conduct necessary negotiations. Among them was Shimon Ornstein, whose later stay
in Prague was to involve him in the Slansky purge.

To complicate matters, a group of Palestinians, operating
independently of the *Rechesh* buyers, roamed the capitals of
Eastern Europe using their personal and political contacts to
secure additional aid. Mordechai Oren of the left-wing
Zionist movement, Hashomer Hatzair, and Shmuel Mikunis,
a leading member of Israel's Communist Party, *MAKI*, were
the most noteworthy among these roving ambassadors.

Born in Galicia in 1905, Mordechai Oren emigrated to
Palestine in 1929 and became a leading left-wing activist,
eventually helping to found the broadly Socialist *MAPAM*.
After 1945, he made political tours, meeting Communist and
trade union leaders, and attending various conferences
throughout Europe as an unofficial spokesman for the Zionist
left. His contribution to the success of the official *Rechesh*
team was enormous. While the Haganah, in an effort to
remain above politics, especially the politics of the extreme
left, dissociated itself from Oren and Mikunis, they, particularly Oren, proved themselves very useful in providing
personal contacts with members of the Czech government.
Referring to this period, Oren writes:

> In Prague, in the middle of 1947, as a delegate of the
> Histadrut, I took part in a meeting of the FSM. From there
> I left for other countries: Poland, Hungary, Bulgaria.
> During my stay I worked in three basic ways: I contacted
> various centres of my movement. I explained the meaning
> of our political fight in Palestine to political contacts

within and outside the government, and I used every opportunity to explain our struggle at the mass level through the radio and the press. . . . In this way I met with syndicalist leaders and talked to responsible groups of workers on the problems raised by our fight.[2]

By the time of Israel's independence, Oren had had interviews with many government officials including such notable Soviet leaders as Mikhailov and Petrenko in Ankara, Gussev in London, Yakovlev, Miranov and Dluginski in Warsaw, and Kuznetzov in Berlin. There is little doubt that Oren's contacts helped the *Rechesh* mission to secure the urgently needed weapons and aircraft. Nor should the efforts of Mikunis, whose later articles in the Comintern publication *For Lasting Peace for a People's Democracy* (15-4-1948) served to clarify the Kremlin's position with regard to Israel, go unnoticed. Between May 1948 and the end of February 1949, Israel received from Czechoslovakia almost 44 million rounds of ammunition, rifles, light and heavy machine-guns, as well as consignments of surplus Messerschmitt fighters and spare parts.[3]

There was no reason to suppose that the Communist coup d'état of February 1948 would materially affect the activities of the Israeli purchasing mission in Prague, particularly since it included several left-wing members as well as a free-floating front of independents like Mordechai Oren. Yet the importance lay in the close ties the Communist coup had now established with Moscow, and the disquieting events in progress there.

There is little doubt that, during the early stages of Russia's support for a partitioned Palestine and the State of Israel, hostility to Zionism rather than to the state itself inspired Soviet policy. The appearance of Golda Meir in Moscow as Israel's first ambassador created a sensation, not merely because she was only the second woman in the diplomatic corps (the first being Mrs Pandit), but more particularly because she represented the reborn Jewish state. Her arrival acted as a catalyst for the upsurge of Jewish identification among Soviet Jewry, many of whom jubilantly surrounded Israeli officials at every public occasion and forced their way into every Embassy party. A number of diplomats and Soviet personalities, among them Mrs Molotov, publicly and privately admitted their Jewish background and offered their hopes for Israel's future.[4] When the Israeli delegation appeared at the only synagogue in Moscow for the Rosh Hashanah services and found themselves mobbed by enthusiastic crowds of about 30,000 to 50,000 people, the Kremlin, faced with what appeared to be a reawakening Jewish national consciousness, became apprehensive. The signal indicating official opposition to any further displays of Soviet Jewry's involvement in the renascence of Jewish statehood was Ilya Ehrenburg's article in *Pravda* (21-9-48) which redefined the official distinction between the 'mystic' Zionists and the current Soviet support for a Jewish homeland in Palestine.[5] This warning evidently failed to impress Moscow's Jews, for when Mrs Meir and her staff went to attend Yom Kippur services, tens of thousands of emotional worshippers again packed the synagogue and overflowed into the streets. Another warning, an article in *Einigkeit*, the Yiddish Communist paper, was equally unavailing. Russian Jews started to apply to the legation for visas, requesting its co-operation in obtaining exit permits. The Soviet authorities responded by banning all emigration to Israel and by arresting and deporting those who persisted. As early as December 1948, other satellite nations began to join the familiar anti-Zionist line.

Contrary to Soviet hopes, the new Israeli government, headed by David Ben-Gurion, announced that it would favour neither East nor West. Israel's position of non-commitment was facilitated by political, financial and military assistance from both blocs.[6] At the end of the Arab-Israeli war in 1949, Israeli-Soviet relations took a new turn. Diminishing Soviet support for Israel and denial of loan applications, coupled with a constant flow of economic aid from the United States and American Jewry, contributed to Israel's deviating from her course of non-commitment to a closer alliance with the Western bloc.[7]

The majority of the members of the *Rechesh* team, having successfully completed their purchase of essential military supplies, were recalled to Israel, leaving a normally staffed

Embassy under the direction of Ehud Avriel. Eastern bloc relations deteriorated quickly as a result both of Israel's failure to accord Soviet interests the expected preference and of the centrifugal tensions within the Soviet Empire itself. Tito had already led Yugoslavia towards its 'separate path to Socialism', and the Greek civil war had resulted in an anti-Communist victory and the establishment of the Truman Doctrine. The economies of the satellite states, unlike those of the Western European recipients of Marshall Aid, were chaotic. The devastation wrought by the war, coupled with nationalization, notoriously poor planning at the directive level, and one-sided trade pacts which funnelled goods to the Soviet Union, brought the satellites to the verge of bankruptcy. A 'hard-line' shake-up, designed to divert public opinion and, at the same time, bring the satellites under tighter control, was Moscow's answer to a deteriorating situation.

Czechoslovakia's dire economic situation in particular necessitated a radical re-appraisal of her market priorities, and, despite heavy Soviet pressure to harness the floundering Czech economy to decidedly unfavourable trade agreements,, the West remained an increasingly attractive trade alternative. Lenin's NEP experiment with 'partial capitalism' might well have been the ideological precedent guiding the Economic Planning Commission in Czechoslovakia. The Commission, for example, agred upon a division of foreign trade in the proportion of 55 per cent to the West and 45 per cent to the Socialist states and entered into promising negotiations with Western firms whose factories in Czechoslovakia had been nationalized following the February coup.[8] In addition, hard bargaining by the Ministry of Foreign Trade with other satellite states over import-export agreements at world market prices plainly indicated the new Czech government's intention to uphold the nation's economic interests irrespective of Moscow's directives. Stalin did not fail to draw political conclusions from such independent action, especially after Yugoslavia's fateful defection of the previous year. Although Rudolf Slansky's widow, Josefa Slanska, maintained in the introduction to her memoirs that '. . . it [the trial] appears to have been completely pointless in its horror . . . and its actual motivation can probably be understood only by a psychiatrist or a psychopath ...',[8] there is little doubt that Stalin demanded a purge to re-establish Moscow's control over its satellites. The best summary of the basic issue involved in the purge of the most prominent Czech and Slovak Communist is offered by Eugene Loebl who states: '... It is obvious that the trial condemned one of the [Czech] Party's basic political concepts, that of giving expression to the interests and the necessity of a Czech socialist organization in the CSR, an idea that ... was incompatible with those held by Stalin, Beria and perhaps others too.'[10]

The fact that the 'hard-line' shake-up which resulted included a large measure of antisemitism, however, was independent of these events and was rather a product of the Byzantine manoeuvring in the Soviet Union, coupled with the time-honoured Eastern European stratagem of using latent antisemitism as a political weapon. The sudden and unexplained death of Andrei Zhdanov on 31 August 1948 resulted in a major struggle for succession and, in the ensuing infighting, antisemitism was used as a political weapon. In late October 1948, General Antonov, the Jewish Chief of Staff of the Red Army, was replaced by a non-Jew, General Shtemenko. The Yiddish newspaper *Einigkeit*, the Yiddish theatre in Moscow and other Jewish institutions were suspended. For the first time small but ominous verbal changes appeared in the usual slogans. Now the adjective 'homeless', never applied before 1949, was added to 'cosmo-politan' which left no doubt that it was the Jews rather than any other minority group who were being indicted.

The underlying issues, culminating in the Slansky trial, were further obscured and complicated by an internal power struggle between Rudolf Slansky and Klement Gottwald. Slansky, of Jewish origin, had played a major part as the Central Secretary of the Czech Communist Part at the seizure of power in February 1948. He had also helped to supervise the aid supplied to the *Rechesh* team in Prague. Klement Gottwald, President of the Czechoslovak Republic, while endeavouring to please Stalin, also tried to concentrate as much political power as possible in his own hands. Political intrigue was not new to either man; for on 14 March 1951, the ambitious Gottwald, with Slansky's hesitant concurrence, had forced the resignation of their colleague, Vladimir Clementis, the Foreign Minister, a loyal party member whose only failing seems to have been his membership of the Czech Government in exile in London during the war years.

Political purges which linked high-ranking defendants to an alleged 'Zionist-Titoist-Anglo-American espionage' conspiracy, began almost simultaneously in various satellite countries, starting with the trials of the Hungarian and Bulgarian leadership. In 1949, the Hungarian Foreign Minister, Laszlo Rajk, was placed on trial and accused of enigmatic anti-party activities involving 'Titoist deviationists' (although, or perhaps because, his political rival, the secretary of the Hungarian Communist Party, Matyas Rakosi, had probably been more sympathetic to Tito before 1948) as well as veterans of the Spanish International Brigades and 'Zionist groups'. In the summer of 1949, he was found guilty and executed.

Similarly, the veteran Bulgarian Communist leader, Traicho Kostov, was accused in the same year of participation in a 'Titoist-Zionist' conspiracy. As in the Rajk trial, the proceedings were initiated by a political rival, Vulko Chervenkov, who used Kostov's own incautious protests against Soviet exploitation to eliminate him. The Bulgarian trial was unique inasmuch as it mentioned for the first time an allegedly Zionist witness—albeit an absent and imaginary one—and also because it provided one of the very rare occasions when an accused 'traitor', in this case Kostov, told a shocked court room that his confession had been extracted by torture and that he was innocent of all charges.

It was in this tense atmosphere that several Israelis, Mordechai Oren and Shimon Ornstein among them, travelled to and from Prague in mid-1951. Mordechai Oren, on another of his political tours, this time to attend the Congress of the Communist World federation of Trade Unions in East Berlin, returned in October 1951 to Prague for the last leg of his journey. There he met a Soviet diplomatic representative, hoping to persuade him to allow Jews from East Germany and the Soviet zone of Austria to emigrate to Israel. Unsuccessful in his efforts, he made leisurely arrangements for his journey home, left on the night train for Vienna, and at three in the morning of 1 November 1951 was stopped at the Czech-Austrian border and asked to complete a few formalities. The few minutes' delay mentioned by the secret police were to occupy Oren and the Czechs for four and a half years.

Shimon Ornstein, one of the original members of the *Rechesh* mission in 1947-48, had become a member of the Israeli Czech Embassy, and frequently travelled between Prague and Israel on official business. In his recently published memoirs, Ornstein describes the daily editorial outbursts against 'Anglo-American espionage and Zionist groups'; his growing apprehension of remaining in Prague; the minor, inexplicable incidents which later proved to have been the work of the dreaded STB (Czech Secret Police); and the cancellation of his visa by the Ministry of Foreign Trade in October 1951.[11] Oren, strangely impervious to this atmosphere, and Ornstein spent much of that last month together, discussing the growing tension which culminated in the announcement by President Klement Gottwald that the recently dismissed party leader Rudolf Slansky was believed to have been the agent of a foreign power and that, to prevent his escape, he had been placed under arrest. Oren and Ornstein made plans to leave Prague on 31 October, and to meet again in Austria. Following Oren's departure, Shimon Ornstein and Shimshon Purmand, another Israeli, who happened to be in Prague buying textile machinery for Israel, left by car for Znaim on the Austro-Czech frontier. Both men were in good spirits, going home after having successfully completed their business, and neither suspected anything but incompetence when they were detained at the border pending authentication of their exit visas. Following many hours of argument, Ornstein and Purmand decided to drive to the nearby town of Znaim where they could more comfortably await the outcome of such bureaucratic inefficiency. For the next thirteen days, Shimon Ornstein made daily trips to the local police station and made indignant calls to the Ministry of Foreign Trade, the Ministry of the Interior, and the Israeli Embassy in Prague, demanding to know the reason for the delay. He was confidently assured by all officials that he had no cause for concern and his normal exit visa would be forthcoming. No one yet knew that his colleague Oren had already been in STB custody for nearly two weeks. Punctually at midnight on 13 November, six STB men, in long leather coats, entered their room and placed Ornstein and Purmand under arrest. The remainder of that night and part of the next day were spent in driving back to Prague and, upon reaching the outskirts of the capital, both were blindfolded and remained so during the ride to their destination and throughout the entire next day of brutal preliminary interrogation. They were transferred on the evening of the 14th to another destination, the name of which Shimon Ornstein learned only twenty-two months later when he was finally brought to trial and sentenced to life imprisonment: Ruzyne Prison, headquarters of the Czech Secret Police.

Since the charges against Slansky and his colleagues were based on their participation in 'Zionist-Anglo-American espionage organizations', it was necessary for the state to produce foreign witnesses—preferably left-wing Zionists—to corroborate the charges. It therefore became the task of the STB to mould the three arrested Israelis, Oren, Ornstein and Purmand, into the missing link between Slansky and the 'Trotskyite-Titoist-Zionist' spy ring. It took exactly one year of relentless interrogation, mental and physical torture, and an assortment of inhuman techniques designed to reduce the witnesses to dazed and obedient puppets.

A problem arose, however, when Shimshon Purmand, one of the three arrested Israelis, turned out to be a Persian Jew living in Israel who had never completed the formality of securing Israeli citizenship, which was essential for his suitability as a witness. Nevertheless, he rotted in a Czech STB prison for a whole year and was released only after the successful conclusion of the Prague show trials. Evidently the Secret Police were afraid that he might give the show away were he released too early. The other two, however, were considered perfectly suitable for the parts allotted to them: both were citizens of Israel, Zionists and life-long socialists, enjoying the personal and political friendships such militant devotion to the cause inevitably engendered. One was a left-wing Zionist, an unofficial roving ambassador who had spent the majority of his adult life going from conference to conference in an effort to influence government and trade union officials to aid the Zionist movement. At the moment of his arrest, Oren was a member of the pro-Communist MAPAM Party in the Israeli Parliament. Ornstein, born in the Carpatho-Ukraine and educated in Leipzig, had been a Communist pioneer in the Hashomer Hatzair Movement, a soldier in the British Army, a member of the Israeli *Rechesh* mission and an assistant commercial attaché of the Israeli Embassy in Prague. The prisoners were thus deemed more than suitable for their role as star witnesses for the prosecution.

The interrogation of the two men, now simply known as No. 2132 (Mordechai Oren) and No. 2392 (Shimon Ornstin)—who never saw each other again until the trial—began immediately. To describe the tortures they endured, although they detailed them to this writer, surpasses his power of evocation. They were dressed only in prison pyjamas, winter and summer, brutally beaten at every opportunity, irregularly fed, forced to remain awake through interrogation sessions which continued for days on end and taken many times through a mock execution—never knowing nor eventually caring, when the procedure might be real. Their treatment at the hands of the STB reduced them to such a state of disorientation that the smallest spark of human kindness asumed tremendous proportions. In his memoirs, Ornstein related that

> . . . I was again blindfolded and dragged out by the sleeve; this, incidentally, was also one of the torture methods the jailers had acquired for themselves. They grasped the sleeve in such a way that it tightened painfully on the arm until the circulation was stopped. During all the time I spent in Ruzyne, I met only one jailer who had not adopted this brutal method—and I shall always keep a soft spot for him in my heart.[12]

The interrogation sessions, occurring at all hours of the day and night, were the central focus of their imprisonment. Everything else was merely designed to 'break' them, thereby facilitating these sessions. The prisoners quickly sensed the

importance of these interrogation periods and the reminis-
cences of both men revolve around the silent war—the 'chess
game of questions and answers'—with the interrogator whose
name neither knows to this day. The early sessions consisted
of beatings and humiliation and slowly progressed to brain-
washing periods designed to make the witnesses themselves
believe in Slansky's participation in a conspiracy; no mean
feat considering that both men knew Slansky well for nearly
two decades. One session, for instance, was spent translating
and retranslating Slansky's name (which was derived from his
birthplace, Slanky, a short distance from Prague) into the
German 'Saltzmann', and from there into the Hebrew
equivalent 'Malchi' and back. Having thus 'established' that
Slansky's code name in the Haganah (which, in fact, no
longer existed by 1951) was 'Malchi', it was now only a
question of weaving a plot of traitorous activities around this
basic link. After months of repetition and torture, the two
witnesses began to believe the story themselves.

Days became weeks, and weeks became months. After more
than a year in prison, the STB felt that, having finally
reduced the two Israelis and the other witnesses to the point
of abject submission, they could begin the Slansky Trial. It
was, of course, a well-rehearsed play, in the course of which
nearly forty broken prosecution witnesses—Oren and Ornstein among them—filed into the courtroom and recited their
lines. In this tragic comedy, each witness accused Slansky and
his fellow defendants of the most heinous crimes committed
in the service of American imperialism, Zionism and Titoism,
crimes which were part of a grand conspiracy to sabotage
Czecholovakia's 'harmonious relations' with the socialist
camp. Then each of the fourteen defendants—including
Slansky—admitted these crimes and pleaded guilty, throwing
themselves on the 'mercy of the People's Court'. In the words
of *Práce* (23-11-52) the accused: ' . . . not only confessed to all
their "crimes", but asked the court to give them the death
sentence. One, the noted Communist journalist, Andre
Simone (Otto Katz), pleaded "I have been a writer, and a
beautiful saying refers to writers as architects of people's
souls. What sort of architect have I been—I who have
poisoned souls? Such an architect of souls belongs on the

gallows. The only good service I can still render is to serve as a warning to all those who . . . are in danger of following the same path to hell. The stiffer the penalty, the more effective will the warning be".' It must be remembered that, like the witnesses, the defendants had been tortured into submission. Ornstein later recalled that after twelve months of intensive interrogation Slansky was a broken man, dragging what appeared to be almost a lifeless body into the courtroom.[13] He admitted every fantastic charge, beginning with his code name 'Malchi' and ending with his admission of the authenticity of the *Protocols of the Elders of Zion*. All defendants at the Prague show trials were found guilty; most of them were hanged without delay.

The witnesses were returned to their cells for nine more months of torture and interrogation before they themselves were tried. One day in August 1953, a representative of the Czech Prosecutor General's Office entered the cell of prisoner No. 2392, carrying a bulky document headed *Protocol for Purposes of Trial*. He read to the sick and dazed prisoner the charges he was to face: espionage, sabotage, attempted overthrow of the Czechoslovakian People's Republic, and participation in a Zionist conspiracy. Each charge carried the death penalty—yet the prisoner agreed to sign. Today, sixteen years later, Ornstein describes his reasons in this way:

> After 21 months of interrogation, you reach the conclusion that there is no 'out', no help anywhere; that your future and your fate are determined by the Secret Police, and not by a Court of any other public body. You are quite willing to surrender even your right to physical existence—if this will only help to free you from the house of terror called Ruzyne . . . The prisoners in this 'spy factory' are rapidly crushed and ground to dust, and I was crushed like them . . . [14]

Mordechai Oren, the second Israeli witness, explained his reason for signing a similar admission of guilt: 'It was a question of signing or going out of my mind. Had the alternative been death, I might have acted differently.'[15]

Soon afterwards, their own show trials were held; Ornstein's in August and Oren's in October. They were accused of being leaders of a gang of saboteurs and foreign agents—some of whom they had never seen before until sitting with them in the dock. It is interesting that, before his trial and after a particularly informal session, Ornstein was told by the interrogator—the nameless individual about whom Ornstein is currently finishing his second book of memoirs entitled the *Grand Inquisitor*—: 'Believe me as a Communist, and I give you my Communist word of honour, that you will not hang and will see your family again.'[16] He was true to his word, for although the prosecutor demanded the death penalty, both Oren and Ornstein were given life sentences. In August 1953, they were transferred to the Mirov prison to serve their terms.

One year later, in mid-1954, Shimon Ornstein was suddenly removed from Mirov and returned to Ruzyne prison in Prague. There he was once again taken to the Grand Inquisitor who informed him that the Attorney-General of the Republic of Czechoslovakia had decided to expel him and that the following day he would be on a plane for Israel. After a long conversation with the Grand Inquisitor, the most informal since his arrest nearly three years before, Shimon Ornstein was released.

In one of the ironic oddities of the event, the second witness, Mordechai Oren, continued to languish in prison after Ornstein's release, and even after the release of other surviving defendants in the original Slansky trial. Finally, on 8 May 1956, Oren was told that he would be released and after a few days' delay the Czech Foreign Ministry telephoned the Israeli envoy to announce Oren's immediate release on 12 May. Accompanied by the envoy, Oren left Prague for Zurich the next morning, wearing the same suit in which he had come to Prague in 1951, and after a day in Zurich, flew on to Israel to face a triumphant reception.

For Oren and Ornstein the terror was over. They had been arrested, tortured and interrogated until they had obediently accepted their role as witnesses and criminals, they had been sentenced to life imprisonment, only to be released after a year, all for no reason apparent to them.

It is interesting to consider the effects of their experiences on their political views; for each now faced in his own heart the ideological conflict between a life-long dedication to the socialist cause and the realities of Communist brutality and injustice. Mordechai Oren resolved this conflict almost immediately and in the conclusion of his speech to several thousand left-wing followers after his return home to Kibbutz Mizra he said:

> When I was released I examined the papers that had been returned to me. I found that my party membership card, which had been so important to me, had been confiscated. I would like to end my speech with the following two small requests: that I be given a new party membership card, and that I be allowed to return soon to public life to take part in the great construction work, the Zionist-halutzic and the socialist revolutionary struggle.[17]

Shimon Ornstein had never been a public figure and upon his return to Israel attempted to pick up the threads of his private life. Unlike Oren, he wrote and spoke very little about his experiences. Nonetheless, he too was forced to resolve the ideological conflict produced by his imprisonment. Perhaps the best indication of his decision may be seen in his account of the final talk with the Grand Inquisitor just before his release. The informal conversation centred around the role of the secret police in a socialist society, at the end of which Ornstein came to the conclusion that the responsibility for the injustices and terror rested not with the political system or even the leader, but with the existence of the secret police, a 'State within the State'. He concluded that:

> Only when a fundamental change has taken place in the internal regime of Communist states and the single party system has been abolished will the Secret Police's power collapse. Of course, there must also be an absolute division of power between the judicial and executive branches of government making an independent judiciary possible. There is no other way of change in such a system . . . The Secret Police practice of uncovering opposition activity and intermittently disappearing from view, makes people forget its existence; but it is always there, ready to carry out the bidding of the ruler, that is, the ruling party. Without destroying this satanic power, all talk of freedom and liberty are so many words and nothing else.[18]

Perhaps the most ironic event of all came thirteen years after Ornstein was first arrested, and ten years after he was released from Ruzyne prison, when the High Court of the Czechoslovakian People's Republic, on 7 February 1964, reversed the judgment against him, as they eventually did with the majority of surviving defendants and witnesses, indicating that it had all been a 'tragic mistake'. He was offered a modest sum in compensation, which could only be used towards purchasing certain Czech national products, such as glass, beer or pianos. He was officially rehabilitated.

On 3 March 1953 Stalin died. Hardly had he been buried in the *sanctum sanctorum* next to Lenin, when the nine Jewish physicians, imprisoned two months earlier on charges of murdering Politburo members, were exonerated and released. Throughout Eastern Europe imprisoned Zionist leaders and Jewish cadre members were given their freedom (except for the two Israeli witnesses who still had not faced their own trials at the time).

Yet amidst the jubilant expectations of the post-Stalin 'thaw', a much more significant change was taking place. It had become clear to Jewish activists throughout the Communist world that there had been a breach of faith by a party which, despite its doctrine, was capable of such antisemitic outbursts. Perhaps the greatest disillusionment occurred in the Israeli Communist Party, which underwent a series of splits and was reduced to a level of relative impotence among Israel's political parties. Analysing the period from the standpoint of Soviet-Israeli relations, the Slansky trials mark the first official indication that in the Middle East the USSR was henceforth to embrace the anti-Zionist, pro-Arab cause.

NOTES

1. Presented to the author by Munya Marder, Tel Aviv, August 1969.
2. Mordechai Oren, *Prisonnier Politique à Prague* 1951-1956 (Julliard, Paris 1960), p. 118.
3. See Arnold Krammer, 'Arms for Independence: When the Soviet Bloc Supported Israel'. *Wiener Library Bulletin*, Vol. XXII, No. 3, Summer 1968 (London), pp. 19-23.

4. Marie Syrkin, *Golda Meir: Woman with a Cause* (New York 1963), pp. 229-230.

5. A section of Ehrenburg's memoirs are devoted to his detailed explanation of these actions in which he goes to great lengths to refute all accusations that he had any part in initiating the antisemitic purges which followed. Ilya Ehrenburg, *Post-War Years, 1945-1954* (New York 1967), pp. 124-135.

6. See Walter Eytan, 'Israel's Foreign Policy and International Relations', *Middle Eastern Affairs* (May 1951), pp. 155-160.

7. Norbert Nieswiski, 'Israel between East and West', *Eastern Quarterley* (October/December 1953), pp. 49-53.

8. Eugene Loebl, *Sentenced and Tried: The Stalinist Purges in Czechoslovakia* (London 1969), pp. 20-24.

9. Josefa Slanska, *Report on my Husband* (New York 1969), xi-xii.

10. Eugene Loebl, *Sentenced and Tried*, p. 20.

11. Shimon Ornstein, *Aliyah b'Prague* (Adventure in Prague), (Tel Aviv 1968), pp. 17-39.

12. *Ibid.,* p. 62.

13. *Ibid.,* p. 121.

14. *Yedioth Ahronoth* (Tel Aviv), 26 April 1968.

15. Walter Z. Laqueur, 'The Oren Case: A fellow-traveller comes home', *Commentary*, Vol. 22, August 1956, p. 112.

16. Ornstein, *op. cit.,* p. 137.

17. Quoted in Walter Z. Laqueur, 'The Oren Case', *loc. cit.*

18. Ornstein, *op. cit.* pp. 184-185.

Israel and China—
A Missed Opportunity?

Meron Medzini

According to some students of current affairs, Israel committed one of her most serious foreign policy blunders in 1955,
when the government let slip the opportunity of establishing
diplomatic relations with the People's Republic of China.
One of the most articulate protagonists of this view is David
Hacohen, Israel's first Minister to Burma, and in 1955 head
of an Israeli trade delegation to China. Similarly, Professor
Michael Brecher, an authority on Israel's foreign policy,
publicly stated that he thought Israel's China policy wrong.[1]
Moshe Sharett, the late Premier and Foreign Minister,
disagreed, but until the publication of the relevant official
documents and his own diaries, historians will have to wait
for a further explanation.

At one time, however, both Peking and Jerusalem, each for
reasons of their own, showed limited interest in establishing
closer ties. Both seemed anxious to improve first their trade
and then diplomatic relations. But, by the spring of 1955, the
two governments, owing to changed circumstances, appeared
less eager to widen their contacts, and the few steps taken to
extend them lacked all sense of urgency. Their policies were
influenced by many outside factors which, although totally
unconnected with the main issue, finally determined their
decisions. The growing Chinese awareness of the importance
of the Arab world apparently overrode the purely commercial

benefits which relations with Israel were expected to yield. In the case of Israel, fear of incurring American displeasure and the absence of any certainty that closer relations would really be to her advantage, determined her views and actions. The available evidence suggests therefore that the charge that the Israeli government mishandled the China issue is unfair, if only because Israel, in view of conditions prevailing in 1955, had very few options left.

One of the fourteen governments which recognized the newly established People's Republic of China between 1 October 1949 and 31 January 1950, Foreign Minister Sharett cabled Chou En-lai, informing him of the Israeli government's decision to 'recognize your government as the legitimate regime of China'. Nothing was said in this cable about the establishment of diplomatic relations. The Chinese Premier acknowledged it ten days later, expressing his gratitude and conveying to Israel the good wishes of the Chinese government. Israel recognized China for purely technical reasons. Recognition was not considered a mark of political approval, but merely an acknowledgement that the government in question was in effective control of the country for which it spoke. Having herself faced the problem of recognition a year earlier, Israel attached importance to this principle, even though she knew that in this particular case its application might not be viewed with favour by the United States.[2] She was moreover encouraged to take this step because of her intended policy of neutralism or non-alignment in the Cold War.

Non-alignment as a political ideal and attitude was the direct result of Israel's recent history and rise to statehood when East and West voted in the UN for the partition of Palestine and so facilitated creation of the Jewish state. Israel wished to retain the support of the two great blocs, while remaining independent of both; she feared that any obvious preference for one side might lead the other, not merely to withdraw its backing, but actively to support the Arab cause. Moreover, in the early years of her existence as a state, the tasks of building the nation, absorbing hundreds of thousands of immigrants and strengthening her defences dictated a policy of neutralism. For years, Prime Minister David

Ben-Gurion had been reiterating that only the United States and the Soviet Union could bring the Arabs to make peace with Israel. Under the circumstances, there was no wish to estrange the Russians whose political support might become as decisive as was their military aid in 1948. This policy had the backing of Israel's left wing, of *Mapam* and the communists—who in 1949 held 23 of the 120 seats in the Knesset.

Both these parties regarded the Chinese revolution as another and a contemporary version of the admired Russian revolution. *Mapam*, strongly neutralist, opposed the American inspired Middle East Defence Organization then being discussed in Washington and London. Foreign Minister Sharett strove to satisfy *Mapam's* demand for neutrality and his own and Ben-Gurion's desire to preserve Israel's freedom of action on specific issues. In the words of Sharett, 'Israel will in no case side with one great bloc in the world against the other'.[3] Recognition of China would therefore conform with Israel's policy of preserving her freedom of action. Yet the hundred days between China's request for recognition and Israel's response revealed the government's hesitations and doubts. Press inquiries on the subject elicited evasive and conflicting replies from official spokesmen now asserting that no such request had been received, and now that the government had not yet been able to discuss it.[4] *Mapam* and the communists pressed the government and their political correspondents, after prodding Foreign Ministry spokesmen, received such information as 'this is not a burning issue', 'mutuality remains a basic principle in our policy', etc.[5] Following the example of Britain, the Scandinavian countries, India and Indonesia, Israel finally recognized Peking. Israel, in the words of the Director General of the Israeli Foreign Ministry, 'not only had no special reason to be grateful to the Formosa regime, but could not doubt that the People's Republic of China was the de facto government on the Chinese mainland. China's internal regime was none of Israel's concern, any more than it was of Switzerland's or Sweden's.'[6] Israel also hoped that her recognition might facilitate the immigration of Jews from China. From September 1948 until March 1949, an Israeli Vice-Consul worked in Shanghai under the Nationalist régime and from 1950 to

1952 two local Jews were nominated as honorary immigration officers to arrange the migration of Jews wishing to go to Israel.[7] Former Russian Jews who held either Czarist or Soviet passports had to obtain a clearance from the Soviet Citizens' Association before they could be granted Chinese exit visas. Israeli diplomats accredited to East European capitals and to Moscow were asked to enlist the help of the local Chinese embassies in an effort to resolve the problem, but of the 25,000 Jews who were in China in 1948, 24,000 were still there in 1964.[7]

After the recognition, Israel waited for 'additional and clearer signals from China suggesting an exchange of representatives'. Meanwhile the Israeli left began to establish ties with the Chinese Communist Party, Israeli delegates attended a Democratic Women's Congress in Peking and laudatory articles on China appeared in Israel's left-wing press. Both *Mapam* and the communists continued to assail the government for failing to support the admission of the People's Republic to the UN. In August 1950 they asked the government in the Knesset to explain its attitude. Replying, Foreign Minister Sharett stated that

> whenever the Israel government was asked to take a stand on the matter of the People's Republic of China, her position was clear . . . when Israel had to decide whether to vote for or against, or abstain on the matter of China's participation in United Nations discussions, the State of Israel, together with a fourteen-nation minority, voted to admit China to that discussion.

When the question of China's admission came before the United Nations General Assembly in September 1950, Mr Sharett spoke for Israel:

> Much of Israel's conception of democracy may differ from that upheld by the new Chinese government. . . . Israel is among the sixteen states which have recognized this government. My delegation feels that it would be unwise for the United Nations, in disregard of compelling realities, to bolster up a regime of the past, which has lost its hold on the territory and people it claims to represent. If the new

regime in China is ready sincerely to uphold its obligations under the Charter, prospects of peace in Asia and throughout the world would be enhanced by its admission.

This was before the Chinese intervention in the Korean war and Israel, together with sixteen other nations, voted on 19 September 1950 for China's admission, which she again supported in the following year. From 1952 onwards, however, she began to abstain on this issue.

At that time, the attitude to China was clearly dictated by expediency. When voting for her admission in 1950 and 1951, Israel was subscribing to the principle of the UN Charter, which China had no intention of upholding; and though Israel in 1951, together with the majority of UN member states, had condemned China as an aggressor, she nevertheless voted a few months later for admission. The Korean war broke out (25 June 1950) before Israel or China had taken any steps to establish diplomatic relations. It is interesting to note that while the war delayed the establishment of contacts until 1953, basically and, judging by what happened later, it did not harm Israel's image in the eyes of Chinese leaders. In fact, the war, so crucial in the evolution of Israel's foreign policy and her retreat from neutralism, did not inhibit the emergence of closer Israeli-Chinese links in 1953-55. Since her support was sought by both the United States and the Soviet Union, the Korean war compelled Israel to adopt a definite position with regard to the Far East, something she had been trying to avoid. At home, *Mapam* and the communists suggested that the Korean war was a continuation of the liberation of China, and they accused the Americans of backing the reactionary forces in South Korea and of conspiring against the North. It did not take the Israeli government long to associate itself with the United Nations Security Council position,[8] a step, no doubt, influenced by Israel's own experience in 1948 when the Arab attack on her went uncensured by the UN. On 2 July 1950, Israel informed the UN Secretary General that 'in fulfilment of its clear obligations under the Charter, Israel supports the Security Council in its efforts to put an end to the breach of the peace in Korea'.[9]

In an effort to reaffirm its belief in the United Nations and to satisfy the United States without antagonizing the Soviet Union and left-wing elements at home, the Israeli governemt tried to steer a very cautious course in the UN. It nevertheless soon became evident that the pro-Western orientation of Premier Ben-Gurion, Foreign Minister Sharett and Abba Eban, his Ambassador to the United States and the United Nations, nullified earlier attempts to remain an uncommitted neutral. The Korean confrontation was the only time when Israel was actively engaged in the Cold War crisis and tried to play a role in its resolution. Even before Chinese troops had entered Korea, Mr Sharett told the General Assembly that the problem was 'how the UN was to move towards the condition of stability . . . which was indispensible both for the unification of Korea and the establishment of a democratically elected all-Korean government'.[10] When the UN asked members to assist the forces fighting in Korea, Israel felt that participation in the actual war would be unacceptable at home as well as to the Soviet Union and the Eastern European countries (still a source of massive Jewish immigration into Israel). Pleading her own security needs and limited manpower resources, Israel sent no soldiers but contributed medical and later food supplies for civilian relief to the value of $100,000. Having drawn closer to the West, she voted in favour of a resolution enabling the United Nations forces to cross the 38th parallel and proceed north because, as Ambassador Eban argued:

> . . . it seemed politically essential to give the United Nations forces the indispensable latitude to consolidate their position, to ensure their substantive control of Korea and to prevent or reduce the threat of renewed aggression. Thirdly, and on the purely moral side, the concept of the 38th parallel seemed already to have lost its validity following the initial violation by the aggressor,'[11]

But, while endorsing the crossing of the 38th parallel, Israel warned against too deep a penetration into North Korea 'lest this advance provoke the Chinese to react'. Mr Sharett later maintained that a promise given to Israel to halt UN forces well away from the Chinese borders had not been kept.[12]

When Chinese forces had entered the war an entirely new situation had arisen.

Late in November 1950, a diplomatic mission from the People's Republic of China arrived in New York. Early in December, Mr Sharett, together with the representatives of Britain, India, Pakistan and Sweden, met the Chinese delegation at Trygve Lie's house. During the ensuing debate on the significance of the Korean war, the Chinese denounced all foreign intervention and asserted that this was a civil war similar to that fought by Chinese revolutionaries. Mr Sharett, arguing that in this instance world peace and the future of the United Nations were at stake, 'broached the principles of the cease-fire resolution which the General Assembly later adopted'.[13] It consisted of a three-stage plan for ending the war, which called for a cease-fire, the evacuation of all non-Korean troops from the peninsula and a continued discussion of Korea's future, to which Communist China was to be a party. The Chinese rejected this plan, even though Israel suggested the admission of Peking to the UN and negotiations on the future of Taiwan. When similar suggestions by other countries were also rejected, Israel despaired of her conciliatory efforts and followed the majority in declaring China an aggressor. The new policy, first announced by Mr Sharett in a press conference in late December, was elaborated by Mr Eban, who told the United Nations in January 1951 that:

> the armed forces of the People's Republic of China had been engaging in hostilities against United Nations forces hundreds of miles beyond Chinese territory and had three times refused to heed the General Assembly's call for a cease-fire. Such action was indisputably illegitimate.[14]

A week before delivering his speech, Mr Eban had rejected Peking's demands for negotitions without a prior cease-fire and called it 'a strange position', while Mr Sharett was moved to express his dismay at China's 'serious threat to world peace'.[15]

Predictably this policy came under fire in the Israeli Parliament. Although the government brushed aside left-wing accusations that it was toeing the American line, it was obvious that Israel's policy of non-alignment was slowly giving way to a more pro-Western orientation. The Korean war and Israel's experiences of great power diplomacy at the UN had made it clear that she could not aspire to a meaningful role, since, in view of the Middle Eastern confrontation, any Israeli initiative was automatically rejected by every Arab state. Having learned her lesson the hard way, Israel from then on remained silent on similar issues. However, anxious not to alienate China completely, after having declared her an aggressor, Israel wanted the General Assembly to avoid any action prejudicial to further conciliation attempts. On the basis of her own experience, she hoped for an immediate cease-fire followed by 'something in the nature of an armistice with a view to reaching a final settlement'.[16] In May 1951, Israel joined forty-three other UN members in·voting for an embargo on the shipment of arms and strategic war materials to mainland China and North Korea.[17] From then on until the·end of the war (July 1953) she remained largely inactive or followed the American line. Reasons for turning inwards were the deteriorating situation in the Middle East and her own economic and security preoccupations which the inauguration of a pro-Western policy seemed to engender.

Because of the Korean war and her slow swing towards the West, Israel made no attempt to discuss the development of relations, diplomatic or commercial, with Peking until late in 1953. In fact, she was not diplomatically represented in the area until David Hacohen opened the Israeli legation in Rangoon about that time. There is little evidence, on the other hand, to show that the Chinese Foreign Ministry had any definite policy towards the Middle East. The absence of formal and informal ties between the Chinese Communists and the Arab world, even before the establishment of the People's Republic, Peking's preoccupation with the prosecution and later the termination of the Korean war, China's absence from the United Nations and the small number of her diplomatic missions abroad, all indicated that she was unlikely to accord the Middle East a high political priority. At that time, the Chinese may not even have clearly differentiated between Israel and her Arab neighbours, particularly

since both had opposed her in the UN. There was certainly
no love lost between Peking and the Arab states, which until
the mid-fifties followed the Western line in their approach to
the Far East. In fact, the Arab League had decided in August
1950 not to recognize Communist China, while most of the
Arab states maintained diplomatic relations with the Nationalist regime. It is likely that in its early years Communist
China's attitude to the Middle East was pragmatic rather
than guided by any preconceived policy. While Peking might
have been trying to gain a minor diplomatic victory over the
United States by initiating diplomatic relations with Israel,
such a move might also have been construed as an attempt to
acquire a lever against the Arabs. But if Israel hesitated, so
did the Arabs. When, in June 1954, Chou En-lai passed
through Cairo on his way to the Geneva Conference, he was
not received by Egypt's leaders. In contrast, that same year
Moslems from Nationalist China on a pilgrimage to Mecca
were received in Cairo by President Nasser and in Riad by
King Saud, both of whom criticized the 'anti-religious crimes
of the Communists'.[18] The Nationalists tried to extend their
contacts with the Arab states, if only to prevent them from
recognizing Peking, and to capitalize on the anti-Communist
sentiment still prevailing among the more orthodox Moslem
nations. Diplomatic missions were established and trade
encouraged. Having given Israel a de facto recognition in
early 1949, Taipei shunned diplomatic contacts once Israel
had recognized Peking and, in an effort to woo the Arabs,
consistently voted against Israel in the United Nations.
Meanwhile, there were no visible signs from Peking that it
was interested in establishing closer ties with Israel, until the
latter part of 1953 when, for various reasons, the position
changed.

The appointment of David Hacohen as Israel's first Minister Plenipotentiary to Rangoon was one such reason. Hacohen came from the labour movement, was not a professional
diplomat, but had been a close friend of Mr Sharett, who had
become Prime Minister after Ben-Gurion's temporary retire-
ment. In many respects the most suitable man to develop
Israel-China relations, Hacohen in December 1953 met the
doyen of the Rangoon Diplomatic Corps, China's ambassador

Yao Chu Ming, whom he described as a close friend of Chou En-lai. 'Ming', Hachohen reports, 'was interested in finding out why we chose to send a Minister to Burma and wondered whether we had ever considered a similar strengthening of ties with China.'[19] Ming also informed Hacohen that he was the first Jew he had ever met. Without any specific instructions regarding China, Hacohen said Rangoon was chosen because of its proximity to China, India, Pakistan and Thailand. He also mentioned Israel's strained financial position, but left he door open for further contacts. He was encouraged to do so by the Soviet chargé-d'affaires. In January 1954, Hacohen was told by Ming that

> the government of China has ordered me to inform you that it welcomes the opening of an Israeli Legation in Burma and . . . wishes to establish trade relations with Israel. We mean imports from Israel to China. We should like to know the goods, prices and quantities you would be prepared to supply.[20]

Economic motives were apparently another reason for China's overtures to Israel, which had two ends in view. The first was to overcome the American 'Battle Act' and the UN embargo which restricted China's trade and led her to cultivate her commercial links with non-communist nations. As early as 1952, China had begun to sign a series of unofficial 'trade agreements' with various Japanese companies. It was hoped that Israel could be induced to sign similar agreements to supply either directly or through a third party some of the urgently needed capital goods. Moreover, she might also become a clandestine staging-post for American and European goods ultimately destined for China. Hence the emphasis on trade and the subsequent invitation to Israel to send a commercial mission to Peking, where attempts after the Korean war to gain wider acceptance in the world at large and in Asia in particular may also have played a part in the approaches to Israel. China's objectives were to weaken the American front, undermine the Nationalist regime, prevent the establishment of SEATO and persuade Asian nations to break with the West. Epitomizing this policy, Chou En-lai said in New Delhi in 1954:

All the nations of the world can co-exist peacefully, no matter whether they are big or small, strong or weak, and irrespective of the social system each of them has. The rights of the people of each nation to national independence and self-determination must be respected. The people of each nation have the right to choose their own system of government without interference from other nations. Revolution cannot be exported.[21]

In her drive for the 'five principles of peaceful co-existence', China had signed a treaty with India and was negotiating others with various Asian nations. The Geneva Conference also provided her with an opportunity to expand her diplomatic contacts in Asia and elsewhere. From 1950 to 1953, Peking had exchanged diplomatic representatives only with Finland and Pakistan, but after the Geneva Conference formal contacts had been considerably extended. Diplomatic relations were established with three European states in 1954 alone. Viewed in this light, it seems highly unlikely that the approaches to Israel were entirely due to the initiative of the Chinese ambassador in Rangoon. It is more plausible to assume that he had general instructions to widen China's international contacts. Similar overtures were reported by Israeli diplomats from Moscow, other East European countries and, after 1954, from London.

The Chinese interest in trade with Israel seems to have taken Hacohen by surprise. He was, of course, fully aware of the UN embargo voted for by Israel; and he wondered whther Israel could accept such trade and how it might be transacted. At the time shipping routes also presented problems with Egypt blocking the Straits of Tirana and barring Israeli shipping from the Suez Canal. The Soviet chargé-d'affaires suggested that Israel could ship goods to Odessa for despatch via the Siberian overland route. Although Hacohen doubted whether his government would approve of such transactions, he nevertheless wanted to follow up the suggestion in direct talks with the Chinese, preferably in China. He consulted Jerusalem, which, probably unable to follow or understand fully China's changing tactics, reacted evasively to the new situation. The Israeli communists continued to urge greater initiative in furthering relations with China. In March 1954, Mr Sharett replied to a question in the Knesset, 'We have not forgotten Peking'. Asked whether Israel was prepared to take the necessary steps, he answered diplomatically: 'The government of Israel assumes that there will be progress in this direction at the appropriate time.' Pressed further, he declined to elaborate, except by repeating 'at the appropriate time'.[22] Undoubtedly, United States attitudes largely influenced official Israeli thinking; after all, Israel could hardly ignore the Eisenhower administration's hostile feelings towards China. She had to be careful not to offend John Foster Dulles, the chief architect of the 'isolate China' policy and so endanger vital interests for the sake of the marginal, indeed doutful, benefits of the Chinese connection. American support was crucial, whereas China, not even a member of the UN, and at the time without influence in the Arab world, could hardly provide Israel with the required military, economic and political support. Moreover, the feelings of American Jewry had also to be considered. But above all, as the Israeli Embassy in Washington pointed out, nothing should be done to exacerbate the somewhat strained relations with the Secretary of State. While Mr Eban saw little profit in Far Eastern adventures, David Hacohen, Mr Sharett's childhood friend and colleague, was urging him from Rangoon to move a little faster. In the end, Jerusalem decided to explore the Chinese offer, and Hacohen was instructed to inform Ambassador Ming of Israel's willingness to despatch a mission to China—'in itself an act which demonstrates the thaw in the attitude to China'.[24]

At a meeting in February 1954, Hacohen dwelt on the trade problems: the embargo, trade routes, samples, prices, etc. He insisted on a visit by an Israeli mission to discuss these matters. He also suggested the possibility of both countries appointing trade commissioners in their respective capitals. When Hacohen met Ming again in late March, no reply had been received from Peking. The Chinese ambassador assured Hacohen that the delay was not intentional and hoped Israel would not conclude that 'the interest China has in establishing commercial and diplomatic ties with us has ceased to be vital'.[24] This was the first time diplomatic relations were mentioned. Hacohen met Premier Chou En-lai in June 1954 as he passed through Rangoon on his way to Geneva. At a Chinese embassy reception, Chou expressed his hope that Hacohen would visit China, and that he himself would, after his return from Europe, be able to attend to the matter of the Israeli mission.[25] A formal invitation to an Israeli delegation authorized to negotiate trade and other agreements was received by Hacohen in September 1954. China, Ambassador Ming explained, would be pleased to bear the expenses involved, and the delegation could stay as long as it liked. As Hacohen was about to join the Israeli UN delegation, it was decided to wait for his return to settle details of the visit.[26] When Chou En-lai delivered a major foreign policy statement to the National People's Congress ten days later, he mentioned that 'negotiations were being conducted to establish normal relations with Afghanistan and Israel'.[27] This was the only time the Chinese Premier publicly mentioned the normalization of diplomatic relations.

All this was duly cabled to Jerusalem, and Hacohen set out on his journey, convinced that the establishment of full diplomatic relations with China was only a matter of time. On his way to New York, he discovered that four days earlier (20 September 1954), Israel had supported the American 'moratorium resolution' designed to prevent the discussion of China's admission to the UN. Foreign Ministry officials told him that there had been a misunderstanding, and that Israel had no intention of offending China. He was also given to understand that the Israeli UN delegation had contravened instructions and was now looking for various excuses to justify its vote.[28] A cable was thereupon despatched to the Chinese embassy in Rangoon in which Israel admitted that her UN delegation had voted contrary to its instructions, pointing out, however, that this vote, far from barring China's admission, only supported a procedural resolution suggesting the time was not propitious for a debate bound to lead to China's defeat. If the Chinese government was offended by the Israeli vote, it did not become apparent, for in January 1955 an Israeli trade mission set out for China.

Headed by David Hacohen, it included Daniel Lewin, head of the Asian Division of the Foreign Ministry, Meir de

Shalit of that Ministry, Joseph Zarchin, head of the Export Division of the Ministry of Commerce and Industry, and Moshe Bejarano, former Commercial Attaché at the Israeli Embassy in Moscow. Before the mission left, Foreign Minister Sharett, anxious to allay American misgivings, minimized the importance of the visit, assuring the Knesset that, while China had not invited the Israeli delegation, 'it was agreed between the two sides that Israel would despatch a mission to China, whereupon the Chinese government announced that during their stay in Peking the members of the delegation were to be their guests'.[29] This luke-warm send-off was probably not lost on the Chinese government. The delegation finally arrived in Peking on 31 January 1955 after having toured Canton for three days. As emphasis of the commercial rather than the political aspect of the visit, it was received by Li Jen Min, the Deputy Minister of Commerce in charge of foreign trade, and second and third level Foreign Ministry officials. At the first meeting, Li welcomed the delegation and recalled the fact that Israel was one of the first nations to recognize the People's Republic. He welcomed the mutual desire to establish commercial contacts,[40] and explained the workings of China's foreign trade, stressing his country's interest in 'developing normal trade relations with the whole world. States with differing regimes, although loyal to conflicting principles could live in peace and freely develop cultural and trade relations.'[31] The next phase of the visit was devoted to a tour of Peking, Tientsin, Mukden and other areas where the Israelis visited factories, agricultural farms, schools and social institutions and met local officials. Final talks were resumed in Peking in mid-February.

Discussions centred on the goods China wanted, means and modes of payment, transportation and the possibility of trading through third countries. Li stressed that China and Israel 'must avoid political entanglements and think only of the economic benefits to be derived from an agreement'.[32] In the talks, officials representing government-controlled enterprises told the Israelis that China wanted to purchase chemicals and fertilizers, spare parts, trucks, industrial diamonds, tyres and dentures, all in considerable quantities. An aide-memoire signed on 19 February stated

1. Both parties desire to develop mutually beneficial commercial relations on the basis of equality;

2. Both parties have explained the problems facing foreign trade in their respective countries, studied the list of goods handled by foreign trade departments and examined other commercial issues;

3. Both parties agreed that the talks and information exchanged have created a basis for the development of closer trade links.

4. Both parties have agreed to inform their governments of the atmosphere permeating the Peking talks and to continue the development of trade relations both through existing channels and those still to be established.

5. The Israeli delegation has expressed on behalf of its government the hope that the government of the People's Republic of China will send a commercial delegation to visit Israel as the official guests of the Israeli government.

The Israelis failed in a last-minute effort to amend Paragraph 5 to incorporate a declaration of Chinese willingness to send such a delegation.[35]

This document, the only tangible result of the visit, is remarkable for its vagueness and for the lack of any specific progress. The Chinese cautiously refrained from making any commitment, either political or economic. It was obvious that the Chinese government—by limiting the scope of the Israeli mission exclusively to trade matters—tried to avoid any political involvements which could harm future ties with the Arabs.

The lack of Chinese enthusiasm suited the mood of the Israeli Ministry for Foreign Affairs. Jerusalem was not unduly saddened by this setback. As the situation along Israel's borders deteriorated and, except for French support, she found herself more and more isolated, fear of American resentment naturally perturbed the government. The Soviet Union had by then joined the Arab camp, and Jerusalem was anxious not to offend Washington, particularly over initiatives offering at best uncertain benefits. This was the time of the bombardment of the off-shore islands which produced the US Senate's Quemoy Resolution; and knowing John Foster Dulles' views, Mr Sharett was not prepared to back any new initiatives in East Asia. China's cool response to the Israeli mission seemed to have strengthened his hand, and he decided to await the arrival of the Chinese delegation before tackling the problem of diplomatic representation. His attitude contrasted sharply with the urgency of Hacohen's report, which insisted that diplomatic relations could be the first step towards wider commercial, cultural and other links with China. They were, in his view, so important that he was ready to return to Peking. He also hoped that the visit of an Israeli mission to China had impressed other Asian nations, particularly India and Indonesia, and strengthened Israel's standing there. He emphasized the need for diplomatic relations in this part of the world, particularly in view of the forthcoming Bandung Conference.[34]

In April 1955, Jerusalem replied that the composition and despatch of China's mission would test the extent of her interest and sincerity. This was the solution favoured by Mr Sharett and fitted his principle of mutuality. He feared that if Israel were to offer the establishment of diplomatic relations before the visit of a Chinese delegation, China might not respond to the overture at all, and Israel might lose prestige.[34]

It is known that 'Relations with China' once appeared on the cabinet agenda, but was dropped at the last minute because of warning signals from the Israeli Embassy in Washington, then engaged in highly delicate and protracted negotiations with the Eisenhower administration for the sale of arms. Hachohen argued that China's interest in diplomatic relations had been expressed publicly by Chou En-lai in September 1954, and by the Chinese ambassador in Rangoon in October in his reply to the Israeli note apologizing for the unfortunate UN vote. In this communication, Ming said China assumed that as Israel 'intended to establish and maintain mutually friendly relations with China, she would henceforth adopt a correct attitude towards China and the UN'.[35] Hacohen saw in this an affirmation of the Chinese desire to proceed towards a closer relationship. He feared that undue insistence on protocol and conventions was ruining the chance of establishing such relations and felt that the risk of incurring Washington's wrath was somewhat exaggerated. Hacohen may not have realized that since his absence from home Jerusalem had become increasingly concerned with Egypt, Jordan and the great powers rather than with China and Burma.

By 1 April 1955, he sadly noted in his diary that Israel might have lost the chance of forging links with China, due partly to what he termed a 'psychological inability to take decisions'. He was, of course, right: Israeli policy-makers were reluctant to rush decisions on any major problems; moreover, they were far less ready to commit themselves on peripheral issues, and to them China certainly was peripheral. While his personal belief was that the Bandung Conference and the impending arrival of Nasser and other Arab leaders might well end any hope of establishing relations with China, his instructions were to hold back.

The first intimation of China's support for the Arab cause came in April. At the New Delhi Cominform Peace Conference, the Chinese delegation, headed by Kuo Mo-jo, supported a resolution calling on Israel to accept the return of the Palestinian refugees. Chou En-lai, on his way to Bandung, was due in Rangoon in mid-April, and Ming asked Hacohen whether he wished to see the Premier. He sought Jerusalem's guidance and was told to inform the Ambassador that Israel was still considering the question of diplomatic representation. Under the circumstances Hacohen preferred not to meet Chou, though why he was so convinced that Chou would raise the question of diplomatic relations remains puzzling. After all Peking had shown no overwhelming desire to pursue the matter. Hacohen was, however, correct in his assumption that Nehru would act as a go-between in an attempt to bring Nasser and other Arab leaders closer to Chou En-lai's position. Undeterred, he complained to Ambassador Ming about the Chinese vote in New Delhi, and was informed that it was the result of insufficient knowledge and of the one-sided information the Chinese delegation had received about the Arab-Israeli conflict.[36]

Evaluating Chou's Bandung support for the Arab cause and

his call for the solution of the Palestine problem on the basis of the UN resolutions, Hacohen wrote:

> The attitude of more friendly nations with normal diplomatic relations with us, and well aware of the meaning of the UN resolution on the refugees, is more surprising than that of Chinese who know less about it. . . . Under the circumstances prevailing in Bandung, for us almost tragic, and in view of Russia's support for the Arabs and China's campaign to gain for herself Arab backing, particularly since they had not yet recognized her, Chou's words have to be weighed carefully. He expressed his sympathy for the suffering refugees, but without a word of condemnation for Israel.[37]

Jerusalem had not yet given up hope and, after the Bandung Conference, the head of the Foreign Ministry Asian Division notified his opposite number in Peking on two occasions that Israel was now ready for diplomatic relations.

China had by then apparently decided not to do anything to antagonize the Arabs, and her reply was evasive. Diplomatic relations with Israel, previously considered an important step in her endeavour to overcome isolation, now seemed much less so. After Bandung, it was the Arabs who were judged to be the more useful partners. Like Jerusalem, Peking doubted the value of entering into diplomatic relations whose benefits were at best marginal and might offend potential allies. No Chinese delegation ever visited Israel. Repeated enquiries from Rangoon and elsewhere elicited only evasive replies. When Egypt recognized Peking in May 1956, it showed that the policy of shunning Israel was beginning to pay off. After the Sinai war all contacts between Israeli and Chinese diplomats abroad were severed.

NOTES

1.   See David Hacohen, *Yoman Burma* (Burma Diary), Tel Aviv, 1963. Professor Brecher's Interview was in Ha'aretz, Tel Aviv, 1971.
2.   See Ernest Stock, *Israel on the Road to Sinai*, Ithaca, 1967, pp. 36-42.
3.   *Divrei Haknesset*, 15.6.1949.
4.   *Ma'ariv*, Tel Aviv, 9.1.1950.

5. *Al Hamishmar*, Tel Aviv, 5.1.1950.
6. Eytan, *The First Ten Years*, New York, 1958, p. 171.
7. See *Israel Government Yearbook*, 1950-51.
8. On 4 July, Foreign Minister Sharett told the Knesset that the Government of Israel accepted the validity of the Security Council proceedings on the Korean problem, and regretted the absence of the Soviet Union from the discussions. *Divrei Haknesset*.
9. *Security Council Official Records, Supplement*, June-August, 1950, p. 52.
10. UN General Assembly Official Records (hereafter UNGA), 5th Session, First Committee, 4.10.1950, p. 45.
11. *Ibid.* 13.12.1950, p. 543.
12. *Divrei Haknesset*, Vol. VIII, p. 854, 23.1.1951.
13. See Trygve Lie, *In the Cause of Peace*, New york, 1954, p. 353; *Divrei Haknesset*, Vol. VII, p. 465 and Vol. VIII, pp. 853-855.
14. UNGA, First Committee, 13.1.1951, pp. 492-494.
15. *Divrei Haknesset, loc. cit.*
16. UNGA, First Committee, 26.1.1951, pp. 558-560.
17. Resolution 500 (V), 18.5.1951.
18. *China Handbook*, Taipei, 1956.
19. Hacohen, *op. cit.*, p. 34.
20. *Ibid.*, pp. 61-62.
21. Jen Min Ji Pao, 2.7.1954, in SCMP 841, 3-4.7.1954.
22. *Divrei Haknesset*, Vol. XVI (b), p. 2361, 10.8.1954; Vol. XVI (a), p. 2614, 14.7.1954.
23. Hacohen, *op. cit.*, p. 91.
24. *Ibid.*, p. 158.
25. *Ibid.*, p. 244.
26. *Ibid.*, pp. 304-5.
27. Harold Hinton, *Communist China in World Politics*, Boston, 1966.
28. Hacohen, *op. cit.*, pp. 318-19.
29. *Divrei Haknesset*, Vol. XVII (a), p. 104, 15.11.1954.
30. Hacohen, *op. cit.*, pp. 386-387.
31. *Ibid.*, p. 390.
32. *Ibid.*, p. 403.
33. *Ibid.*, p. 416.
34. *Ibid.*, p. 434.
35. *Ibid.*, p. 435.
36. *Ibid.*, p. 449.
37. *Ibid.*, p. 458. For the speeches of Chou, see *China at the Africa-Asia Conference*, Peking, 1955.

Crisis Management
in the Russian Press, 1967

Compiled by Jane Degras

It is difficult to assess to what degree Pravda and the rest of the Russian press have become prisoners of their own slogans. In the early stages of the 1967 Middle East crisis and in the period immediately preceding it, the survival of Syria's shaky regime—for the USSR pre-eminently 'the vanguard of Socialism'—seemed to be Russia's primary concern. When a wave of emotional Pan-Arabism, backed up by regional defence agreements, assured the continued existence of Syria's unpopular, if quasi-socialist establishment, Russia, having attained her objective, was no longer interested in aggravating the situation. The crisis was consequently soft-pedalled. In view of Arab dependence on Russian armaments and much else, the Moscow establishment may also have had some exaggerated ideas of its ability to control the situation. This would explain why the crisis was still underplayed when the East German press was already giving vociferous and unqualified support to Arab arguments.

This is not to say that Russian editors were unprepared for the course events took under the impact of Arab warmongering. A further twist to the blanket denunciation of the 'imperialist American world conspiracy' was all that seemed to be required.

Preoccupied with the Syrian situation, *Pravda's* columnist Igor Belyaev (16 May) wondered why, if Israel according to

President Eshkol 'felt entirely safe', she had to indulge in sabre rattling.

'In Tel Aviv (wrote Belyaev) they like to talk peace and simultaneously to threaten the security of their neighbours. Only the day before yesterday the chief of the Israeli army boasted that Israel's specially trained commandos were ready for action against Syria. . . . As a result of all this the situation on the Israeli-Syrian border became so tense that the Syrian delegate to the UN had to inform the Secretary General of Damascus' grave concern'.

This wanton Israeli intransigence, Belyaev had no difficulty in explaining, stemmed from the fact that 'the present Syrian government, opposing as it does the rule of foreign monopolies in the Near and Middle East, embarrasses Washington'—to be exact, certain 'imperialist circles' there, who were anxious to create new difficulties for Syria when the Damascus and Aleppo uprisings they had instigated failed to bring down the government. They persuaded Israel 'to take it upon herself to organize fresh anti-Syrian actions. After all, it is not for nothing that Israel received American military equipment including heavy tanks'. Somewhat disingenuously putting the cart before the horse, Belyaev wondered why, since 'Israel, according to Levi Eshkol, enjoys complete security'.

The gathering crisis was, during the following days, relegated to the obscurity of minor paragraphs on the foreign news page. Short and inconspicuous reports quoted *Al Ahram* (*Pravda*, 18 May), or the routine statement by the Syrian Defence Minister Assad (*Pravda*, 21 May) that 'Israel's policy of adventurism, even though backed by imperialism and the guns of the Sixth Fleet, is doomed to collapse and total defeat'.

But on 22 May *Pravda* accorded the confrontation front page treatment. Its political commentator, Victor Maevsky, after analysing the situation at length, arrived at predictable conclusions. Events in the Middle East, he maintained, could not be viewed in isolation. 'They are closely interconnected with the crimes of the American aggression in Vietnam . . . and their provocative preparations in Cuba.' In fact all this was part and parcel of Washington's concept of 'local conflicts', and 'little wars' which are to underpin 'America's imperialist positions in various parts of the world'. In the Middle Eastern context, according to Maevsky, this means that Syria, whose 'anti-imperialist outlook displeases Washington, may in the next few days become the object of further provocation. The USA are unscrupulously encouraging Israel's military intervention on Syrian territory'.

Barely five days before the conclusion of the Husain-Nasser defence treaty, Maevsky subscribed to the somewhat outdated idea that conspiratorial imperialism plans to use 'neighbouring countries who, on the pretext of assisting her, are to occupy Syria and support the counter-revolutionary elements who have so busily been undermining the authority of the Syrian government'. The article ends with the usual warnings against the 'dangers of such a course', and an appeal to 'intensify the struggle for peace and security and against imperialism and reaction'.

Izvestia (23 May), in an editorial headlined 'The Common Denominator of the Tensions', regarded the coincidence of 'anti-Cuban declarations in Venezuela, threats from Tel Aviv, orgies of police brutality in Greece, and the screech of American planes over Hanoi' as 'suspicious'. America is blamed for all these global efforts to put the clock back.

Pravda's commentator, Oleg Skalkin (25 May), however, focused attention more specifically on the Middle East without casting much new light on the situation. He castigated 'the American hypocrisy of expressing concern at the deteriorating Middle East situation' while all the world knew 'that the CIA and nobody else instigated the anti-Syrian conspiracy'. Still clinging to the official line, although it was increasingly overtaken by events, Skalkin inveighed against imperialist efforts to 'sow discord among the Arab countries by making use of reactionary Arab feudalism'. Skalkin was nevertheless confident that such manoevres were bound to fail. Referring to the Soviet statement of the same date on the Middle East crisis, he concluded with the stern warning that 'the maintenance of peace in the region represents a vital Soviet interest'.

On 26 May the *Pravda* front page featured foreign reports under the headline 'The Tension Mounts'. A Turkish news agency was quoted as saying that the American forces in

Turkey were being alerted. Further down, the declaration of the UAR Defence Minister, Mahmud Riad, was briefly mentioned. It stated that attempts by Israeli shipping to enter UAR territorial waters would be regarded as an act of aggression.

Izvestia (27 May), continuing to regard the UAR as the main source of tension in the Middle East, delivered itself of a long blistering attack against the Sixth Fleet under the telling title 'Little Rock in the Mediterranean'. The American naval task force, it was suggested, 'indulged in looting forays beyond the wildest dreams of that old British pirate Drake. . . . Indeed, compared with its record, even the darkest chapters in the history of piracy pale into insignificance'. The Sixth Fleet, *Izvestia* concluded, 'must retire beyond the Straits of Gibraltar and return to its American home ports. This is demanded by the tens of million inhabitants of Southern Europe, North Africa and the Near East, who insist that their skies and their seas remain uncontaminated'.

Two days later, *Izvestia* (29 May) in similarly intemperate language denounced Golda Meir, the former Israeli Minister of Foreign Affairs, for describing the Soviet attitude to Israel as 'devoid of shame, conscience, or anything remotely reminiscent of human justice'. Such revealing verbatim quotation allowed, perhaps unintentionally, interested citizens, such as Jews and liberal intellectuals, a glimpse at the Western view of the Soviet position.

From 1 June onwards, *Pravda* seemed to think that the balance of events inclined towards war. On that day, commentator Maevsky 'emerged with the impression' that somebody was ready 'to light the torch of war in the Middle East'. The irresponsibility of certain circles in Israel, he noted, 'cast doubt on the sincerity of their protestations of restraint'.

On the next day the resolution of the (largely banned) Middle East Communist parties under the headline 'Arab Countries are on Guard', sounded somewhat more optimistic. Moshe Dayan's appointment as Minister of Defence appeared in *Pravda* (3 June) under the headline 'The Situation is Fraught with Danger'. These apprehensions perhaps justified the resolution of the *World Council for Peace (Pravda,*

4 June), in which Israel was exhorted 'to refrain from acts of aggression against either Syria or the UAR, and from allowing herself to become involved in the imperialist power game'.

Other East European countries, notably Yugoslavia, did not back the Arab cause quite so unreservedly, and *Politika* (Belgrade, 4 June), approaching the issue in a more concilatory spirit, wrote: 'The radical call for force in order to deny Israel's right to exist, to which no doubt the form, weight and direction of her actions contributed, obviously does not represent a solution likely to remove current difficulties. The insistence of one side on imposing its own conditions would multiply rather than reduce the obstructions still barring the way towards a consolidation and normalisation of relations. It would therefore seem that in the moment of success one should be more wary of one's own mistakes than of the adversary's intentions—and who could now doubt the political and moral success achieved by the Arabs? Under prevailing circumstances the Arab countries should therefore produce a plan so phased as to dovetail each new step into the next, along guide lines designed to promote a political solution. Such a plan would allow emotions to cool down and would also prevent one becoming, as Lenin put it, "the prisoner of one's own catchphrases".'

Warsaw's *Polityka* (1 June 1967) also expressed pained surprise at some Arabs' attitudes. Reporting on conditions in the Gaza strip, the paper's own correspondent found himself out of sympathy with the prevailing refugee mentality. Listening to complaints about the inadequacy of UNRWA funds, said to have compelled some refugees to accept domestic employment in the town of Gaza, the reporter commented: 'This seemed quite reasonable to us. After all, people can't just sit and idly wait for decades on end'. With something akin to shocked incredulity at the Arab propensity for semantic equivocation, the correspondent noted their contention 'that nobody intended to exterminate Israel physically since it would disappear from the face of the earth together with the era of neo-colonialism, exploitation and imperialism. The Arab world (the argument ran) would like to co-exist peacefully with the Jewish people, but had no chance of doing so in view of Israel's manifest Zionism'.

Nothing, however, more clearly illustrates the complete reversal of the Soviet response to near-identical contingencies than a comparison between the official Russian declarations of 1948 and 1967.

The USSR Declaration of 25 May 1967, as published in *Izvestia* of the same date:

During the last few weeks, a situation has developed in the Middle East which, judged by the criteria of peace and international security, gives cause for grave concern. After Israel's armed attack of 7 April on the Syrian Republic, the ruling circles in Israel continue to inflame the war psychosis in their country. Leading statesmen, among them the Foreign Minister Eban, openly advocate large scale 'punitive' expeditions against Syria, demanding that she be dealt 'a decisive blow'. The Defence and Foreign Affairs Committee of the Knesset (Parliament) authorized the Government on 9 May to initiate military operations against Syria. Israeli troops stationed on the Syrian border were alerted. The country was mobilized.

It is quite obvious that Israel would not have been able to take these steps without encouragement, direct or indirect, from certain imperialist circles, anxious to re-impose their oppressive colonial rule on the Arab region. Under prevailing circumstances these circles regard Israel as the main instrument for bringing to heel those Arab nations who pursue independent national policies and resist the pressure of imperialism. Israeli extremists apparently believed they could invade Syria and deal her a blow without let or hindrance. But their calculations have badly miscarried. The Arab nations—the UAR, Iraq, Algeria, the Yemen, Kuwait, Sudan and Jordan—declared their solidarity with the Syrian people in their heroic struggle to preserve their independence and sovereign rights, and they avowed their determination to come to the aid of Syria should Israel attack her. The UAR, honouring obligations under a mutual defence agreement, took steps to repel the aggression. The government of the UAR, in view of the fact that in this situation the presence of

UN forces in the Gaza strip and in the Sinai peninsula would favour the instigators of military provocations against Arab countries, requested the UN to consider the withdrawal of its forces from the region. A number of Arab nations expressed their willingness to put their forces under a joint Arab command in order to repel the Israeli aggression.

It will be remembered that, on the occasion of her armed aggression of 7 April, the government of the USSR had already warned Israel that she would be held fully responsible for the consequences of her aggressive policies. Apparently reason did not prevail in Tel Aviv. Israel proved herself once more the cause of a dangerous intensification of tension in the Near East.

The question arises whose interest does the State of Israel serve by pursuing such policies? If Tel Aviv counts on playing the colonial overseer for the imperialist powers over the peoples of the Arab East, the fallacy of such a calculation is self-evident in an age in which the nations of whole continents have shaken off the shackles of colonial subjugation in order to build an independent life.

For decades, the USSR supported the peoples of the Arab countries in their just struggle for national liberation and against colonisation, and has in many ways helped the progress of their economies. Nobody should be under any illusion; whosoever unleashes an aggression in the Near East will be confronted, not only with the united forces of the Arab countries but also with the determined resistance of the Soviet Union, and all peace loving nations. The government of the USSR is convinced that the people are not interested in the unleashing of a military conflict in the Near East. A conflagration would only serve the interests of a handful of colonialist oil monopolies and their stooges. Hence, militant action will only benefit the imperialist powers whose policies Israel supports.

The Soviet Union watches the development in the Near East very attentively. It bases its own policy on the assumption that the maintenance of peace and security in a region which borders the Soviet Union is a national and vital concern to the peoples of the USSR. Giving full consideration to current developments, the USSR is doing everything and will continue to do everything within her power to prevent any breach of Near Eastern peace and security, and to protect the legitimate rights of its people.

Excerpt from Mr Gromyko's Statement to the Security Council of 21 May 1948:

'It is very difficult not to agree that the military operation in Palestine, in which eight States, the majority of which are members of the United Nations, are more or less involved, constitutes a threat to peace. . . . The USSR delegation cannot but express surprise at the position adopted by the Arab States in the Palestine question, and particularly at the fact that those States—or some of them, at least—have resorted to such action as sending their troops into Palestine and carrying out military operations aimed at the suppression of the national liberation movement in Palestine.'

Neues Deutschland and Israel

A Diary of East German Reactions

Of all the Soviet bloc papers Neues Deutschland, *the official East German Government and party organ, was the most vicious in its attacks on Israel in the run-up to the Six Day War of 1967. Its ferocity was only matched by the venomous onslaughts of the West German neo-Nazi* Deutsche National-Zeitung *and* Soldaten-Zeitung. *Such identity of views, far from being a political novum, ominously recalled the early thirties when Nazis and Communists repeatedly joined forces in their efforts to undermine the Weimar Republic, and the human liberties and dignities it stood for.*

That any German state, irrespective of its political persuasion owes the survivors of Hitler's extermination camps some special consideration seems not to have occurred to the rulers of the German Democratic Republic. Or if so, as some of the articles specifically repudiating charges of antisemitism tend to indicate, the idea has speedily been disowned.

Whether the violence of the East German 'Hate Israel' campaign represents psychologically an over-compensation of repressed guilt feelings, or politically a welcome opportunity to score off the Federal Republic and to capture Arab markets and sympathies, is of comparatively minor interest. What stands out is that a German state once again supported powers openly committed to the extermination of Jews. Moreover, this Communist state, forever pre-occupied with the manifestations of surviving Nazism in West Germany, has branded that country's substantial restitution efforts to the citizens and state of Israel as 'aggression'.

On this issue too, the Communists of the Neues Deutschland, *and the neo-Nazi readers of the* Deutsche National-Zeitung *and* Soldaten-Zeitung *are fully agreed. There is, however, one salient difference between the two papers and their respective readerships: while the* Deutsche National-Zeitung *and* Soldaten-Zeitung *addresses the lunatic fringe,* Neues Deutschland *is official and matters.*

114

17 May

Neues Deutschland first mentioned the Middle East Crisis in an inconspicuous 3½″ single column agency report from Cairo. It read: 'Israeli troop concentration at the Syria and Lebanon frontiers have cause Syria's Minister of Foreign Affairs to write to the UN armistice commission drawing its attention to the danger of renewed Israeli aggression against the Arab States. In the complex anti-Syrian schemes, organized and financed by the American Intelligence Service CIA, Israel is said to have been assigned the part of the *provocateur.* Israel's open war threats have produced a very serious situation.

The influential Cairo paper *Al Ahram* reports that the forces of the UAR are ready to repulse any Israeli aggression against Syria, and that units of the UAR police have been alerted.'

18 May

Under the headline 'Syrian Army Alerted' a 2″ news flash from Damascus on page 7 reported the mobilisation of Syria's armed forces. These, according to a government declaration, 'were being reinforced by several brigades of the People's Army, so as to be ready to counter any Israeli attack'. The paper also mentioned briefly that Algeria and Iraq had declared 'their active solidarity with their Syrian brethren'.

19 May

A 6″ double column article on page 7 quoting Western news agencies, summarises the UAR's letter to U Thant demanding the speedy withdrawal of the UN force. The arrival in Cairo of Syria's Deputy Prime Minister, Dr Ibrahim Makhous, was mentioned as a token of 'a growing movement for Arab unity'. In this context, the letter addressed by the Algerian President Boumédienne to Syria and UAR was quoted verbatim: 'Israeli troop movements and their concentration at the Syrian border, as well as the threats of the imperialist lackeys in this region, reveal the existence of a comprehensive plot to subvert the Arab revolution.'

The fact that Kuwait and Iraq mobilized their forces and put them under a unified Arab command, was briefly mentioned, along with a declaration of the *Federation of Arab Trade Unions* condemning 'the colonialist and imperialist forces, among them the USA and West Germany, for their backing of Israeli aggression'. The Cairo *Al Gumhuriya* was quoted as reporting 'that Bonn had purchased in the USA $300m worth of armaments which were in part to be passed on to Israel'.

21 May

Under the headline 'USA and Bonn encourage Israel's aggression' a 5″ double column article on the foreign news page (p.7) referred to the Syrian Defence Minister's accusation against the USA's efforts to involve Israel 'in war-like adventures'. The Minister was also said to have protested against 'West Germany's colossal financial aid which made Israel's arms purchases possible'. An article from the Algerian *FLN* paper *Revolution Africaine* then focused attention on 'secret negotiations with the Israel Ambassador regarding the extension of Bonn's aid'. Representatives of both governments, the paper asserted had discussed a further extension of West Germany's credit grant beyond the 1966 level of £20m annually. The agreement, significantly contributing to Israel's military and economic strength, was to run for 10 years and included provisions for £320m worth of military equipment.

22 May

On a front page a 2″ double column under the heading 'U Thant—Israel aggravates the situation', reported that on his way to Cairo, U Thant 'declared the situation in the Near East to be more dangerous than at any time since 1956. He made the statement in view of the anti-Syrian threats recently uttered by prominent Israeli politicians. Moreover it has become known that Israel has mustered troops at the Syrian border. The Secretary General recalled that Israel had for years obstructed the work of the armistice commission.' A three line reference to Egypt's mobilization concluded the front page dispatch.

Neues Deutschland readers learned on page 2 of 'unbridled

agitation against U Thant and Nasser'. As a typical example
of West Berlin's press 'foaming at the mouth', the *Morgenpost*
was to have denounced the Secretary General, saying that 'U
Thant has meekly given in to the demands of the imperialist
Nasser'. 'Shamelessly standing facts on their head' the
Morgenpost was then rebuked for describing 'the politicians of
the UAR and other Arab states, who are at present taking
steps to safeguard the security of their countries, as the
initiators of terrorist activities'. At the same time the *Morgenpost* had allegedly praised the provocative activities of Israel,
which has, as everyone knows, received considerable financial
and military assistance from Bonn for the building up of an
aggressive army *(Aggressionsarmee)*.

23 May

'Further strengthening of the Arab front formed to repel
Israel's aggressive threats against Syria', from a double
column 6″ news report on page 7. It states that Iraq's armed
forces were ready to give instant ground and air support and
would on request be stationed on Syrian territory. News of
similar assurances to the UAR was said to have been
welcomed by President Nasser when it reached him at
advanced Air-Force Headquarters in the Sinai peninsula.
The report also mentioned Lebanon's partial mobilization,
and a declaration that Libya would regard any attack against
an Arab country as an attack against herself. It also reported
that 'to complement Israel's aggressive preparations, the
American Sixth Fleet has been concentrated east of Cyprus'.
    The papers of the West German Springer Publishing
Corporation were again castigated for their attempt 'to divert
attention from Israel's aggressive machinations by their
attacks on U Thant'. The Springer press, *Neues Deutschland*
claimed, 'denigrates the efforts of the Secretary General of the
world organization to meet the dangers of a conflagration in
the Near East. It had accused the "brown-skinned Burmese
ditherer" of being reluctant to accept political responsibility,
of "failure to take risks", and of "surrender", arguing that
"his strangely coloured neutralism benefits only the Soviet
Union".' Having given further examples of the Springer

press's objectionable anti-U Thant bias, *Neues Deutschland*
took exception to its spade-calling references to 'the power
struggle of the Egyptian dictator' or the 'terrorist activities of
Syrian extremists'.

24 May

'GDR solidly behind the Arab countries', was the front page
headline over an 8″ double column situation report giving
pride of place to the GDR policy declaration 'The prevailing
policy of aggravating tension (runs the statement) has led to
developments in the Near East which threaten the peace of
the region. In their desperate efforts to maintain their
neo-colonial influence, to undermine the national integrity of
Arab nations, to inhibit their social progress, while continuing to exploit their oil wealth, imperialism and reaction have
had recourse to crude military provocations. Tensions have
been dangerously intensified by Israeli troop concentrations
on the Syrian border, and also by aggressive actions against
other Arab countries. This demonstrates again the part Israel
plays as one of imperialism's military bases threatening the
Arab nations and states.'

The GDR emphatically condemns such imperialist
machinations against Arab countries. Opposing the anti-Arab
policies of the government of the West German Republic, the
government and the people of the GDR are ranged today as
in the past firmly behind the Arab states and peoples in their
defence against imperialist provocations. The GDR strongly
condemns the vile calumnies the West German Federal
Republic's imperialist press levels against the representatives
of Syria, the UAR, and Secretary General U Thant.

The journey through five Arab countries from which Otto
Winzer, the GDR's Minister for Foreign Affairs, has just
returned gave further proof of the anti-imperialist alliance
existing between the GDR and the Arab nations. Increasing
resistance to the common imperialist enemy, will further
strengthen the alliance in future.

The GDR demands that the West German government
should immediately suspend military aid to Israel. The GDR,

in common with all peace-loving anti-imperialist forces, will
see to it that peace in the Near East will be safeguarded and
defended.'

Considerable prominence was also given to the official
Soviet warning that 'those taking part in unleashing an
aggression in the Near East would have to reckon not only
with the united might of the Arab countries but also with the
determined opposition of the Soviet Union and all peace-
loving nations'. Other verbatim quotations from the Soviet
declaration referred to Russia's view that 'the maintenance of
peace and security in a region immediately bordering on the
Soviet Union is regarded as a matter of vital importance to
the interests of the people of the USSR'. They emphasized
Russia's contention that 'a warlike conflict would only benefit
a handful of colonial oil monopolies' and that Israel had only
succeeded in creating an atmosphere of war-psychosis
'because she was directly or indirectly encouraged to adopt
such a stance by certain imperialist circles only too anxious to
return Arab lands to the system of colonialist exploitation'.

An 8″ double column on the foreign news page features
further reports from the Middle East under the headline 'U
Thant off to Cairo talks because of Israel's threats.' The
fateful closing of the Gulf of Aqaba appeared as a sub-title
under the above headline and reads: 'UAR closes Gulf of
Aqaba to strategic war material.' But the main emphasis was
on the *ADN* agency message from Cairo that U Thant
'intends during his three day visit to discuss with leading
UAR personalities the tense Near Eastern situation provoked
by Israel's aggressive preparations against Syria'. The arrival
in Cairo of Syria's Prime Minister one day after that of the
Secretary General was briefly mentioned and so was the
agreement between Egypt and Iraqi leaders to 'combine the
material and moral resources of the two countries'.

The all important Aqaba issue was tucked away in a 15
line paragraph. Officers of the Egyptian custom service at
Sharm El Sheikh were ordered, it said, 'to enforce the boy-
cott regulations laid down by the Arab League' which, it
explained, included oil. A London dispatch reported that
'whereas the US Sixth Fleet has in support of Israel's
aggressive preparations been concentrated east of Cyprus,

Great Britain, is trying to dissociate herself from Israel'. The point was made that contrary to the USA, Great Britain no longer regards the tripartite declaration of 1950 as binding.

Under the heading 'The Springer hate campaign', *Die Welt* was berated for trying 'to prepare West German public opinion psychologically for an intervention by Bonn'. The paper had argued that 'Europeans could not possibly desert the USA in the Middle East *detente* in Europe'. *Die Welt* was also condemned for advocating NATO solidarity in support of Israel.

25 May

A 4″ front page paragraph noted that 'Arab unity and readiness to ward off any Israeli threat collectively is growing day by day', and that 'Western attempts to increase tension by threats of force against the UAR culminated in an effort to convene the Security Council which was however indefinitely adjourned.' For details readers were referred to the foreign news on page 7. Here, more than a quarter of the page featured the latest developments under such headings as 'Arabs united against conspirators, Dangerous plot against the peace of the Near East,' 'Israel's aggressive threats part of a global strategy,' and 'Bonn pours oil on fire.' Much was made of the solidarity declarations from Algiers, Morocco, the Yemen, the Sudan and Kuwait as well as of the utterances of the various Arab dignitaries who had hurried to Cairo to assure Nasser of their personal support. This apparently was also extended to the Syrian People's Army, reported as daily attracting more volunteers from workers, farmers, employees and students.

The West 'in contradiction to its protestations of peaceful intent was, however, hotting up Near Eastern tensions by military threats'. The USA was accused of having 'threatened the UAR with the use of force, should it exercise control over ships bound for Israel at the Gulf of Aqaba'. The only mention of the Security Council's meeting on the previous day came in a reference to the contention of the Soviet delegate, Professor Nicolai Federenko, that 'there was no adequate reason for convening the Council and that this was done by the representatives of the West to dramatize the situation'.

The other dispatches endeavoured to show how the local conflict fitted into a global overall plan. According to *Neues Deutschland* the plot was engineered in the following manner:

> On 12 May President Eshkol issued his provocative declaration against Syria; on 14 May the Chief of Staff Robin stated that Israel was training special armed commando groups for action against Syria; on 15 May a great military parade was held for the first time in Jerusalem at which the most modern equipment was displayed. This military parade was in flagrant contravention of the UN resolution of 1947 . . .

Dwelling once more on the movement of the US Sixth Fleet, *Neues Deutschland* alleged that 'the Tel-Aviv government assumes once again the role of the imperialist spearhead against the independent state, for obviously the dangerous step taken by Tel-Aviv cannot be understood in isolation. It is part and parcel of a carefully conceived design, a plot which the governments of Washington, Tel-Aviv and Bonn have hatched out in order to stop progressive developments in the Middle East.'

Bonn figured as the other main villain in this world conspiracy, and a 12″ column was entirely devoted to the financial, economic and military assistance it extended to Israel. Adenauer and Strauss, one learned, were the architects of the secret agreement about arms gifts worth £30m. But the most important aspect of the military co-operation was said to be Bonn's help in developing Israel's nuclear industry. By the middle of 1965, according to *Neues Deutschland*, more than 50 German nuclear scientists and 400 armament specialists were working in Israel.

The vilification of the Springer press continued. *Neues Deutschland* indignantly repeated the charge that one of the Springer papers referred to U Thant as 'the brown-skinned Burmese ditherer'.

26 May

A $3\frac{1}{2}''$ single column, front page paragraph noted the 'wide interest which the GDR's official declaration had received in the UAR. American troop movements 'designed to exacerbate the Middle East situation' were also reported, particularly the fact that 2,500 'leathernecks' (American marines) had left Naples 'to be available for aggressive operations'. The same anti-American mood dominated a 10'' double column on the foreign news page under the headline 'USA global strategists fan tensions in the Near East.' 'News of American threats of force (wrote the *Neues Deutschland*) against Arab countries make it clear who in fact pulls the strings in order to aggravate the Near Eastern situation.'

> It is the US Government which has prodded Israel to embark on this dangerous course. Israel figures in their schemes as a military base, and plays the part of a willing handmaid. The current confrontation in the Near East was deliberately engineered by the USA. It is part and parcel of President Johnson's global strategy. This global plot aims at stopping and reversing progressive developments throughout the world, a goal pursued by Washington with particular savagery in Vietnam, in the Dominican Republic, in Greece, and in collusion with the West German Government in Europe through its attacks on the status quo. The non-capitalist path of the UAR, Syria and other countries in the Near East has for a long time been a thorn in the flesh of the Washington, Tel-Aviv and Bonn league (the latter acting mainly as an arms supplier). These countries are to be forced into the American sphere of influence. It would suit this global strategy concept admirably if here in the immediate neighbourhood of the social camp a new 'limited armed conflict' could be unleashed. As the main enemy of the people in this Near Eastern crisis, the imperialism of the US stands clearly revealed; it alone, in the interest of its global strategy, endangers the peace and security of the world.

Among the others news from the Middle East, Indian and Czech support for the Arab cause was given some prominence.

27 May

Under the headline 'USSR unmasks US hypocrisy,' Soviet denunciations of American policy were made front page news. Tass described American references in the security Council 'to international law and the principles of free navigation as sheer mockery, since in their agression against Vietnam, the USA have trodden every norm of international law underfoot'.

A Damascus agency message reported that Syria has informed all diplomatic missions of the 'dangerous situation brought about by Israel's role as one of imperialism's military bases'.

28 May

A 5″ single column front page paragraph reported the Egyptian demand for a Security Council meeting in order to debate what the Egyptian delegate describes 'as Israel's agressive actions which endanger the peace and security of the Near East as well as of the world'. Under the cross heading 'US Sixth Fleet threatens Arabs', eight lines mentioned an *Izvestia* editorial accusing the American naval task force of 'brazenly menacing Arab nations with its guns', adding that 'the Sixth Fleet constitutes a perpetual threat to the independence of the Mediterranean people'.

Almost half the foreign news page was given over to the crisis. The Arab position, as the Algerian UN delegate Bovattoura described it during a press conference, was reported at some length. 'The Arab states (he is quoted as saying) expect from the UN that it will respect the legitimate decisions of the UAR as well as the resulting political and legal consequences and that it will repudiate any attempt to question them.' Hinting at de Gaulle's plan—without, however, mentioning his name—Bovattoura emphasized that 'the day of great power trusteeship over the small nations is long past. Interference with the sovereign interest of the Arab states will no longer be tolerated. Threats, whatever their nature, will be resisted, even those Washington tries to exert by the dispatch of the Sixth Fleet.'

An article by Rolf Günther, the paper's Cairo correspondent, stressed the growing Arab unity. 'Developments in the Near East,' he wrote,

> make it daily clearer that what is happening here is a confrontation between all the Arab states and the global strategy of the US brand of imperialism ... With this strategy the Americans believe themselves 'entitled' to engineer uprisings, *putsches*, and wars, anywhere in the world where [the exploiters'] 'liberty and democracy' are in danger. In the Middle East, Israel has been assigned the task of providing a military base against the progressive development of the Arab states.

This was followed by a recapitulation of the events leading up to the crisis which, for the first time, brought out the fact that the entire Arab posture stemmed from unverifiable intelligence reports. After analysing what Günther considered the abortive and the anti-religious revolt designed to overthrow the Syrian government early in May, he continued: 'Notwithstanding the American setback on 12 May, members of the Israeli government, enthusiastically egged on by the head of the cabinet, provocatively threatened to attack Syria and to overthrow the Damascus government. One day later, news of Israeli troop concentrations on the Syrian border is received. Thereupon the UAR Chief of Staff goes to Damascus to co-ordinate defence measures. On 16 May, Egyptian armed forces are alerted, and the UN are at the same time requested to withdraw their forces from the Gaza strip and the country's eastern frontiers where they were stationed by permission of the Cairo government. This happened the day before 17 May, the day for which, as well informed circles in Tel-Aviv were able to establish, the attack on Syria was planned. This attack was to deal the progressive Arab movement a deadly blow ... ' It was, however, averted because, as Günther explained, 'the deployment of Egypt's armed forces at her eastern frontiers demonstrated the real power relations and the hopelessness of an Israeli attack'. Indeed, 'Israeli-American probing for the weak spots in the fabric of Arab unity proved a fiasco. All it achieved was to precipitate a closer coming together of these states to meet the common danger.' While Günther did not rule out the possibility of the crisis 'becoming even more acute', he nevertheless concluded on a note of unintentionally ambiguous optimism.

Those who experience here in Cairo the demonstrations of militant zeal, who watch the younger generation march off to the recruiting centres and training camps, realize that the people stand more firmly behind their government than ever before. The UAR has the powerful backing of all socialist and progressive forces. Such worldwide support renders the Egyptian people as invincible as they were in 1956.

On the same page, a 6″ column levelled stereotyped denunciations against 'the Bonn-inspired hate campaign' in the West German press.

29 May

A 3 ″ single front page column featured the appeal by Syria's Communist party to fraternal parties all over the world 'to support the Syrian people in their attempt to frustrate Israel's aggression backed by American imperialism'. Yugoslavian support for the UAR was also mentioned.

On page 2 a 3″ double column again belaboured the Springer press for its 'hate campaign against the Arab states'. This agitation of the West German press 'systematically fanned by Bonn' had continued unabated. Springer's Sunday paper *Welt am Sonntag* was severely taken to task for describing President Nasser as 'the Führer on the Nile'. Apart from being criticized for suggesting that Arab countries are 'prepared to wage total war' and try to 'keep a stranglehold on Israel', the Springer paper was also condemned for publishing 'spiteful caricatures ridiculing the President of the UAR'.

30 May

Under the headline 'Unshakable Solidarity between the GDR and the Arab nations', assurances of militant support (*Kampfesgrüsse*) which the Central Committee of the SED had dispatched to the Government of the UAR, the Central

Committee of Syria's CP, and to the Executive of the Baath
Party, took up a quarter of the front page. In slightly differing
words the 'dear comrades' were informed that, 'in the hour of
a dangerous threat to liberty, progress and independence', the
SED's Central Committee was sending militant greetings to
its Arab friends. It indignantly condemned the imperialist
war preparations of the USA, West Germany and Israel. It
hoped that 'the united exertions, inspired by the fraternal
unity and solidarity of all anti-imperialist forces, would
succeed in safeguarding the peace, in decreasing tension and
in forcing the imperialists to retreat'. Nasser's praise for
Walter Ulbricht and the people of the GDR, and his
denunciation of the Federal Republic at his Cairo press
conference also made the front page. President Nasser,
according to *Neues Deutschland*, found it 'impossible to forget
for one moment that West Germany had secretly and behind
his back presented Israel with tanks, planes, guns and other
weapons'. He also considered it misleading 'to describe
Bonn's attitude in the current crisis as neutral. The entire
West German press sides with Israel, and is full of anti-Arab
innuendo.' Nasser's elaboration of the subject in reply to
questions from a *Neues Deutschland* correspondent filled a
quarter of the foreign news page. The presidential contention
was that 'when battle is joined between us and Israel, the
result of these [arms – *ed.*] gifts is predictable. The blood of
our sons is going to flow. Weapons in Israel's hands, tanks,
planes, aiming at our sons, that is the result. How can we ever
lightly forget it?'

The subject was not closed without the inevitable vilification of West Germany's press. Under the headline 'Furious
Yelping, Springer press steps up Arab hate campaign', *Neues
Deutschland* dismissed references to Nasser as 'the dictator on
the Nile', or 'Egypt's Dictator' as 'Nazi-type calumnies', or
'deliberate attempts at character assassination'.

31 May

Taking up a 12″ double column on the front page, East
Germany's reactions to the crisis were given pride of place
under the headline 'Republic outraged by imperialist plots in

the Near East'. Responding to what the paper called 'a wave of solidarity with the Arab countries menaced by imperialist global strategists', the executive of the East German Trade unions had sent the All Arab Trade Union Federation (ICATU) the following goodwill message: 'The workers of the GDR are outraged by the military conspiracy of the American and West German imperialists who, backed by the ruling circles of Israel, are plotting against the peace, freedom, independence and social progress of the Arab countries. The Trade Unionists of the GDR stand solidly behind the Arab peoples.' Similar messages were sent by the GDR's Afro-Asian Solidarity Committee and numerous trade union branches and other official institutions.

President Podgorny's Kabul declaration that the 'USSR sides with the Arab countries and peoples whose national independence the imperialists are trying to undermine by organizing dangerous military provocations', was also featured on the front page along with the continuing campaign against Springer. All his papers were attacked for their pro-Israeli attitude, none more fiercely than *Die Welt* which dared to suggest that young Germans ought to volunteer for service in Israel. These polemics were continued on the foreign news page, more than half of which dealt with the Middle East confrontation. A detailed (8" single column) account of the misdeeds perpetrated by the Springer press, entitled 'Spoilers of the broth' (*Sudelköche*) began: 'The scribblers writing for Axel Caesar Springer dip their pens deeper into the muck wells as soon as the Middle East is mentioned. The direction in which they will squirt their poison has been unmistakably indicated by Bonn's official backing of Israel's aggressive preparations . . . ' Allegations regarding 'the billions of economic aid consisting of planes, tanks, torpedo boats and rocket ramps' led to the by now familiar denunciation of the attitudes and language of the Springer press

It took Rolf Günther, the paper's Cairo correspondent, a quarter page to prove 'how and why' the UAR's right to the Gulf of Aqaba was incontrovertible. The reasoning behind his argument would be perhaps best exemplified by the following passage: 'If Israeli ships could use the Straits of

Tiran for ten years, this was solely due to the fact that, as a result of the Suez aggression, the UAR has been prevented from exercising her full rights. Hence, the UAR has currently done nothing but remove the last vestiges of the 1956 aggression and resume her full national sovereignty. . . . ' Under the cross heading 'No return to 1956', Günther concludes:

> This then is the position and these are the facts. Therefore, anyone threatening to force the Straits of Tiran would be responsible for increasing the pressure of tension to such a degree as to render an explosion inevitable. The UAR has international law on her side. She has vowed to fight for her sovereign right and shown her determination to do so. There is no going back, and a return to the status based on the remnants of the Suez aggression is no longer possible. The demonstration of Arabs' solidarity has shown the imperialist aggressors that a policy of strength will be of no benefit to Washington's global strategists.

1 June

Headlines like 'We stand firmly by our Arab friends', 'Massive protests against the machinations of the American global strategists in the Near East sweeps the Republic', 'Bonn hopes for escalation', and 'Arab countries denounce West Germany's hate campaign', dominated a good quarter of the front page. The 'wave of protests' included a message from the executive of the *Freie Deutsche Jugend (FDJ)* to its opposite numbers in the Arab countries. They were assured of the East German youngsters' 'solidarity with the Arab nations confronted by American global strategists and their Israeli lackeys'. East German journalists also dispatched similar messages to their Arab colleagues. *Neues Deutschland* was pleased to note that while the Arab press greatly appreciated East German attitudes, it strongly criticized 'West Germany's hate campaign', which it claimed led to an official demarche by Jordan and Lebanon. Polemics against 'Bonn's strong pro-Israel bias' also filled three 14" columns on the foreign news page. The sincerity of West Germany's repudiation of Egypt's charge that it was responsible for Israel's rearmament was strongly questioned in an editorial. 'This impudence (the paper states) matches the malevolent obstinacy with which Bonn has for the last 15 years been supporting Israel financially, economically, militarily and morally. Every Arab knows that West Germany delivered £320m. worth of goods and equipment, trained 5,000 Israeli soldiers, supplied heavy armament to the value of £30m. as a gift, helped with nuclear research, in short, encouraged every aggression.'

By contrast 'the Soviet Union's unflinching attitude to the imperialist threat of aggression in the Near East' was, as one of the headlines indicated, 'appreciated by Syria's press'. According to Damascus: 'Whether the imperialists like it or not, the Arab nations will move closer to the Soviet Union and the Socialist camp.'

New political developments are rarely treated by *Neues Deutschland* as straight news, but are generally served up in a thick sauce of ideological exegesis. The important fact of King Husain's sudden understanding with Nasser, and the signing of a mutual defence treaty was barely mentioned, even though the consequences were triumphantly emphasized: 'While King Husain's surprising arrival aroused much spiteful comment from the global strategists in Washington and Bonn, the actual signing of the defence agreement caused, according to political observers, great consternation among American and West German government officials.'

2 June

Front page prominence was given to Walter Ulbricht's message to President Nasser, handed over in the Hallstein-doctrine-defying words of the *Neues Deutschland* by 'Ambassador Dr Scholz, the GDR's representative in the UAR'. In his address, Herr Ulbricht said 'he felt moved to assure' the President, Government and peoples of the UAR of the GDR's solidarity with them. Retracing the familiar outlines of the 'all-embracing conspiracy of the US imperialists and of Israel', Herr Ulbricht, after enlightening Egypt's President on what must by now be the exceedingly well known 'aims of the notorious global strategy', namely 'to divest the Arab nations of their social progress, liberty and independence, and to deprive them of their native wealth and resources', proceeded to expose and abuse the Federal Republic. He argued that by 'extending over a long period of time economic and military aid . . . [here follow familiar details—*ed.*] the West German government had gravely transgressed against the Arab nations. Even now irresponsible politicians and public opinion media in the Federal Republic are busily fanning the war psychosis. Assurances to the contrary notwithstanding, the West German government continues to extend aid, not excluding military aid, to Israel. The GDR regards it therefore as her duty to expose these essentially imperialist tendencies in West Germany and to oppose them.' Having offered this original contribution to the Arab cause, Herr Ulbricht concluded his goodwill message with the customary long-winded denunciation of 'imperialist manoeuvres'.

Under the sinister heading 'Bonn approves the dispatch of war material', readers were informed of 'Bonn's full cabinet backing for the shipment of arms in support of Israel's aggressive circles'. The arms turned out to be '20,000 *Bundeswehr* respirators'. Undeterred by the unusual terminology in which gas masks rank as 'arms', *Neues Deutschland*, with the courage of its perverted semantics, proceeded to describe their delivery as 'aggression aid'.

Another feature on this page dealt with the 'Death Merchants', West German officials who, like the then Defence Minister Franz Josef Strauss, allegedly converted 20% of the German restitution deliveries into armaments.

3 June

This time it was the projected international attempt of keeping the Straits of Tiran open which caused 'a storm of protest in our Republic'. The apprentices at the state-owned Köpenik broadcasting station and the members of the collective '13 August' made the front page with their fulminations against 'the military assault on the independence of Arab nations now being prepared by the American imperialists supported by the reactionary Israeli army'.

Bonn which, as far as *Neues Deutschland* was concerned, remained one of the chief instigators of the crisis, was castigated for dispatching 'another shipment of war material', to wit a further 20,000 army respirators to Israel. These were needed, the paper declared on the authority of the Arab League's Bonn office, for the use of Israeli troops. 'Israel (*Neues Deutschland* says) has recently purchased considerable quantities of poison gas from Great Britain with intent to use it against the Arab nations; the Arab nations, on the other hand, have no stocks of poison gas.'

Headlines over the three column section devoted to the Middle East crisis stated: 'UAR asserts her sovereign rights over territorial waters. Emphatic warning to imperialist 'maritime powers'. USA and Great Britain anxious to find pretext for aggression. French government's refusal to participate' set the tone and theme for the subsequent reports. A declaration by the UAR Foreign Minister, Mr Riad, warning the maritime powers against '19th century gunboat diplomacy' was reprinted at considerable length.

> The interests of the states describing themselves as maritime powers are exposed to grave dangers if they participate in an act of aggression ... These countries must realize that they are neither called upon to exercize protective rights over the territorial waters of other nations, nor are they entitled to interpret international law in a manner which benefits only imperialist interests.

A short report on Anglo-American attempts at organizing an international initiative to keep the Straits of Tiran open emphasizes their view that 'in the last resort the use of force cannot be excluded'. In an article, 'The moment of truth for friend and foe', the paper's Cairo correspondent Rolf Günther was pleased to note how, in Egypt's estimation, 'the GDR ranks among those who in these fateful days have proved themselves friends of the Arab Nation'. With regard to Bonn's Middle East policy and standing, Günther concluded: 'It has been weighed and found wanting.'

4 June

Headlined 'Springer's incitement to nuclear war in the Near East—Nuclear arms to threaten Arabs—Israel's open aggression', a 6″ single front page column commented on an article in *Die Welt*, 'the Springer paper closely connected with the Bonn Government'; this discussed Israel's prospects of building a limited nuclear strike force and the strategic implications of such an eventuality, and is regarded as 'an admission of Bonn's complicity'.

A Tel-Aviv news flash reported Minister Allon as saying that 'unless the UAR accept Israeli terms, armed conflict is inevitable'.

The exchange of further goodwill messages between the GDR establishment and its institutions and their Arab equivalents filled almost two 12″ columns on page 6, where the various positions and official declarations regarding the inviolability of the Straits of Tiran were once more recapitulated punctiliously, and under headlines almost identical with those used on previous days.

A 16″ single column article initialled G.P. entitled 'Look who's talking!' repudiated West German charges of East German antisemitism.

The West German Kiesinger-Strauss Government (G.P. remarks) has by virtue of its aggression aid to Israel become one of the most dedicated stokers of Near East tension... Much as they try to conceal their complicity, President Nasser's recent exposures have for ever branded the West German government in the eyes of Arab and world opinion with the Cain's mark of abetting aggression. To divert attention from their own guilt, the Bonn warmongers have had recourse to that hoary gangster trick of blaming their own misdeeds on somebody else—to be specific, on the GDR. At the same time they ingratiate themselves as 'the friend and defender of Jews'. Words like 'humanity' and 'human duty' suddenly drip like mellifluous honey from the lips of Springer's propaganda writers whenever West Germany's aiding and abetting of this aggression is mentioned.

But woe betide those who, like the government and the people of the GDR, dare to expose these intrigues for what they are—means and methods by which one nation is being helped and encouraged to fall upon its neighbour. They immediately... turn into veritable angels of innocence and wail that we, the so-called GDR, provoke antisemitic passions, we debase the German people's moral credibility, and other such lies.

But let us look somewhat closer at the people who criticize us. The lilywhite garb of innocence in which Bonn prostitutes herself is in fact the funeral shroud of millions and millions of Jews who were sent by the selfsame people to the gaschambers of Auschwitz and Maidanek . . . These then are the people who want to teach us human kindness! The Bonn establishment uses this infamous crime, this murder of six million Jews as a blind for the perpetration of a new outrage.

Our position on this and indeed on any aggression is clear . . . the fact that we condemn the contemplated aggression by the Israeli bourgeoisie against the Arab nations does not make us the enemy of the Israeli people. This position has stood the test of history. For the German anti-Fascists who build the GDR as their own state—opposed by the militarists and antisemites, but respected by all peace-loving nations—have themselves in the years of Fascism trodden the path of suffering under and resistance to the murderers . . . And in order that this shall never happen again and that the German name shall once more be honoured, our Republic has—in contrast to West Germany—eradicated Fascism and militarism, the twin brothers of antisemitism, root and branch.

5 June

News of a further Ulbricht message, this time to the President of Syria, dominated the front page. Perhaps because it covered the well-known ground of the ultimate benefit imperialism hoped to reap from its global plot . . . 'to destroy the freedom and independence of the Arab nations, to obstruct their social progress, to continue in the interests of imperialist power and expansionist policies exploiting the regional oil wealth and to withhold it from their rightful owners, the Arab peoples', the full text of the message was relegated to the second page. So were excerpts from a high level radio discussion in which the Deputy Foreign Minister, Dr Wolfgang Kiesewetter, and a candidate member of the

East German Central Committee, Paul Markowski, felt constrained to refute charges of antisemitism. Dr Kiesewetter stated: 'We oppose the ruling circles in Israel who, in league with the imperialist forces, attempt to strangle or arrest the Arab freedom movement.' The Candidate Member of the Central Committee was prepared to examine GDR attitudes to Israel closely, since 'the Jew-baiters of the Nazi Reich and the West German Nazis are now attempting to brand the GDR as antisemites'. Such calumnies flatly contradicted all known facts, Markowski insisted. 'After all, we have shown that we exterminated antisemitism root and branch.' Moreover, the policy pursued by the GDR was one of peace, and this surely corresponded to the region's 'most deeply felt interests'. He stressed the fact that the 2.2 m. Jews living in Israel were only a fraction of

> the 13m. people of Jewish extraction all over the world
> . . . who would strongly object to being identified with the
> class and government now ruling Israel. This is definitely
> engaged in pro-imperialist, reactionary power policies of
> the chauvinistic and nationalistic variety. There are in Israel
> people—and let it be said, it rebounds to that country's
> honour that they exist—who oppose such policies.'

Another speaker dealt with West Germany and the 'libellous attempt of its press to blame the prevailing tensions on the Arab nations'. He held the Federal Republic responsible for supplying one-third of Israel's military equipment and asserted that 'the recently delivered gas masks were not intended to be used by civilians but by specialized units pursuing aggressive objectives in Arab countries'. The Central Committee Candidate Member recalled in this context 'imperial Germany's traditional urge towards the Near East. The attempt to secure a basis for military operations by establishing footholds, and by gaining political and economic influence through exercising control over raw materials: that was the real objective, the essence and the deepest motivation of their policy.'

6 June

Predictably, the transition from hostility to open warfare was featured on the front page as 'Israel began aggression against Arab nations'. The first Cairo communiqués and their claims of 'repelled attacks', 'bitter defence battles', 'Israeli forces thrown back . . . ' received considerable attention. However, there were also hints to the sophisticated reader that things in fact looked grimmer than Cairo cared to admit. Under the cross heading 'USA prevent UN decision' a Tass report explained the American refusal to accept a cease fire appeal demanding an immediate return to the positions originally held. According to Tass 'the American object was to delay the call for a cease fire until Israeli troops had managed to gain control of the Straits of Tiran and to penetrate into the Gaza strip and the Sinai peninsula'. '

Great prominence was given to the official Soviet declaration which unhesitatingly branded Israel as the aggressor. 'On 5 June, 1967 (it begins), Israel started military operations against the UAR and thereby committed an act of aggression.' Noting the various Arab countries who had come to the aid of Egypt, the declaration also dealt with the less obvious help for the other side.

> The adventurism of the rulers of one country—Israel—encouraged by open and secret actions of certain imperialist circles is therefore responsible for the outbreak of a military conflict in the Near East. With the unleashing of aggression against neighbouring Arab countries, the government of Israel has trodden the UN Charter and the elementary rules of international law underfoot.

While war news and the 'waves of protest sweeping the GDR' took up one quarter of the second page, almost the entire foreign news page dealt with the various aspects of the conflict. Here West Germany figured as one of the main instigators and culprits with the inevitable and apparently indefatigable Springer 'propagating world war'. Another headline read: 'Bonn knew timing of attack' and underneath 'Registration of West German mercenaries already under way.'

A 'situation report' was sent in on the eve of the war by the Cairo correspondent Rolf Günther. Its aggressively optimistic undertones made it particularly interesting reading. Günther regarded the conclusion of the defence pact with Jordan as 'indubitably the most important event in the week under review. Friend and foe agree that this event materially changed the power relations in favour of the national Arab forces.' The system of unified command structures now linking Egypt with Syria and Jordan 'made it possible to close the defensive ring round the bridgehead of Israel'. The completion of these arrangements represented, according to Günther, 'the second great victory of the national liberation movement in the Arab East. The first, averting an open threat of aggression against Syria, had led to the removal of the last vestiges of the 1956 aggression. It demonstrated a change in the military power relations on a world scale. The second victory indicated that a powerful and popular anti-imperialist movement was taking root in the region. This pressure from below has been responsible for the fact that the tendency towards united action has become predominant.' This unity of the progressive anti-imperialist forces in the Arab world had in Günther's submission, 'endangered all British and American positions. These positions, should they further aggravate the situation, will not survive a conflict.'

'Anti-Zionism' in
Polish Communist Party Politics

Adam Ciolkosz

'Three difficult weeks' (8-28 March 1968), as the Minister of
Education Henryk Jablonski described the unrest in Polish
universities, were preceded by a series of events in Warsaw
connected with the staging of Adam Mickiewicz' intensely
patriotic drama *Dziady* (Forefathers' Eve) which represents
the apogee of Polish poetry. It was produced under Kazimierz
Dejmek's direction in the Warsaw National Theatre on 25
November 1967 and banned by the Ministry of Culture after
thirteen performances, the last of which, on 30 January 1968,
turned into a protest march by students to the monument of
Mickiewicz, where flowers were laid. The students were
backed by the Warsaw branch of the *Polish Writers' Union
(ZLP)* which, after a stormy meeting, had adopted a
resolution demanding the withdrawal of the ban. One after
the other nearly all Polish universities became involved in the
protest movement; there were sit-ins in Warsaw, Cracow
and Wroclaw, and the number of arrested reached 2,730.
Two resolutions sum up the nature of the students' and
writers' complaints. The first, passed by *ZLP* (29-2-68), reads:
'The interference of the government departments in charge
of culture and art has considerably increased over the years in
both scope and intensity and extends not only to the contents
of literary works but also to their dissemination among and
acceptance by the public; such a situation endangers the

national culture, restrains its development, deprives it of its authentic character and condemns it to permanent sterility. Prompted by patriotic care, we call upon the authorities of the Polish People's Republic to restore, in accordance with our age-old tradition, tolerance and creative liberty.' The second resolution, adopted by the students of the Warsaw Polytechnic (13-3-68), demanded that Article 71 of the Polish Constitution guaranteeing freedom of the press, speech, assembly, etc., be respected and implemented.[1]

The *Polish United Workers' Party (PZPR)* was not slow in accepting the challenge. The counter-attack came in three speeches delivered by Jozef Kepa, First Secretary of the *PZPR* Warsaw Committee (11-3-68), Edward Gierek, then the *PZPR*'s First Secretary in the Katowice Voivodship (14-3-68) and Wladyslaw Gomulka, the First Secretary of the *PZPR* Central Committee. Gomulka's broadcast and televised speech (19-3-68) was reprinted in all daily papers and as a separate pamphlet. It outlined the Party's and the Government's policy and was meant as a declaration of intent of the utmost political importance. Nevertheless, it should be analyzed together with the speeches by Kepa and Gierek who as supporters of Gomulka, were at that time unlikely to voice opinions not shared by the General Secretary. All later speeches and publications did little more than reiterate and elaborate the ideas formulated by Kepa, Gierek and Gomulka.

Five distinct elements in the alleged conspiracy against the 'people's power' stand out from the chaotic and overlapping maze of accusations. The first category was represented by 'various posthumous children of the *ancien régime*' (Gierek's description), or people having as their ideal 'the restoration of a bourgeois and anti-Soviet Poland' (Gomulka). They included pre-war left-wing Pilsudskists, like the writer January Grzedzinski, and Catholics loyal to the hierarchy, like the writer Stefan Kisielewski.

The second category consisted of 'cosmopolitans' and 'imperialist lackeys', such as the poet Antoni Slonimski.

The third category was made up of 'modern revisionists'. In this context it is worth remembering that Gomulka was the first in the 'socialist camp' to identify this heresy when he asserted in his speech (15-5-1957) that in the present situation revisionism represented the main ideological danger within the Party.[2] At the time the philosopher Leszek Kolakowski was castigated as a prominent example of revisionist attitudes. Kolakowski still figured in 1968 on Gomulka's list of miscreants; but this time the list was much longer and the charge graver. In his speech Gomulka denounced the large body of Warsaw students who supported two young scholars, Jacek Kuron and Karol Modzelewski. The group's views, Kepa alleged, 'includes a collection of nearly all anti-socialist notions which in the recent, and in the not so recent past, have been formulated by foreign and native revisionists as well as by thinkers and theoreticians of the Fourth International'. Although it should be obvious that revisionism, whether ancient or modern, cannot be reconciled with Trotskyism—since the one excludes the other—this unlikely mixture was nevertheless concocted for the *PZPR*'s domestic use. Useful as it may have been, it nevertheless proved insufficient and accordingly Kepa and Gierek, for good measure, raised the bogy of Zionism. This question will be dealt with later.

Kepa's attack was also directed against Roman Zambrowski and Stefan Staszewski, once prominent communist leaders whom Kepa had described as 'consummate political gamblers experienced in the intricacies of political infighting, now removed from influence, discredited in the eyes of the Party and the opinion of society'. Not far removed though; for at the time these views were expressed, Zambrowski was the Vice-Chairman of the Supreme State Chamber of Control.

From these accusations, inventions and insinuations a complete, although utterly fantastic picture gradually emerged; a *coup d'état*[3] was being prepared in which Roman Zambrowski was the central figure, the instigator and pretender to power. His son Antoni served as a link to the dissenting revisionist and Zionist student groups. The students' unrest caused by the banning of *Dziady* was to be the spark to ignite the flames of the *coup*. But the conspiracy itself had far-reaching aims and was meant to serve a higher purpose: the revisionists made common cause with the

Zionists, and the Zionists represented a link with the Israelis, who, in their turn, were allies of the German *revanchists* in Bonn. They, as everyone knows, were the lackeys of the American imperialists and warmongers. Their objective was to introduce, if not at once, then step by step, a bourgeois democracy in Poland and to separate Poland from the 'Socialist camp', thus isolating her from the Soviet Union. Hence, the 'patriotic' phrase which was repeated time and again by leading Polish communists in their speeches and articles—whoever turns against socialism turns against Poland. In this vein, Gomulka pronounced (19-3-68): 'The guarantor of socialism in Poland and of the alliance with the Sovet Union is first of all our Party; anybody who opposes our Party and the socialist system undermines the foundations of Poland's national existence'. There was nothing new in this contention, which in fact amounted to the threat of armed Soviet intervention if the rule of the *PZPR* were to be seriously challenged. Gomulka had made the same dire predictions, using literally the same words, in his speech on the eve of the *Sejm* general elections of January 1957. When it was doubtful whether the *PZPR* would win a majority, he did not hesitate to intimidate the electorate with threats of Soviet reprisals and the resulting loss of Poland's independence, should *PZPR* candidates fail to gain a decisive victory. At that time the possibility of Soviet intervention, with events in Hungary still fresh in everyone's memory, made a great impression and produced the desired result. Now, however, nobody in his senses could believe that as a result of the applause for Dejmek's direction of *Dziady*, Soviet troops would enter Warsaw. Gomulka's threat coincided with the events in Czechoslovakia, where considerably more important matters were at stake, but he was obviously frightened by the prospect that events in Czechoslovakia could be re-enacted in Poland. Hence, Gierek's intemperate threat 'to break every bone . . . of the frustrated enemies of People's Poland'[4] was not a hollow menace. Even before Gomulka made his speech a wave of reprisals had begun to purge the establishment of all shades of opposition. Strangely enough, the villain of the piece, the elder Zambrowski, although deprived of his official post and expelled from the party, was never arrested or interrogated. It had all been a sham, and everybody knew it.

The heterogeneous and contradictory composition of the opposition, its alleged links with Israel, the German Federal Republic and America's CIA, so untiringly evoked by the communist leadership, failed to make any sense or to lend itself to anything more specific than the blanket denunciation of being 'enemies of the people'; an accusation reminiscent of the Soviet Union at the height of the Stalinist period. Although reprisals on a Stalinist scale are at present impossible even in Russia, the absurdity of the witchhunt has survived. Who constitutes an 'enemy of the people' is decided by the First Secretary and the Political Bureau. The selection is, however, not completely arbitrary. The animus is, above all, against people of moral integrity and an independent mind, against the intelligentsia, whether old or young, Gentile or Jewish, within the ranks of the Party or outside it. The leadership of the Party now represents, according to Stefan Kisielewski's speech at the Warsaw writers' meeting,[5] 'a dictatorship of the ignorant' *(dyktatura ciemniakow)*, who needed the enemies of the people because they were unable to fight the opponents and critics of the regime on an intellectual and political plane. In short, they needed bogymen.

Expulsions from the Party long ago ceased to arouse fear; on the contrary, in the eyes of the general public they have become something of a distinction. The new method is to deprive those anathemized of their employment. As a rule, this method is aimed at men who are or have been until quite recently luminaries of Polish science, leading members of the Party or government bureaucracy, or industrial managers. Most of the purged, but by no means all, are the object of general compassion and sympathy. In some cases, however, their removal from public office is greeted by a general sigh of relief and regrets that this particular piece of surgery had not been applied much earlier. The regime's technique is to have some really guilty people to swell the ranks of the innocent thousands. If the purge, therefore, represents a somewhat chaotic picture and lacks a consistent pattern, it is because too many accounts have been settled simultaneously, and because the campaign's deliberate absurdity is one of its essential characteristics.

In these conspiratorial fantasies, anti-Zionism has played a significant part. Its immediate roots can be traced back to Gomulka's speech at the 6th Polish Trade Union Congress (Warsaw, 19-6-67), delivered in the hectic atmosphere immediately after the Six-Day War which, whatever its political aspects, had inflicted defeat on the military protegé of the Soviet Union and compromised her reputation. At that time Gomulka propagated the ambiguous slogan: 'Every Polish citizen can have one fatherland only, the People's Poland'. Had he spoken of 'Poland', the meaning would have been unequivocal. The slogan 'People's Poland', however, suggested the idea of a definite political system, of a 'People's democracy'. In any case sympathies for Israel were at that time widespread in Poland, and Gomulka's speech could not produce a change of climate. Nor could it be changed by Tadeusz Walichnowski's *Israel a NRF* (Israel and the German Federal Republic (Warsaw 1967), a book which received wide publicity and rapidly went through three printings. This book, published by the communist *Ksiazka i Wiedze*, was meant to be a scholarly documentation of the alleged conspiracy between the students' revolt and the alleged sinister manipulators behind the scenes, and by sleight of hand managed to equate the State of Israel with Zionism and Zionism with Jewry, suggesting all sorts of underhanded activities hostile to socialism, or at least to the kind of socialism practised by countries under communist rule.

In his speech of 19 March 1968, Gomulka divided the Polish Jews into those attached by reason and emotion to Israel, who sooner or later would leave Poland, the cosmopolitan ones who consider themselves as neither Poles nor Jews and who should avoid activities requiring national identification, and those who regard Poland as their sole homeland. While opposing Zionism and Jewish nationalism as a political programme, the Party was, as the First Secretary explained, also opposed to antisemitism, defined as 'rejection of Jews simply because they happen to be Jews'. This was, however, a purely theoretical distinction. From many other pronouncements of *PZPR* leaders and activists, not least from the 'pioneering' speech by Kepa, it was to be inferred that every Jew who expressed sympathy with Israel was a 'Zionist', particularly when he welcomed the Israeli victory in the Six-Day War. It was obviously quite unthinkable that a cosmopolitan Jew, or a patriotic Polish Jew, could have sympathies with Israel, or rejoice at her triumph over the Arab armies. It was, of course, just feasible that patriotic or cosmopolitan Poles of Catholic persuasion could succumb to similar sentiments, although it emerged from Gomulka's speech that only Jews are of the stuff cosmopolitans are made of.

Tarring the Jews with the revisionist-cum-Trotsykist brush proved even more damaging. Gomulka had no compunction at suggesting such sinister Jewish conspiracies. 'On 3 March of this year,' he alleged, 'a score of people, mainly Jewish or Jewish born students known for their revisionist pronouncements and views,' assembled in Jacek Kuron's flat. Even had that actually been so, the very fact of stigmatizing the participants as 'Jewish born', allowed the listener and reader to draw definite conclusions of the kind which Gomulka himself had defined as antisemitic. Following the First Secretary's lead, other *PZPR* speakers adopted the same tone, embellishing their speeches with strictures on 'wreckers', easily identifiable by their distinctly Jewish sounding names. The official Polish Press Agency in its communiqué of 25 March, reporting the dismissal of six Warsaw University professors and lecturers, accused them of protecting the rebellious leaders of 'the well organized group of students or former graduates from Warsaw University, mainly of Jewish extraction'. 'Mainly of Jewish extraction', has since become a stereotype in the communist vocabulary.

This thinly veiled antisemitism drew its appeal and plausibility from two separate sources. The first of these focused on the part played by Jewish Communists in the 1944-56 era. They were, as the Minister of Education Henryk Jablonski explained,[6] the men who, in the formative years of our people's statehood, were promoted because they were less likely to be influenced by Polish nationalism'. He went on to say that, as a consequence of the political changes of October 1956, many of them lost their leading positions. Their families were easily affected by a sense of opposition. In other families the general conditions of existence favoured the growth of bourgeois ways of life and offered an opportunity for the emergence of oppositional sentiments hostile to the transformation which Poland was undergoing.

> 'Against this background,' the Minister explained, 'the seemingly paradoxical phenomenon may have arisen that some of these families became disenchanted with the policy of our country, while they increasingly identified with the interests and policy of a state which occupies a particularly advanced place in the imperialist camp [the United States—ed]'.[7]

This theory conveniently explains why parents are responsible and must be punished for the alleged misbehaviour of their children.[8] Moreover, the ethos of the Stalinist era is somehow linked to the cosmopolitan inclinations of Polish-Jewish communists, suggesting that it was permissible before, but not after October 1956 to have been immune from Polish nationalism.

A stalwart of the pre-war period, Andrzej Werblan, Chief of the Department of Science and Learning in the *PZRP* Central Committee and himself a Jew, asserted: 'It should be openly admitted that the ethnic composition of the *Communist Party of Poland (KPP)* in the essentially Polish territories has not been correctly balanced. Proportionally, the *KPP* has had wider influence among the Jewish national minority than among the Polish population'. As a result, Werblan alleged, the *KPP* held a simplistic, cosmopolitan interpretation of internationalism which found its expression both in a certain indifference to the national obligations of the Left and in a tendency to subordinate these aspirations mechanically to international tasks and duties instead of trying to 'harmonize the two'. Whereas those former members of the *KPP*[9] who remained on Polish soil managed in 1942 to rebuild the Polish revolutionary movement through the *Polish Workers' Party (PPR)*, the majority of the former *KPP* 'actives', particularly the Jewish communists, had left for the Soviet Union. 'This acccounts for the disproportionally large number of Jewish militants among the leaders and organisers of the *Union of Polish Patriots (ZPP)* as well as among the leading

political officers of the First Polish Army', then being formed
in the Soviet Union. Cut off from Poland during the war,
they were afterwards 'unable to achieve a correct understanding of what the nation needed, and of the new tasks facing the
Party. The attitude of these activists was marked by sectar-
ianism and dogmatism'. On their return, they considered
themselves somehow superior to the fighters who stayed in
Poland. They felt called upon to lay down the political line
which the newly born People's Republic was to follow.
Ignorant of their own oversimplifications and their cosmopolitan deviations in interpreting socialism, they took it upon
themselves to adjudicate between the claims of internationalism and nationalism.

The *PPR* approach immediately after the liberation, when
Gomulka was its First Secretary, was marked, according to
Werblan, by a deep understanding of the peculiarities of the
Polish nation, its needs, aims and mentality, but in 1948
Gomulka and other initiators were criticised for their
'rightist-nationalist deviation'. They had even been accused
of antisemitism, whereas in fact they realised quite correctly

> that no society would be willing to tolerate an excessive
> representation of a national minority in the leading
> councils of the nation, particularly in departments con-
> cerned with national defence, security, propaganda and
> diplomacy. . . . Every society rejects such privileges with
> disgust.

Here all the arguments used by Polish nationalists in the
1918-39 period were revived including those advocating a
numerus clausus for the Jews. Werblan singled out Jakub
Berman, Roman Zambrowski and Hilary Minc among those
particularly responsible for 'simplifications and deviations',
studiously avoiding, however, any mention of Stalin who in
fact decided all major Polish appointments of the post-war
era. Nor was the 'Aryan' Boleslaw Bierut, surely Stalin's
most loyal Polish *Gauleiter,* mentioned. In any case, Werblan,
like Jablonski, equated Stalinism with the cosmopolitan
tendencies of Polish-Jewish communists and a predilection
for Stalinist methods is again identified with a particular
ethnic background. This led to his ineluctable conclusion:

> Experience has proved that the majority of the newly created cadres were ideologically alienated and were easily led along the path of revisionism. Many adopted Zionism and emigrated, usually after having broken with all things Polish.[10]

Jewish communists, Werblan asserted, were not only prone to disassociate themselves from the communist party in its post-October period, but many of them also achieved 'a personal union' between revisionism and Zionism. This is hardly surprising in view of the important role Jews played among the revisionists. Moreover, reactionary tendencies shared by revisionist, cosmopolitan, Pilsudskist and retrograde Catholic groupings had induced them to form an alliance. Starting from their positions among the students and writers, they attacked as their first objective the political superstructure of socialist society, namely its political system, in the hope that they might eventually replace the socialist by a bourgeois democracy. What distinguished the *PZPR* leadership from the revisionist groups in the post-October period, was the nihilistic and demagogic character of the latter. They attacked the essence of socialism, while the *PZPR* leadership [under Gomulka—ed.] confined itself to criticizing the errors of dogmatism and defended the leading role of the Marxist-Leninist Party.

Jablonski's and Werblan's criticism of Polish Jews was confined to their alleged influence on internal party developments. Both attempted to explain recent events in terms of Leninist ideology and politics. Another version, simultaneously presented, dealt with the Jewish problem outside the party. It can be fairly described as the racialist version of which Stanislaw Kociolek's speech in *Sejm* (11-4-68) provides a representative example. Kociolek, a supporter of Gomulka, was the *PZPR*'s First Secretary in the Gdansk Voivodship. According to Kociolek, the experience of the past had shown that internationalism and the ideologically and morally important struggle against Polish nationalist selfishness and narrow-mindedness 'has been exploited as an alibi for definite group interests by a national minority, in order to achieve an excessive concentration and representation in the key areas controlling and directing the national effort'. But now, Kociolek added, under Gomulka's guidance we are throwing off the humpback of the nationalist misrepresentation of internationalism, and of the nationalist defence of group interests. . . . There can be no philosophy of humility towards any *Herrenvolk* thrown up by history.

The charge that Jewish communists had been unable, because of their race, to harmonize Polish national interests with the true spirit of internationalism, was in this way extended to equate all Jews with a *Herrenvolk*. This was on a par with the preachings of the Right-wing extremists of pre-war Poland. There was no contradiction between what Jablonski and Werblan were telling party stalwarts, and what Kociolek was preaching to the simple-minded general public not particularly interested in the subtleties of Party dialectics. They might not care much for the Party's leading role in the 'People's State'; on the contrary, they might well wish that the Party and all its works, its internal conflicts and factions would disappear from the stage of history. Nevertheless, it was expected they would listen and pay attention to talk about *Herrenvolk*, particularly if the warning comes not from sinister and discredited hawkers of hatred, as in pre-war times, but from officials in prominent positions; not from antisemitic fascists but from communists with a reputation for objectivity towards Jews. This, it seems, was the motive behind the manoeuvre which, however, failed to catch on.

Subsequently, the communists began posing as the defenders of Poland's national honour against Jewish attempts to denigrate it. Every speech or article in the Jewish press, whether from London, Paris, New York, or Tel-Aviv, lending itself to representation as such an attempt was seized upon and publicized in the communist-controlled press. Although the communists failed to convince the country that the party was the best guardian of Polish interests, they nevertheless succeeded, at one remove, in stirring up much resentment against those foreign Jewish speakers and journalists who were unable to differentiate between antisemites, including the communist variety, and the overwhelming majority of the Polish nation.

From 11 March 1968 onwards, first in Warsaw and then

throughout the country, meetings against the 'brawling' students were organized, first in the factories and mines, then in the public squares of cities, towns and villages and finally as vast regional rallies. 100,000 people were said to have demonstrated in Katowice and in Cracow, while 150,000 people paraded in Lodz. Not one of these demonstrations took place after working hours, not a single one on a Sunday, but all were staged during working time in lieu of work. This means the whole nation had to pay with millions of wasted man-hours for this show of alleged solidarity between the nation, the Political Bureau and Gomulka. These rallies were characterized by a note of organised hysteria previously not noticeable except perhaps during the 1944-48 period prior to Gomulka's fall. It consisted of the chanting of 'Wie-slaw' (Gomulka's pseudonym under the Nazi occupation), the display of such slogans as 'We believe in thee, Wieslaw', or 'We are with you, Wieslaw', and the carrying of Gomulka portraits. All this seemed to indicate the resurrection of the 'personality cult'; this time, however, the 'personality' was Polish, even though the pattern of the cult was Muscovite and Stalinist.

The banners, as usual, conformed to the instructions from above, and the slogans they carried must therefore be considered to have represented the Party line. Most of them referred to Zionism. 'Down with the Zionists', they proclaimed, or 'Zionists to Israel', 'Purge the Party of Zionists', 'Purge the Government of Zionists'. The concept of Zionism was, however, completely unknown to the general public, at least before the *PZPR* embarked on its latest campaign. And why should it be known? Half of Poland's population was born after the outbreak of the Second World War, and its, at most, 30,000 Jews (0.1% of the population) no longer formed an identifiable minority. Poles knew about Israel, and the Israeli-Arab conflicts; but they were justifiably ignorant of a non-existent Zionist movement in Poland. To enlighten them, *Trybuna Ludu* (15-3-68) published a feature 'What is Zionism?' which it continued (19-3-68) under the title 'Zionists on themselves'. The dates of these articles are significant: first, a wave of anti-Zionist slogans and resolutions flooded the country and then a series of 'explanations' as to the meaning of Zionism was launched. It is, therefore, fairly obvious that the March demonstrations could not have been spontaneous; people were ordered to take part just as they were on May Day or 22 July parades. The anti-Zionist slogans must also have been prepared by the Party organizations. The published photographs of the various rallies confirm this suspicion for the inscriptions were everywhere the same. To the demonstrators the inscriptions on the banners could only mean one thing: to rid the Party, the government and the country of Jews. 'Jews back to Palestine!' was the message preached by the pre-war Fascist *ONR (National Radical Organisation)* which—although in a totally reprehensible way—responded to a real minority problem, whereas its latter-day imitators have not even that excuse. They invented the issue in order to strengthen party cohesion. This they achieved, but strangely enough by giving whole-hearted support to Gomulka, a man known to have reached the closing stages of his career.

PZPR, The Polish Communist Party, faced immensely difficult problems. Apart from economic stagnation, the most intractable was perhaps the decline of the party's ideological credibility, an increasing disavowal of its doctrinal and political premises. The number of convinced communists in the ranks of the *PZPR* was in all probability smaller than that of the pre-war members of the KPP, which was insignificant enough. The fires of a new fervour, kindled during the 'turning point' of October 1956, have long since been extinct, and nobody worked harder to extinguish them than Gomulka himself. The attempt to give the *PZPR* a new ideology was closely connected with the activites of the so-called 'Partisans' group, led by General Mieczyslaw Moczar. He was the spokesman of that *Nationalist* communism (not to be confused with *national* communism) of which antisemitism forms an integral part. The peculiarity of this nationalism was its utter dependence on Soviet Russia as the guarantor of Poland's strength and development. It was an eastwards-looking nationalism. As far as the methods of government were concerned, Moczar and his 'partisans' favoured strong-arm tactics. They represented the forces anxious to end any drift towards liberalism and social-democracy within the Party and government. Moczar and his 'partisans' created for themselves a solid power base in the ex-combatants' organization *Union of Fighters for Freedom and Democracy (ZBoWiD)*, some of whose aspects (respect for Poland's historical grandeur) appealed to Polish national sentiments more than the discredited, plain, uninspiring and tedious communist internationalism of Gomulka. Patiently but consistently, Moczar and his 'partisans' infiltrated the party and its affiliated organisations. Their secret organization *Pion (Plummet)* covered the entire country and carried out directives given by the centre. In 1968, Moczar was playing a waiting game, biding his time, and preparing for his hour to come. He had markedly improved his position when, at the plenary meeting of the *PZPR* Central Committee on 9 July 1968, he was promoted to be one of the eight secretaries of the Central Committee with responsibility for security. Gomulka's actions certainly suited Moczar's interests. He had already accepted Moczar's ideological, political and tactical dispositions. At a time when Dubcek's Czechoslovakia was moving ahead, Poland under Gomulka had moved backward.

Two characteristic examples of the then prevailing chaos may be mentioned: Professor Adam Schaff resigned (or rather was advised to resign) from his post as Director of the Philosophy and Sociology Institute of the Polish Academy of Sciences. Like Professors Kolakowski, Baczko, Bauman and Zolkiewski he was one of the principal targets in the campaign against 'philosophical and sociological revisionism', but at the same time he was allowed to remain a member of the *PZPR* Central Committee, as well as of the Commission preparing the Fifth Party Congress. The heated and abusive feud concerning the meaning of socialism and socialist economy between the weekly *Polityka* and the daily *Trybuna Ludu*, both of which supported what they took to be Gomulka's policies, also highlighted the general confusion. The style and quality of their arguments was somewhat reminiscent of those in China's cultural revolution. Incidentally, the editor of *Polityka*, Mieczyslaw Rakowski, was one of the spokesmen of the October 1956 line, whereas the newly appointed editor of *Trybuna Ludu* Stanislaw Mojkowski, was a devoted Catholic before the war. He replaced Leon Kasman, a Polish-Jewish communist who during the Second World War fought on Polish soil against the Germans as one of the communist partisans.

But to look back at the students, professors and writers, and the semi-legendary 'events of March'. 'Public order has been restored', asserted the *Trybuna Ludu* (31-3-68), recalling the famous *L'ordre règne à Varsovie;* glib misapprehensions which have punctuated Polish history. Time and again they have spelt the defeat of Polish freedom and progress. Time and again they have proved to be false prophecies not, fortunately, borne out by events. *Trybuna Ludu's* assertion only meant that Poland's once revolutionary *Communist Party,* the present *PZPR,* had become a reactionary instrument of the established order, and a model of a new communist variant: that of antisemitic communism. This, however, is not the end of the story. The future will in the long run be shaped by the young people whose leaders had languished in Gomulka's and Moczar's prisons. The belief that inspired them, their sense of reasoned dedication as expressed by one of the students at a mass meeting in the courtyard of Warsaw University is unlikely ever to be forgotten or disowned:

> In fighting for Mickiewicz' play we fight for the independence, freedom and democratic traditions of our country. In so doing, we also fight in defence of the working class, for there is no bread without freedom, no learning without freedom.

NOTES

1. *Zycie Warszawy,* Warsaw, 26 March 1968.
2. At the plenary meeting of the *PZPR* Central Committee. Wladyslaw Gomulka, 'Wezlowe problemy polityki partii', *Nowe Drogi,* No. 6/96, Warsaw, June 1957.
3. Kazimierz Kakol in the Warsaw weekly *Prawo i Zycie* (24-3-68).
4. At the *PZPR* rally in Katowice, 14-3-1968. *Trybuna Ludu,* No. 74/6901 15-3-1968.
5. At the meeting of the Warsaw branch, Polish Writers' Union, 29-1-1968. 'Zebranie warszawskich literatow', *Kultura,* Paris, No. 4/246, April 1968.
6. Henryk Jablonski, 'Zaburzenia studenckie w marcu 1968 r.', *Nowe Drogi,* No. 5/228, May 1968.

7.   *ibid.*

8.   One of the most interesting cases was the expulsion of Ozjasz Szechter. *Trybuna Ludu* explained on 24 April 1968 that Szechter was the father of Adam Michnik, one of the main organizers of the March events in Warsaw University'. Prudently, *Trybuna Ludu* passed over in silence the fact that the same Szechter was responsible for a new Polish translation (the fourth) of *Das Kapital* which appeared as the twenty-third volume of Marx and Engels' collected works in March 1968—a few weeks before its translator and editor was expelled from the Party.

9.   The *KPP* was disbanded by the Communist International at the beginning of 1938.

10.   Andrzej Werblan, 'Przyczynek do genezy konflikitu', *Miesiecznik Literacki*, Warsaw, June 1968.

Neo-Stalinist Antisemitism in Czechoslovakia

W. Oschlies

Since the Six Day War, and particularly after Golda Meir's plea in March 1970 to let Soviet Jews emigrate to Israel, Eastern Europe has once again been engulfed by a noisy 'anti-Zionist' campaign. The motive of and directives for such a campaign, reflected in hundreds of declarations, articles, speeches, letters to the press, etc have been set out in Yuri Ivanov's book *Caution—Zionism,* which defines Zionism as follows:

> Zionism, being a reactionary system of ideas and reactionary organizations serving the aims of imperialism, is therefore a manifestation of the class struggle and—like the whole structure of imperialism—is in the throes of a deep crisis. However, the facts showing the trickery of Zionist propagandists lead inescapably to the conclusion that Zionism, its political potential, its room for manoeuvre, its future course and ultimate death are directly related to the political potential, the course and ultimate death of the exploiting classes and to the course and death of imperialism.
>
> In our time, Zionism finds it increasingly difficult to operate. Yet it was and remains to this day an experienced and cunning foe of internationalism and brotherhood among nations, and a dangerous tool of imperialist reaction.

The Czech party stalwarts, over-zealous as ever, who had

153

previously given their enthusiastic support to the Soviet-inspired antisemitic campaign, are once more denouncing 'Zionism as a tool of American imperialism', or as something similarly evil. Even though, compared with the virulence of the Russian attack, the current Czech campaign remains somewhat muted, it nevertheless introduced some specifically Czech approaches to the age-old subject. It is therefore pertinent to inquire what part Czech antisemitism (invariably labelled anti-Zionism) played before the events of January 1968, how far reaction against it was part of the regenerative processes of that year, and what importance it assumed in the cause of the present restoration.

The numbers and influences of Czech Jews have always been and still are greatly exaggerated. The reasons for such a misconception are many and complex; their varied motives were well caught in one of Gustav Meyrink's animal sketches, in which a vulture inquires of a hamster:

'A Southerner then?'
'No, I'm from Prague.'
'So, of the Hebrew persuasion, eh?'
'What me? What do you take me for, Mr Vulture?' protests the hamster, sorely frightened at being confronted with a Russian. 'Me an Israelite, who's been a shabbes-goy for ten years in a Jewish, though poor, family.

The 'so' is a clever dig at a widespread popular misconception. For Meyrink, a former Prague banker, knew only too well that the Jews of Prague were quite a small minority. The notion of a Prague populated by Jews arose first from Jewish identification with the solid and affluent German-speaking minority, and secondly from the existence of some common traits in Czechs and Jews. Both, for example, display a defensive reticence, adroitness in handling authority and a detached, self-mocking sense of humour. These characteristics, while tending to exaggerate the size of the Jewish presence, earned for the Czechs the name of 'Slav Jews'.

The constitution of the First Republic acknowledged Judaism both as a religion and as a nationality, and according to the 1930 census 356,830 citizens regarded themselves as Jewish by religion and only 204,800 as Jewish by nationality.

The main area of Jewish settlement was the Carpatho-Ukraine which, after World War II, was ceded to the USSR. During the Nazi Protectorate and World War II, Czech Jewry suffered atrocious losses. While estimates vary considerably, it must be assumed that at least 80 per cent. of Czechoslovakia's Jewish population perished. No precise information as to their number and condition in postwar Czechoslovakia exists, since official statistical handbooks do not deal with religious or similar affiliations.

When, after an interval of more than twenty years, socio-religious statistics were again collected in 1966, they revealed that in Bohemia and Moravia the Jews had dwindled to a minority representing about .08 per cent. of the population. The estimates in 1970 suggest that about 10,000 Jews were then left in Czechoslovakia.

As long as the Eastern Bloc countries supported the newly founded state of Israel in the hope that it would eventually be turned into a People's Democracy, Zionist organizations were accepted and made to feel at home in Czechoslovakia. They developed a complex internal life of their own, which, together with their strangely assorted membership and their extensive foreign contacts, often caused them to be regarded as weird, but never as hostile. Zionist factions advocating pro-Soviet policies were dubbed 'progressive', while those preferring pro-American foreign and liberal-democratic alignments were duly denounced as reactionaries. However, as the Cold War grew more intense, and Israel increasingly sided with the West, the originally friendly attitude towards Zionist organizations turned to detestation. Moreover, throughout the immediate post-war years and quite independent of official policies, residual grass-roots antisemitism had lingered on in Czechoslovakia.

A 1946-47 public opinion poll revealed that, although the majority of Czechs (67.2 per cent) did not bear a grudge against any particular religious belief, dislike of Jews (15.9 per cent) remained far and away the strongest popular prejudice.[1] This situation was further aggravated by the purges of the early fifties with their pronounced appeal to latent xenophobic and antisemitic—camouflaged as anti-Zionist—hatreds. Looking back at the underlying reasons for the purges in 1968, Professor Eduard Goldstücker, himself one of their victims, gave this explanation:

> About the end of the forties and the beginning of the fifties, Stalin, and in this context I don't just mean Stalin personally, believed in the imminence of a new world war. Given this assumption, the necessary steps had to be taken and measures to protect the hinterland became inevitable. The trials in our country did not therefore focus so much on the individuals, their action and character, as on whether or not they belonged to a group whose loyalty could be regarded as doubtful, or who would otherwise answer the demand for a sacrificial lamb. Hence, anyone who had lived temporarily in the capitalist West came under suspicion, quite irrespective of his individual character or what performance in fact he had done, or failed to do. Emigrés to the West, as well as the men who volunteered to fight in Spain, belonged to this category, later to be joined by Jews occupying prominent positions in party and government.[2]

According to what the Czechs could piece together in 1968, the main purge trial against Slansky and the thirteen other high-ranking accused went through three stages. The first, marked by the arrest of Otto Sling, the Brno party secretary, introduced the new concept of 'forming an anti-party faction', and he was also accused of being an 'imperialist agent'. The purge's second stage, mainly directed against the security forces, culminated in the arrest of Karel Svab, the Deputy Minister of State Security, and volunteers who had fought in the Spanish Civil War (the so-called 'Inter-brigadists') came under suspicion. The third stage, which led to the arrest of Rudolf Slansky, the alleged head of the conspiracy, acquired definitely antisemitic overtones.

These were already implicit in earlier stages, as Artur London, the Deputy Foreign Minister (arrested 29.1.1951, condemned to life imprisonment, but released after a few years) recalls in his memoirs (*L'aveu*, Paris, Gallimard, 1968):

> Major Smola took me by the throat and in a voice shaking with hatred shouted, 'You and your dirty race, we shall

exterminate it. Not everything Hitler did was right; but he exterminated the Jews and that was a good thing. Far too many of them managed to avoid the gas chambers but we shall finish where he left off. . . .' As soon as a new name was mentioned, the interrogators wanted to know whether it was that of a Jew, and the more skilful among them enquired whether the name had been changed and what it was before. If a Jew was involved, the interrogators would see to it that this was mentioned in the protocols, irrespective of whether or not it was relevant in the particular context. The name was inevitably preceded by the obligatory epithet 'Zionist'.

The trials were instituted and supervised by Soviet 'advisers'. To Professor B. Rattinger, a former president of the Association of Communist Members of Parliament and another victim of the purges, these 'Beria men' vividly recalled the Gestapo, 'both by their marked antisemitism and by their methods of interrogation'.[3] Rattinger's and London's accounts anticipate the third stage of the trial, when the Soviet advisers and their Czech disciples built up their case against Rudolf Slansky as the 'head of the conspiracy'.

Although the collecting of incriminating material against Slansky had been expressly forbidden by Minister Kopriva, Czech security officials continued to extort from their prisoners confessions tending to compromise Slansky. These reports were sent to the Soviet Ambassador in Prague, who immediately turned them over to the Soviet adviser in charge of the trial. They then contacted Kopriva, drawing his attention to the 'danger of Zionism' and to the fact that with Slansky the Jews had managed to penetrate a key position. The chief Soviet adviser Vladimir (Bojarskij?)—Russian advisers were only known by their first names and their true identity could rarely be established after 1968—was particularly eager to demonstrate the 'dangers inherent in the world Zionist movement'. On the strength of these fantasies, he succeeded in persuading Klement Gottwald, head of the party and Government, to set up a special anti-Zionist department in the Ministry of Home Security. Predictably, in 'fighting Zionism within and outside the state', it acquitted itself so well that in 1968 Kopriva admitted:

> An increasing volume of evidence revealed that the World Zionist Movement received support from leading officials in the Treasury and Foreign Trade Ministry who had maintained links with the Israeli Embassy which, at the time, was considered an agent of American interests. In this context the names of Rudolf Slansky and B. Geminder were repeatedly mentioned.[4]

Slansky was arrested on 24 November 1951. Major Smola, already known to London as a sincere admirer of Hitler, was put in charge of the case. After the 'head of the conspiracy' had been caught, a new wave of arrests brought in Frejka, Margolius and Simone as the latest members of the alleged plot.

For a long time, Slansky bravely withstood the physical and mental tortures he had to endure. However, he tried to commit suicide when it became clear that the authorities, indifferent to the question of his guilt or innocence, were only interested in obtaining his confession. When the attempted suicide failed, his resistance broke and, almost exactly a year after his arrest, the trial against him and his fellow 'conspirators' was formally opened (20.11.1952). It was scripted to show that representatives of all major government branches were involved in the conspiracy. Slansky, Geminder and Frank stood for the party, Svab for the state security apparatus, Reicin for the army; Clementis and Hajdu for the Foreign Office, Frejka for the economy, Löbl for foreign trade, Margolius and London for the emigrés to the West and the Spanish interbrigadists. With the exception of Clementis, Frank and Svab, all the accused were, as the indictment emphasized, of 'Jewish origin'. These antecedents, according to the prosecution, predisposed them to develop into imperialist Zionist and Titoist agents, and as such to commit 'heinous crimes' and promote their accomplices, mostly Jewish, to key positions. Hajdu's confession made it abundantly clear what the court wished to hear.

My past had already made me an enemy of the cause of

progress and socialism. I was born into a middle-class Jewish family and brought up in the spirit of bourgeois ideology and Jewish nationalism. I had no contact with workers.[5]

Such admissions encouraged the press to anti-semitic comments of unprecedented virulence.

Zionists are the representatives of a reactionary-bourgeois and chauvinistic Jewish movement which, since its inception, has doggedly opposed the cause of progress and of the people. Under the cloak of Jewish national interest, they pursue only their class interest and dirty money-making trickery. Their policies are designed to exploit the entire working class. In the interests of these selfish and extortionist objectives, they organize themselves into international Zionist movements and serve the American imperialists as their most reliable running dogs. In any case, the Zionist organizations with which Slansky was associated were nothing but Fascist shock-troops. It is moreover self-evident that any bourgeois nationalism, including of course its Jewish variant, must inevitably produce fascism.[6]

Such appeals to primitive hatred could only lead to the revival of a Nazi-type antisemitism. Public opinion became so ugly that it was quite usual to hear such remarks as 'Hitler had a lot of them shot but not enough'; 'Hitler ought to have finished them all off'; 'String all those Jewish louts up'. Party resolutions were passed demanding that 'no Jew should be eligible for party office' (Brno); 'No citizen of Jewish extraction should be allowed to become a party member' (Kolin); 'Kick all Jews out, show them no mercy' (Avie Cakovice).[7]

Klement Gottwald gave these outbursts his official blessing when he declared at the December 1952 National Conference of the *CPC*:

Investigations into the activities of the anti-government conspiracy unearthed a new channel for betraying the Communist party and spying on it. This is what Zionism amounts to. Why? Because Zionist organizations of all denominations, particularly after the establishment of the

the State of Israel and its subservience to the United States, simply became an extension of the American intelligence services. They provided in fact an ideal vehicle for infiltrating the workers' movement and the recruiting of agents among the ranks of the Communist Party. The Zionist organizations and their American masters were thus able to exploit shamelessly the sufferings Hitler and the other Fascists inflicted on the Jews. It could almost be said that they were quite willing to make capital out of Auschwitz and Maidanek. Normally, former bankers, industrialists, estate owners or kulaks would hardly have been accepted into a Communist Party, let alone allowed to rise to leading positions. But moved by our dislike of antisemitism and also by our respect for their sufferings after the Second World War, we overlooked their class background when it came to people of Jewish origin and Zionist views. In the past and before the war the dangers were not so grave. But after the war when Zionists and Zionist organizations became the tool of American imperialism the situation changed radically. Nowadays Zionism is a dangerous and cunning enemy.[8]

Jews have now become traitors and were former bankers and estate owners. They exploit the general sympathy for their sufferings to infiltrate and subvert communist parties. This is what, twenty-five years ago, the 'first workers' President of Czechoslovakia' proclaimed, a man whom present-day party stalwarts are busily resuscitating as one of the 'greatest statesmen' in Czech history.

How well this campaign succeeded in keeping immemorial and irrational prejudices alive, became apparent during the brief months of the Prague Spring of 1968. Nothing perhaps was quite so revealing of the prevailing climate of opinion as the declaration which the 'Council of Jewish Communities in Czechoslovakia' felt obliged to issue in May 1968. It stated:

We Czech Jews regard the Czech Socialist Republic as our Fatherland, to whose development we shall always want to contribute. Today, after the distressing experiences of the fifties and despite the injustices we have had to endure, we shall put all our abilities and endeavours at the disposal of our country which is led by men in whom we have every confidence.

The Council also put forward a number of demands, among which the following figured prominently:

An official denunciation of the 'antisemitic manifestations generated by the political trials' accompanied by official efforts at rehabilitation.

Rehabilitation of victims not only of perverted justice, but also of administrative directives which tend to the disadvantage of Jews.

Parity between the pensions granted to victims of racial and political persecution.

Provisions to prevent external events from adversely affecting the status of Jewish communities in Czechoslovakia.

Guarantees for unhampered contact with Jewish communities abroad.

The right to give religious instruction to the young unhindered by administrative interference.[9]

A letter from a Jew published by a Prague evening paper, further illuminated the general situation. It read:

During the last few years a tacit, but persistent, antisemitism has informed official attitudes, and it will take a long time before it can be eradicated . . . In this context the word Zionism is invariably used. Please take your notebook and interview people; I am sure they will tell you what they always tell me: that (a) Jews are out to destroy the socialist countries; (b) Jews aspire to world domination; (c) They want to revenge themselves for the victims of the gas chambers.[10]

The candid press debate of such problems provoked a veritable flood of anonymous letters in which the senders openly vented their antisemitic spleen. Josef Fleissig, a journalist, collected these surprising denunciations and published them under the title 'Jews among *Prace's* editors'. He was driven to undertake this task, he admitted, by the process of his own disillusionment.

I used to think [he wrote] that if there were any Fascists

left in this world, they would by now have become
contented farmers somewhere in the Argentine, or inn-
keepers in the Federal German Republic; but all of a
sudden I realized that we too have our Fascists here at
home. And what choice types they are!

One of the letters addressed to his paper threatened:

> Mr Stern, Fleissig, Kohn, Weiner, Kraus, and however
> many you are, we know all about you. We know that you
> are Jews, that you are parasites living off our people. When
> our patience is exhausted, we will know how to get rid of
> you.

Some of the replies to such menaces were equally telling. One
of the correspondents wrote:

> In reply to this amiable contribution, all I can say is 'Heil
> Hitler'. What impressed them [the anonymous letter-
> writers] so strongly in the Novotny regime was not so much
> its socialism as its social Fascism.

However, these antisemitic outbursts encouraged an alarm-
ingly large number of similar letters such as:

> The time will come when we shall clean up our editorial
> offices again. Having kicked out half your lot, we shall
> revive a decent socialism purged of bourgeois parasites.

Or:

> You he-whores were paid by Hitler; pity he couldn't spare
> the time to liquidate you . . . Obviously the *Prace* has been
> infiltrated by Jews ready to sell the Republic down the
> river.

Fleissig, whose office received about ten such letters, might
have agreed to dismiss them as a somewhat insignificant
minority view, had not most correspondents been at pains to
stress their Party membership and expressed their unshaken
belief in the correctness of their views.

How doggedly Stalinist Party stalwarts fought to maintain
their position was also evidenced by the clandestine leaflet
campaigns denouncing Sik, Kriegel, Cisar and Goldstücker

as being 'bent on destroying the social achievements of our people and on preparing the ground for a Zionist takeover'. Although the official party paper *Rude Pravo* declared, 'Their charges are so obviously ridiculous that it is not worth while to refute them in detail', it nevertheless went on to say:

> The writers of these leaflets will not mislead the honest working masses. They can only produce an effect exactly opposite to the one intended. One particularly repugnant published statement endeavours to encourage race hatred. Anybody daring publicly to spread views so redolent of Hitler's propaganda machine, would be kicked out; and that is why the disseminators of these sheets prefer to operate in the dark.[11]

When an editor of the *Zmedelske noviny* attacked the Stalinist cadre policy, his office received an anonymous letter addressing him as 'you coward' saying 'you smell of filthy Jew rabble'. The paper used this incident (10.7.68) to give its readers a glimpse of how Stalinist antisemitism used to bedevil and brutalize party counsels:

> Some time at the beginning of the fifties, another investigation of party members took place. A comrade, who in fact was a Jew, was being scrutinized. Having served as an air force officer, he had returned from England in 1945. He was being cross-examined by a glib young man who had spent a comfortable war at home. 'Why did you fight in the West, comrade?' The question sounded dangerous and hostile, and the whole atmosphere was so charged with antisemitism that the man answered somewhat sharply, 'Because, comrades, I did not want to end up in the gaschambers'. They immediately snapped back, 'You had better watch that insolent tone of yours, this is a party investigation. . . .' I know of a comrade whom they finished both professionally and with the party simply because they could not understand why he alone should have managed to escape from an Auschwitz-bound transport while millions of other Jews failed to do so.

The article concluded with the author's poignant admission:

'Anyway I have never quite understood how Fascist precepts managed to infiltrate into the Communist Party.'

The reimposition of antisemitism in post-1968 occupied Czechoslovakia would require a second article. Meanwhile it should be noted that Yuri Ivanov's anti-Jewish diatribe *Caution—Zionism*, contained a 35-page epilogue which accused Czech Jewry of counter-revolutionary machinations under Dubcek. Under the Russian-sounding pseudonym Yevgeny Yevseyev, the epilogue's author, was none other than the journalist Svatopluk Dolejs who fifteen years ago had already been unmasked as an agent (of the state security forces). During the 'reform era', he worked as head of the Czech Radio Arab Service and spent most of the time in the Middle East. Reviving the spectre of a 'Zionist conspiracy', his epilogue denounced such leading ex-Party members as Sik, Pavel, Hajek, Kriegel and Goldstücker as plotters. While in power, they were alleged to have established conspiratorial contacts with Jewish foreigners in Prague and with influential Zionists abroad. Among those mentioned were the diplomats serving in the Israeli Embassy until its withdrawal in 1967, the *JOINT*, and the *Jewish Agency*. Other suspect contacts were allegedly established with Sulzberger, the owner of the *New York Times,* the Viennese publisher Molden, and Simon Wiesenthal, the head of the Vienna Jewish Documentation Centre. These were the channels through which CIA money supposedly reached the counter-revolutionists. The Jewish communities throughout Czechoslovakia, according to Dolejs, had provided a network by which foreign exchange and orders from abroad could be transmitted to the 'Kriegel Club' in Prague. Kriegel, a life-long Jewish Communist and veteran of the Spanish Civil War, offered an almost archetypal target for any 'anti-Zionist' attacks in the Stalinist manner. Some of these were based on a forged letter (21.5.1968), purporting to be from Wiesenthal to Czech Jews, appealing to them 'to support liberalization and democratization because this would lead to a better understanding with the Federal German Republic and with Israel'. The letter also asked recipients to 'co-operate in collecting material for documentation on antisemitism in Communist countries'.

The exploitation of race prejudice has since Czarist days

been a device familiar to representatives of the Russian establishment. It remains, however, to be seen whether in the long term it will be a sufficiently powerful argument to persuade people to accept their subjugation; in the face of Czarist oppression it singularly failed to do so.

NOTES

1.   J. Lion, in *Svobodné slovo,* 4 December 1966, p. 5.
2.   Interview, *Slovenské pohl'ady,* No. 2/1968, pp. 37-55.
3.   *Lidová demokracie,* 22 March 1968, p. 5.
4.   Josef Holler, in *Reportér,* No. 25/1968, p. IV.
5.   Report of the proceedings against Slansky and others, Prague, 1953, p. 232.
6.   *Rudé Právo,* 24 November 1952, p. 1.
7.   Václav Brabec, in *Revue déjin socialismu,* No. 3/1969, p. 369.
8.   Klement Gottwald, in *Funkcionár,* No. 24/1952, p. 807.
9.   *Literárni listy,* No. 14/1968, p. 2.
10.   *Vecerni praha,* 14 June 1968, p. 5.
11.   F. Zdobina, in *Rudé právo,* 5 July 1968, p. 3.

Communist Attitudes in France and Italy to the Six Day War

François Bondy

Reactions to the Six Day War by the democratic Left and by the communists in France are of particular interest since certain factors peculiar to France produced some strange, even unique, configurations.

Perhaps the most important was that in de Gaulle's France, foreign policy fell within the domain reserved for the President who was solely responsible for its formulation and execution. During the Middle East conflict, the President initially prescribed a stance of the strictest neutrality, notwithstanding the noticeable groundswell of public sympathy for Israel's cause, and shortly thereafter, he took up a distinctly pro-Arab posture. He adopted this attitude in view both of France's special interests in the Mediterranean and of the position the Arabs held in the Third World whose champion de Gaulle liked to appear. He was also influenced by the fact that Israel was in his eyes a de facto ally of the USA, and that the war could therefore be regarded as a by-product of the American involvement in Vietnam, of which he disapproved.

The debate was further enlivened by the French communists' unquestioning acceptance of the Soviet line. The resulting divisions and differences within the party gave rise to singularly rigid attitudes as well as an unusually frank airing of divergent views in the party press and periodicals. Moreover, many non-communist intellectuals, remembering their struggle against French colonialism, particularly during the Algerian war, were only too eager to discover in the post-colonial regimes of the Arab people proofs of progress, socialism and revolutionary fervour in order to reaffirm solidarities proclaimed in the days of their anti-colonial struggle.

Israel on the other hand, was generally identified with the fate of European Jewry, so that sympathy for her appeared as an extension of the comradely feelings towards Jews fostered by the Resistance—attitudes further reinforced by widespread interest, particularly among the young, in the *kibbutzim* and other aspects of Israeli life. This was reflected in the marked sympathy for Israel shown by the socialist SFIO *(Section Française de l'International Ouvrière).* Its secretary-general, Guy Mollet, and other leading members of the leadership may admittedly have been inclined to regard the issue as yet another belated justification of the action taken during the Suez crisis. This sudden emergence of opposing views seriously affected the electoral alliance between the communists and the *Fédération de la Gauche,* and undermined its credibility as a potential coalition.

The political scene was further exacerbated by the fact that French Jewry's opposition to the country's official foreign policy, suddenly created a 'Jewish problem' of divided loyalties. Just as, to part of the Left, the Israelis were first and foremost Jews and therefore deserving of sympathy, the Jews were to the Gaullist establishment primarily partisans of Israel and hence a lobby serving a foreign power. Since, however, Israel was denounced not as Israel but as an outgrowth of American power, the resulting resentments must perhaps be regarded as a secondary anti-Zionism, which in turn gave rise to tertiary antisemitism. A regression of this artificial tertiary antisemitism into latent primitive forms cannot, of course, be ruled out.

The political issue was also affected by prevailing moods and prejudices. These became particularly noticeable in the widespread resentment against Arabs, rooted, no doubt, in the French retreat from Empire and the expulsion of Europeans from the Maghreb, particularly from Algeria. Hence the general satisfaction felt when a small country of European traditions and standards triumphed over the Arab world. The Left therefore emphasised that in its sympathy for Israel it would gladly forgo the support of certain circles close to the former OAS which despised Arabs and particularly the Algerian *bicots* (wogs) as an inferior race. Another irrational emotional reaction was the emergence of antisemitism mentioned above.

This brief summary touching on some of the problems with which the Six Day War confronted the French Left may give the reader an inkling of the complexity and many-sidedness of its political motivations, and the interplay of facts, myth and clichés. There were jostling each other the stereotypes of the persecuted Jew; the colonising Jewish master-race; the influence of the Jewish press on public opinion; Israel as a model of social progress to its neighbours; Nasser, the social reformer and anti-imperialist; Nasser, the totalitaran dictator and disciple of Hitler; the natural sympathy extended to any David fighting a Goliath, which at first benefited tiny Israel threatened by vastly superior forces, and then veered towards weak Arabs who, owing to Western negligence, remained underdeveloped and were utterly defeated when they collided with a modern technically advanced power. Finally, attitudes were influenced by the general loathing of the Vietnam war and the fact that, in the eyes of the Left, any cause supported by the USA was suspect as forming part of the American imperialist bid for power. Since in this instance, as indeed in all others, the Left had no influence on the formulation of French foreign policy, the presentation and analysis of its internal difficulties may seem somewhat academic. But it is already obvious that the apparently moribund parties of the French Left are bound to become more powerful and may yet play a role in shaping the future of France. Moreover the repercussions of the Middle East war, highlighting irreconcilable dissensions within the French Left, tended to give the other political forces a power quite disproportionate to their weight within the French social structure. The divisions generated by the Middle East conflict had therefore an an important if mainly negative bearing on the contemporary French scene.

In the first book to appear in France after the Six Day War, essentially a discussion between Jean-Francis Held, the correspondent of the *Nouvel Observateur* in Israel, and Eric Rouleau, the Arab expert of *Le Monde*, Held stated:

> Up to the end of the war, Israel remained utterly calm. I noted that our contact with Paris completely unnerved us. In a telephone conversation with my Paris editor, I was surprised to hear myself say, 'You apparently do not understand what it is like here. We are getting exceedingly abusive letters from people violently opposed to the war.' In fact, the French, whether Jews or not, became far more emotional than people in Israel. Moreover, they produced something which did not exist in Israel itself, a violently anti-Arab faction. The Israelis would have raised no objections if I had passed on information which would have outraged Paris. In Tel-Aviv, anything could be discussed without causing the least offence.

The (communist) *Humanité* did not share the general sympathy for Israel. Its editorialist, Yves Moreau, wrote so many aggressive anti-Israel editorials that the satirical weekly *Le Canard Enchainé* referred to him as '*Yves Mort-aux-juifs*'. He maintained *(Humanité* 24.5.1967) that the closing of the Gulf of Aqaba was no more responsible for the existing differences than the Bey's tap of a fan had been for the conquest of Algeria in 1830.

Moreau stressed the Israeli 'people's' though not the Israeli state's right to exist, a significant distinction, which was, however, later dropped. But on 30 May, *Humanité* still suggested that:

> An artificial graft, Israel, notwithstanding the efforts of its pioneers, could not have survived without the dollar support of the USA, whether from public or private sources. American imperialism could not fail to exploit such a situation. . . .

The government's Middle East policy earned the praise of the Communist Party's Central Committee, which *(Le Monde,* 2/3 June) stated:

> It is a fact that the French government believes the

Middle East crisis and the American involvement in Vietnam
to be inter-connected, that it deplores the opening of hostilities by Israel and that it objects to the creation of a *fait
accompli.*

On 3 June, *Humanité* endeavoured to forge a connection
between the Nazis and the Israelis by alleging that the same
German industrialists who produced the lethal gas for the
extermination camps were now supplying the Israeli government with gasmasks. To prove how questionable the Israeli
case really was, *Humanité* (7.6.1967) quoted such right-wing
antisemites as Tixier-Vignancour or Vichy's former 'Jewish
commissioner', Xavier Vallat, who, it was said, supported
Israel:

> . . . Those wishing to see clearly must wonder how
> professional antisemites like M Tixier-Vignancour and the
> Maurras-inspired *Aspects de la France* have suddenly disco-
> vered an unsuspected fondness for Israel and how the men
> of Munich or their successsors can today oppose a peaceful
> solution with the cry, 'No Middle East Munich'. This
> reversal of roles has indeed reached a climax of absurdity
> when last-ditch defenders of the Atlantic alliance such as
> M André François-Poncet, can, notwithstanding their
> record of appeasement, join in this strange new chorus.

Time and again the direct connection between the war in
Vietnam and the Middle East crisis is emphasised:

> . . . The Middle East crisis and the American interven-
> tion in Vietnam are inter-connected. This cannot be
> denied. The only difference is that while in Vietnam the
> Americans intervene directly, they cleverly use the Israeli
> ruling classes in the Middle East to fight Arab govern-
> ments whose intention of controlling their own oil incurs
> American displeasure.

The *Humanité Dimanche,* a more widely read paper than the
daily *Humanité,* published a number of readers' letters criticizing communist policies:

> In whose name do you support Arabs against the Jews
> of Israel? Particulary since Jews all over the world have

suffered enough as a result of Hitler's racism. . . . They too have a right to live! Why do you support the enemies of their country?

Answers to such letters filled whole pages, as did explanations of why communists should feel such sympathy for countries where, contrary to Israeli practice, communist parties are suppressed:

> . . . Communists support every national movement, every party, organisation of personality which actively opposes the forces of imperialism . . .

The reproach that French communists slavishly followed policies laid down by Soviet Russia was met with explanations like:

> . . . It is a fact—and no doubt it is to this that you allude—that, as a general rule, our party's views on international affairs agree with those of the Communist Party of the USSR. But there is no deliberate 'co-ordination', as is sometimes alleged. After all, the policy of our two parties, as indeed of all communist parties, is inspired by the same principles of peaceful coexistence, the right of national self-determination, the rejection of imperialist interference, international solidarity of workers and peoples, etc.

A Jewish communist, Jacqueline Hadamard, in a letter to *Le Monde*, challenged Baron Edmond de Rothschild, who had asked the Jewish people to accept financial sacrifice in support of Israel. *Humanité* (11.7.1967) reprinted this letter using bold type:

> . . . I do not belong to the Jewish people. Like the majority of French Jews, I belong to the French people which has given the world the Declaration of Human Rights, the abolition of slavery, the emancipation of Jews by the statute
> of 1791, and Zola's *J'accuse*. This is where my dignity lies. No, I owe no 'contribution' as a token of my solidarity. Such gifts go to the oppressed, to the persecuted, to the Israeli victims and the innumerable Arab victims. . . .

But Mr Rothschild's letter raises another question: has he never pondered the fact that the Jew who considers himself as belonging to a 'chosen race' is just as racist as the antisemite?

Humanité (22.6.67) shared these views:

> ... It is easy to underestimate the indignation such assumptions often arouse among people of Jewish origin or rather because they are of Jewish origin. Even if—provided they still hold religious views—they feel some slight sympathy for their co-religionists in another country, how could they accept obligations of such a nature?

Up to the beginning of the Middle East crisis, it was generally assumed that France maintained particularly close ties with Israel. Suddenly, the Jews were to learn that they alone, not France, maintained such ties. The communists published as many letters as possible in which Jews criticised Zionism, just as after the arrest of Stalin's Jewish doctors, other card-carrying Jewish doctors had demanded and obtained the condemnation of 'those white-coated criminals'. One of these doctors was again able to oblige *Humanité* (20.7.67):

> ... Six million Jews were not slaughtered by the Nazis so that young *sabras* could on occasion behave like young Hitlerites. Israel's honour rests more safely with Spinoza or Uriel da Costa than with Moshe Dayan and the advocates of a sudden preemptive blow in order to confront the UN with a *fait accompli*.

Humanité was never very eager to reply to the argument that at the time of the creation of the State of Israel the USSR had figured as one of her main supporters. This point was discussed only once in a long *Humanité Dimanche* article (24.6.67) by the party theoretician, André Gisselbrecht:

> ... Why should the withdrawal of USSR support seem so surprising? Accorded while Israel fought for her independence, it was withdrawn after the outbreak of the Korean war (1952), when the Israeli government began to

back all the USA's imperialist ventures including the Vietnam war.

The communist literary magazine *Europe* (July/August 1967), published by the communist Pierre Abraham, admitted that its editorial board held divergent views on the Middle East issue. The journal printed a dispatch, headed however by a qualifying statement, from its Jerusalem correspondent making it quite clear that the city's reunification had given rise to general rejoicing:

> The coffee-house politicans all have their own, mostly contradictory, views as to the details of a future settlement. On one point, however, there seems to be complete unanimity: Jerusalem must never again be divided or mutilated . . . for this is our very soul, our most intimate and profound being. Every year for two thousand years Jews have untiringly vowed 'next year in Jerusalem'. And now the cry goes up: 'This very year in Jerusalem!'

Démocratie nouvelle (No. 6), an orthodox party journal, published a debate between the well-known Arab scholar, Jacques Berque and Georges Friedmann, the sociologist and author of the widely discussed book *Fin du peuple Juif?* (Paris, Gallimard, 1965):

> If we could contemplate the Arab/Jewish problem in isolation, admittedly a difficult proposition, and if we could consider the Israel-Arab relationship as one like others where, in the setting of our contemporary world, a Western industrial civilisation or a Western-inspired society collided with Afro-Asian countries, we would then, I suggest, see the problem in its true perspective. (Jacques Berque)

Such arguments could also have been advanced by any non-communist periodicals.

The left-of-centre socialist PSU (*Parti Socialiste Unifié*), torn by internal dissensions, adopted utterly contradictory attitudes to the Israeli crisis. *L'Action,* under the editorship of Claude Bourdet, supported the Arab cause, while Jean Daniel's *Nouvel Observateur* made determined efforts to remain objective without however jeopardizing a relationship of mutual trust with Arab groups dating back to the Algerian war.

Immediately before the outbreak of the Six Day War, the monthly *Les Temps Modernes* published its bulky special issue, *Le Conflit Israélo-Arabe*. In his introduction, Jean-Paul Sartre said that he could not condemn Israel.

> . . . I can only emphasise that many of us feel this emotional determination which, far from being merely an important featue of our individual make-up, also has its roots in completely objective circumstances and general historical events, which we are not prepared to forget. Hence, we are allergic to anything that bears the slightest resemblance to antisemitism; a proposition to which many Arabs would reply: 'We are not antisemitic, we are anti-Israeli', and no doubt they are right; but can they alter the fact that for us, Israelis are also Jews? . . . The idea that the Arabs could destroy the Jewish state and drive its inhabitants into the sea is anathema unless I am a racialist . . .

Some of Sartre's friends were even more outspoken. Claude Lanzmann, who was largely responsible for the Arab section of *Le Conflit Israélo-Arabe*, made an impassioned speech during a public discussion, reported as follows in *Le Monde* (2.6.67):

> The disillusionment with 'left-wing Arabs' was spelt out in some detail by M Claude Lanzmann who, having called M Yves Moreau of the *Humanité* an 'inane simplifier', recalled the part he himself played in the fight against the Algerian war. He confessed to being 'distressed' by declaration of solidarity with the USSR from Havana, Algeria and Hanoi. 'Shall I', he asked, 'be obliged to shout one day: "Long live Johnson!" because the United States alone opposes the annihilation of Israel? Yes, I would be ready to do it. This is part of the Jewish contradiction. Not my contradiction. But that of socialist countries when they come face to face with the problems of the Middle East. . . . The destruction of Israel would be worse than the Nazi holocaust. For Israel is my freedom. True, I am assimilated, but in whom can I trust? Without Israel I feel naked and vulnerable. . . .'

Predictably, *Humanité* sharply attacked Sartre and *Les Temps Modernes*, although for the last few years the party had tried to observe a sort of an armistice with the philosopher. Under the headline 'Jean-Paul Sartre or the incertitude of the scholars', its leader-writer René Andrieu praised Arab forbearance:

> Despite the excesses of a propaganda which could certainly have done with some pruning, despite the impassioned appeals for a holy war and Shukeiry's threats (which have been, moreover, denied), those in charge, instead of aggravating the situation, did their best to improve the chances of negotiation and stubbornly refused to unleash war.

Just before the publication of the special issue of the *Temps Moderne*, *Le Monde* reported Sartre's Cairo press conference during which the philosopher seemed greatly impressed by his talks with Nasser. Egypt's President, he said, was an outstanding reformer and quite unlike the image presented of him in the West. Hitherto Sartre had clashed with the communists because he stood to the left of them and had criticized their caution towards the central American guerrillas. His journal had also demanded that Soviet Russia should support North Vietnam wholeheartedly and to the point of threatening war. The conflict between his circle and the communists over the Israeli issue was a different kind and, transcending questions of doctrine, concerned human values and responsibilites. The rift between the *SFIO* and the communists, which the Israeli conflict had deepened, was of course politically of greater consequence. The editor-in-chief of *Populaire*, Claude Fuzier, criticised the communists:

> The French Left recognises the Oder-Neisse line. Could it not also recognise the frontiers of Israel, that is, of a state which has been annihilated by history, whose people have been dispersed against their will, and at long last have reclaimed the homelands which have been theirs since ancient times? Jews eager for citizenship rather than for membership of a religious denomination have a right to

the territories of which history has robbed them. *(Le Monde,*
26.5.67).

On the other hand, François Mitterand, the leader of the
Fédération de la Gauche, tried to temper the disagreement with
the communists:

> It is inconceivable that the state of Israel could be
> allowed to disappear. It must be permitted to exist. We do
> not agree with all of her policies; for instance, her
> reluctance to face the problem of the Palestinian refugees,
> but we maintain that nothing could justify her disappear-
> ance as a state. *(Le Monde,* 28.5.67).

The *Fédération de la Gauche* founded a *Comité pour de droit
d'Israel à l'existence,* while an opposing group, including some
well-known Arab experts of the Left, established a *Committee
for the peaceful Solution of the Palestine Problem* under the
leadership of Maxime Rodinson, which campaigned actively
by circulating bulletins and calling meetings. The emotional
identification with Israel's cause was nowhere as outspoken as
in the SFIO. The Mayor of Marseilles, Gaston Deferre,
pronounced the cause of Israel to be just and insisted that
France was her ally. In Toulouse, a long-prepared Franco-
Russian festival was cancelled because of Russia's attitude in
the conflict. Guy Mollet, the Secretary-General of the party,
sent a message of solidarity to *MAPAI,* while the ex-Prime
Minister Pierre Mendès-France wrote to *MAPAM*:

> Our friends of the Federation and I have chosen our
> side. We are for Israel. In our opinion, Nasser is a dictator
> attempting to impose his views by force. Nasser is a man
> who uses force and the threat of force to wipe out Israel.
> Like Hitler, he resorts to diversionary tactics because his
> country faces grave economic difficulty. This is unaccept-
> able. (Gaston Deferre, *Le Monde,* 4.6.67.)

In the National Assembly, Guy Mollet attacked de Gaulle's
interpretation of French neutrality. The pro-Israel attitude of
a socialist and former Foreign Minister like Christian Pineau
was doubtless influenced by memories of Suez. Opposing the
pro-Israelis, other groups tried to narrow the gulf that had
opened between the *Fédération* and the communists.

Some, *(Le Monde,* 24.6.67 reported) among them the socialist deputy from the north, Arthur Notebart, had vainly argued that the official communiqué should take specific note of the part played by the USSR in the Middle East crisis. By adopting such a position, they were told, they would only underline divergences between the *Fédération* and the communists (Thursday's *Humanité* demanded unhesitating support for de Gaulle) and would therefore play de Gaulle's game. While the *Fédérés* would do nothing to hide their differences with the communists, they were equally anxious to discourage any action likely to deepen the rift or lastingly to endanger the unity of the Left.

The part played by *Le Monde* would repay a study. In the initial stages of the conflict, immediately after the blockade of the Gulf of Aqaba, France's most important daily was not absolutely objective and published in its *Tribune libre* views predominantly critical of Israel. Later however, by fully reporting the public debate and publishing letters reflecting all shades of opinion, the paper became an incomparable mirror of public attitudes and views. Within the *PSU,* for which some *Le Monde* editors had a particular liking, opinions on the issue clashed sharply. André Philip suggested an enquiry into the poisoning of public opinion through press and radio. According to him, the editors of papers ranging from *France-Soir* to *Aurore* and *Europe I* belonged to a 'Jewish lobby' which at least should be identified as such. On the other hand, Daniel Mayer, the former Secretary-General of the SFIO, President of the League of Human Rights, and a member of the *PSU,* declared in an impassioned personal manifesto:

I am ashamed of calling myself socialist if this term signifies agreement with the openly warmongering policies of the USSR. I am ashamed of being French since for the second time in thirty years official French policy advocates abandonment of a friendly ally in its hour of need. I am ashamed of belonging to the human race since humanity seems to be unable to prevent a repetition of genocide. To anticipate certain questions, let me add that I am not ashamed of being a Jew. *(Le Monde,* 6.6.67).

He was answered by a number of Jewish academics critical of Zionism and by the left-wing Gaullist, Vincent Monteil, Professor at Dakar, who wrote:

> As to the persistent confusion between Israel representing an imperialist and colonialist bridgehead, and on the other the Hitler-inflicted martyrdom of millions of European Jews, the latter in no way entitles Zionists to become the exterminating angels of Arabs who had nothing to do with Auschwitz or Treblinka. (*Le Monde*, 8.6.67.)

And two Jewish academics declared:

> We feel ashamed to see socialists praise bankers because they are Zionists. We are ashamed to see French Jews behave like Israeli nationalists. (*Le Monde*, 16.7.67.)

In the midst of this debate, the *PSU* leadership had to dissociate itself from the Sorbonne branch of its student association which had denounced any position not unequivocally favouring the Arabs as sheer racism. The students' resolution concluded:

> Finally, the association expresses its surprise at the racist character of certain pro-Israel manifestations and the solid support given to them by individuals and organisations who have willingly condoned American genocide in Vietnam. (*Le Monde*, 2.6.67.)

The *PSU* National Executive replied:

> The *PSU's* National Executive and National Secretariat of its student branches want to make it clear the the *PSU* does not in any way endorse the purely emotional positions taken up by some of its members whose attitudes will serve neither the course of peace nor the people of the Middle East. (*Le Monde*, 3.6.67.)

Among left-wing Arab experts, Maxime Rodinson, one of the most deeply-committed to the Arab cause and who, although a Jew, had previously accepted the 'Zionist conspiracy' argument of the Slansky trial, went on record as saying:

> Personally, I believe Zionism to be the greatest misfortune

in contemporary Jewish history, with, of course, the exception of the Nazi persecution. *(Combat, 22.6.67.)*

He was answered by Vidal-Naquet, a Jewish left-wing historian—

I very humbly admit that I am torn between two contradictory forces. One, merely rational, tries to persuade me that Zionism has been a gigantic historical error, while the other consideration, purely emotional as I will unblushingly concede, argues that there must be some place where Jews are in the majority. This is what I feel, and although unable to justify it rationally, I nevertheless feel it very strongly.

A young Arabist, Roger Paret, who had lectured for three years in Tunis, wrote a widely-read and debated article, which analysed the thought processes of the European pro-Arab intelligentsia who saw in the Arab cause a non-existent revolutionary universalism.

Because they [the intellectuals—ed.] believe that the Palestine conflict presents a pattern familiar to them from the anti-colonialist fight, they have relegated the Israeli presence to the level of colonialist domination and think of Israel in the terms they previously applied to Algeria and Morocco. To them, the Israelis are, therefore, nothing but the last of the colonialists; while they represent themselves quite unblushingly as the uncompromising supporters of a cause which reflects the meaning of history and purposes of the universe. This parallels the universalist views formulated in the age of European enlightenment. The universal laws, however, seem to militate exclusively against the states within the European political and cultural orbit of which Israel forms part, while the phenomena of individuality and of specific identity are, apparently, reserved for non-European cultures. Every man is believed to embody the characteristics of all mankind—except the European; for this purpose an Israeli is a European. *(Preuves, July 1967.)*

It is interesting to note that this article was fully reported in an Algerian press bulletin, while Jewish circles resented its provocative title 'Israel does not exist' and its assertion that victory had not solved any problems.

Between August and de Gaulle's press conference in November 1967, the debate did not progress beyond the positions reached in July. The left-wing Catholic weekly, *Témoignage Chrétien*, was particularly preoccupied with the future of the holy places, whereas the Protestant and equally left-wing *Réforme* disregarded such apprehensions. The so-called left Gaullists—a number of small groups and individuals who form a somewhat diffuse and indefinable spectrum—not only supported de Gaulle's foreign policy wholeheartedly, but regretted the fact that it had not been more ruthlessly implemented, for example, by immediate withdrawal from the Atlantic alliance, and that the regime's economic and social dispensations were not as 'progressive' as its foreign policy.

One of the best-known moderate left Gaullists is perhaps François Mauriac, the aged Roman Catholic writer. He too was one of de Gaulle's uncompromising supporters. Convinced that Israel, although it had struck the first blow, was not the aggressor, he expressed the hope that de Gaulle would soon change course and recognise Israel's just claims. But when de Gaulle's foreign policy swung from neutrality to definite support for the Arabs, Mauriac happily concurred; for, as he argued, 'the alliance with the Grand Turk' represented one of France's great political traditions. Where moral considerations as understood by the ordinary citizen and the demands of world politics clashed, it was, he argued, de Gaulle's task to ensure priority for political considerations.

De Gaulle's press conference (27.11.1967) represented a turning-point. For the first time the President not only talked about Israel but passed value judgments on Jews in general—'*Les Juifs sont restés ce qu'ils avaient toujours été de tout temps, c'est-à-dire un peuple d'élite, sûr de lui-même et dominateur.*'

Although *Le Monde's* home affairs editor, Viansson-Ponté, observed that the phrase sounded less damnatory to the historians than when it appeared in print, this was a case where the sense mattered more than the sound. *Nouvel Observateur* led its correspondence column with a letter from Jean Bloch-Michel, formerly active in the Resistance and nephew of the historian Marc Bloch, shot by the Germans for Resistance activities:

> But it is not of Israel that I want to speak today. France, now that the Algerian war is over, no longer needing the pressure this 'friendly' and allied nation, so usefully exerted on the flank of our former enemy, has shifted her interests to the Iraqi oilfields and she must adapt her feelings to her interests. I know.
>
> But we are not concerned with Israel, but with me personally—a French Jew or a Jewish Frenchman, depending on how you look at it. De Gaulle has just dismissed me. His extreme nationalism has propelled him towards the point which all such nationalisms invariably reach—racialism. The people of Quebec are French, but not I. The people of Quebec belong to that worldwide community united by blood which is the French people, but a presence of 300 years within her frontiers and the identity of my 'history' with that of the country does not prevent me from belonging to another people who, we are told, are 'domineering'. Jewish history, as everyone has known for a long time, is one of oppressive rule exercised over host nations, not only France, but Poland, Russia and, let us not forget, Germany . . .

The former Vichy Commissioner for Jewish affairs, Xavier Vallat, praised this passage of de Gaulle's speech. He did not, however, agree with the President's desire for French Jews to be exclusively committed to France without any feelings of solidarity with Israel; he wanted to deprive Jews of their French nationality and give them Israeli citizenship instead. De Gaulle's remarks nevertheless breached a wall by creating the impression that antisemitism had once again become respectable. An opinion poll organised by the weekly *L'Express* (11.12.67) to discover whether Jews were believed to be a domineering elite showed:

Yes	30%
No	35%
Don't know	21%

But the question whether Israel's behaviour since 1956 had become expansionist and detrimental to the Arabs received the following answers:

Yes	30%
No	47%
Don't know	23%

These figures prove that sympathy for Israel and a dislike for the native Jew were by no means incompatible.

Fourteen well-known Jewish academics, amongst them Raymond Aron and the biologist and Nobel Prize winner, François Jacob, addressed an open letter to President de Gaulle in which they declared:

> It pains us to note that the liberator and President to whom so many of us have in times of the gravest crisis given their whole-hearted support, is in danger of reviving and encouraging, on the basis of erroneous and tendentious allegations, age-old prejudices which have caused such unspeakable suffering in the recent past. (*Le Monde*, 10.12.67.)

In a press conference, Guy Mollet, replying point by point to de Gaulle, said:

> The survivors of the death camps, converging on the land of Palestine still barred to them (who does not remember the tragedy of the Exodus?), were inspired, it seems, by an 'eager and conquering ambition'. If this figure of speech simply signifies the wish to live on after experiencing the miracle of being alive and free, we will not quarrel with it. But, hedged in by pseudo-historic explanations of the Jewish character, it is both unjust and insulting. (*Le Populaire de Paris*, 2.12.67.)

The Paris *New York Herald Tribune*, jointly published by the *Washington Post* and the *New York Times*, featured an article by Joel Blocker, the Paris correspondent of *Newsweek;*

... it is not only French Jews who must act. All men of goodwill—Jews and non-Jews, officials and non-officials—should stand up and be counted, and speak out forthrightly, before the threat becomes a reality. Finally, too, all friends of France, everywhere, must raise their voices on behalf of the principles formulated by the French Revolution—which belongs not only to France but to the world. For it was another great Frenchman, Albert Camus, who, only 20 years ago, showed us unforgettably the real insidiousness of the plague: barely perceptible at first, it can only be effectively fought if early action is taken; once the virus has reached epidemic proportions, the fight has already been lost. (2.12.67.)

He was answered by the Gaullist editorial writer, Georges Broussine, the only French commentator regularly contributing to the *New York Herald Tribune:*

The allegations of antisemitism against President Charles de Gaulle after his press conference strike me as unfair, clumsy and scandalous... Once the Zionist notion of Israel is admitted, then normal relations between states become the rule, with all the ups and downs that that implies. Israeli ambassadors abroad must become normal diplomats and not the de facto leaders of Jewish communities in the countries to which they are accredited.

It would be unthinkable for a great nation like France to let its political choices be guided by the problems of conscience which might be caused for an infinitely small minority of its population, especially since the Israeli government pays absolutely no heed to General de Gaulle's counsels of prudence and moderation... *(New York Herald Tribune,* 4.12.67.)

Yves Moreau of *Humanité* praised de Gaulle's speech, notwithstanding slight reservations with regard to generalisations about Jews:

While leaving the responsibility for certain psychological interpretations applicable to Jews and Arabs alike to him, one cannot but approve of the uneasiness he expressed... *(Humanité,* 28.11.67.)

If French Jewry felt itself offended by General de Gaulle, many non-religious left-wing Jews took exception to Chief Rabbi Kaplan's rebuttal and dissociated themselves from the Rabbi's contention that French Jewry had unanimously made Israel's cause its own. He was told that not all French Jews accepted his definition of them as a part of the Jewish People, and were therefore not in duty bound to accept all aspects of Israeli policy. The historian Pierre Vidal-Naquet pointed this out in an article featured by *Le Monde* (2.12.67.)

Such considerations both affected and extended the problems besetting the Left in its approach to the Israeli/Arab war. The point at issue was: were French Jews as loyal as other Frenchmen, even if the overwhelming majority of them were actively involved in the fate of Israel, and thus found themselves at variance with the official French policy? Apart from the extreme right wing which rejoiced in papers such as the scandal-mongering *Minute* at the attention drawn to the Jewish problem, none of the French parties showed any antisemitic bias. But supporters of the radical Left which regarded de Gaulle's foreign policy as the only right one, were not particularly upset by their attitude to Israel. Many French Jews were essentially in agreement with such opinions as Bernard Levin's who stated that, regarding himself exclusively as an Englishman, he felt neither the obligation nor the need to display special sympathy for Israel. *(Daily Mail,* 2.6.67.)

The whole issue was further aggravated by the French habit of thinking in terms of clear-cut alternatives (a phrase frequently heard in discussions on the topic was *'De deux choses l'une'),* and by a monolithic concept of nationhood fashioned by the Jacobins on the model of absolutism. Monolithic thinking, therefore, had deep roots in the French traditions of both right and left, but it was the Left which this time had to face an unfamiliar problem touching on the structure of French society and even the basic concept of the state itself. As long as France was Israel's close friend and near ally, the relationship between Jews and Israel caused no concern. During the Middle East crisis, however, this became a new issue. A man like Professor Raymond Aron, no Zionist but rather a liberal French nationalist, in the moment of the greatest danger said he could not imagine surviving Israel's destruction.

The interaction of events in the Middle East with emotions regarding the position of French Jews produced problems where hitherto no problems had existed. Slight differences of opinion developed into doctrinal conflicts. The same Baron Rothschild whose name had in left-wing mythology for over a century stood for monopoly capitalism, also represented solidarity with Israel, and the resulting identification of capitalism with Zionism proved an embarrassment to the Left. In this way, the Left was confronted with a number of unforeseen questions for which its doctrines had no answer. Such sudden confrontation with new problems was nothing new—it occurred in 1914 in the clash between internationalism and national defence, in 1936 in the conflict between pacifism and support for the Spanish Republic. In this perspective, the Israeli crisis and its accompanying problems does not represent a new departure, but conforms with a historical tradition in which the actual event, failing to fit its concept of history, compelled the Left each time to rethink its intellectual and political philosophy.

In *Silver Blaze* Sherlock Holmes mentions the 'curious incident' of the dog which did not bark in the night. The most remarkable fact in the attitude of the Italian communists to the Israeli war is that it differed in no fundamental way from that of their French comrades. This seems strange, for all students of the Left during the past years have stressed the difference between the Italian and French approach, pointing out that the Italians show more broadmindedness, more readiness to discuss, a more independent attitude to Soviet Russia's policy. Existing dissimilarities, often more a matter of style than of substance, were due to the fact that in Italy the exigencies of anti-fascism persuaded many members of the politically committed intelligentsia to support the communists, whereas in France the party tended to attract recognised intellectuals who might enhance the party image without, however, yielding to the temptations of independent political thought.

When it was reported in May that the Rome section of the *CPI* had expressed sympathy for Israel, it was often assumed outside Italy that the *CPI* itself had adopted an independent attitude to the Near Eastern conflict. In fact, this was not the case, and the differences between the French and the Italian parties were only slight although some of them were interesting. The Italian communist press accorded more space to Israeli communist resolutions than the French. The attacks on the socialist Nenni who supported Israel just as unequivocally as Guy Mollet in Paris, were on the other hand more savage than in France. The reason is not far to seek. In France the communists and the *Fédération* had entered into an electoral alliance, in Italy the socialists together with the *Democrazia Cristiana* had formed a government and the communists were in opposition. In France, the communists supported the government's Near Eastern foreign policy; in Italy, they could only support the Foreign Minister Fanfani who, unlike the neutralist Nenni, did not want to become party to the resolution of the maritime powers demanding the opening of the Gulf of Aquaba. His approach reflected the well-established traditions of Italian Mediterranean policy, in this case reinforced by Vatican views and by considerations of Italian oil interests. The communists supported what they termed an Italian 'active peace policy' in the Mediterranean which excluded any sympathy for the encircled state of Israel.

This also accounted for their sympathy with the 'progressive Arabs' fighting in the Yemen rarely mentioned in the French party press. *Unità* featured dramatic headlines like 'Sixth Fleet threatens Syria' or 'Growing Imperialist Menace in the Middle East'. It also headlined reports from Cairo about 'America's aggressive intentions', etc. On the other hand *Unità* (29.5.67) reported without polemical undertones a meeting of the World Jewish Congress in Milan and a rally of the Jewish Congregation in Rome, in which prominent anti-fascists participated. Such reports would have been looked for in vain in the Paris *Humanité*. The theoretical party organ *Rinascita* stated:

> The Middle East crisis has produced some absurd and grotesque resolutions and names of people known for their racialist views have again been mentioned; this time on the anti-Arab side. *(Rinascita,* 2.6.67.)

On the day the war started *Unità* (6.6.67) ended its editorial with an appeal for moderation:

> Apart from the need for Israel to adopt a new attitude to the reality of the Arab states, there is also the problem of Arab recognition of the reality of the state of Israel. We have to reconquer peace, not only for the Arabs and the Israelis but for all of us.

A day later, however, Pietro Nenni was attacked:

> It is impossible to close one's eyes to the 'sinister, irresponsible and extremist campaign somehow or other to involve Italy in the conflict. *(Unità, 7.6.67.)*

In Parliament, the communist Emilio Sereni confirmed the need for solidarity with the national movement of the Arab peoples 'if only for reasons of geography' (9.6.67.) A few days later *Unità* (13.6.67) rebuked certain 'friends of Israel', but nevertheless noted that the war was 'a reply to the threat of genocide'. Unlike the corresponding French organs, *Unita* featured a larger number of letters by dissenting readers which were, moreover, not invariably followed by editorial rebuttals. *Rinascita* (9 and 16.6.67) analysed the Left's attitude towards Israel, comparing opinions favourable to Israel with the pro-war agitation of the Italian socialists in 1915 which, it suggested, gave birth to Mussolini's 'fasci'. The paper noted with some satisfaction that dissenting left-wing socialists belonging to the Ricardo Lombardi circle denounced 'Atlantic degeneration'. Emilio Sereni who, perhaps because of his Jewish origin, was called upon to explain the official party line, wrote:

> The fact that there is no leading party or leading country does not prevent the USSR—the first socialist state, militarily and economically superior to the rest of the socialist world, and possessor of an incomparable store of political experience, acquired in fifty years of statehood— from occupying a special position in the working-class movement and among the anti-imperialist, progressive forces of the world. Togliatti never ceased to remind us that we Italian communists have a special relationship to

the communist party of the Soviet Union, which was based, even before it became political, on human, class, emotional and historical sympathies of inestimable importance. In the present crisis, awareness of this relationship has made itself positively felt and helped us to find out bearings in a complex and confusing situation. Among certain party cadres this necessary and decisive awareness has seemed, however, at times somewhat dulled . . .

To which Carlo Galluzzi, also a member of the party's central committee, replied:

. . . All this argues that we have to reappraise the view now gaining ground in our ranks and reflecting certain Chinese theories which accord pride of place to the national liberation movements of former colonial peoples disregarding all other revolutionary efforts, particularly in the socialist countries and by the working class of the industrialised West. Hence we have to overcome the tendency to hold the USSR responsible for everything that happens. For this tendency, while fully acknowledging the importance of the USSR, also reflects a certain desire to misinterpret the real facts . . . (*Rinascita*, 7.7.67.)

Sereni, who was asked to reply to Tel-Aviv comrades who had criticized the *CPI*, did not hesitate to explain that, objectively and in the context of global developments, even the most reactionary Arab regimes must be regarded as progressive:

The limitations, weaknesses, even the errors of the Arab liberation movements cannot, for us, obscure in any way the general progressive anti-imperialist development to which they belong. Even less can we justify the Israeli Communist Party's 'readiness to resist' and its willingness to support a *union sacrée* with an aggressive government. We do not overlook the difficulties which slogans about the 'destruction of Israel', circulated by the liberation movement and even by certain Arab communist parties, pose for the emergence of a strong communist party in Israel . . . But not by erring and even less by capitulating is it possible to overcome the mistakes of others. (21.7.67)

Piero Paolo Pasolini, a writer of the far Left, published in the *Nuovi Argumenti*, which rarely found itself out of line with communist thought, poems written in Israel. In an introductory passage, he admitted:

> Nowadays, reading *Unità* is as revolting as reading the most mendacious bourgeois papers.

In the influential and popular left-wing weekly, *Espresso*, the editor, Eugenio Scalfari and Arrigo Benedetti, his regular contributor and founder of the paper, openly clashed over the Middle East issue. Benedetti, an active anti-fascist greatly respected in literary circles, suggested in his weekly column of 11 June that Israel had shown that democracy and pacifism were not always identical, as the latter often represented only a facile escape from reality. A week later, Benedetti suggested that the Six Day War was a victory for civilisation.

> The Israelis have won because they identified with the modern world, which, irrespective of geographical or other differences, emancipates all people and invariably proves itself superior when attacked by nations clinging to backward and out-dated ideologies. Italy's two largest parties have been manipulated by foreign diplomacies. While the *CPI* soon toed the Soviet line, the *Democrazia Cristiana* took into account the interest of the Holy See and the Pope's apparent preference of the Arab world to the enlightened and secular Israel. There was never any question of Catholic neutrality as between the two warring countries. Among so many totalitarian factors, civilisation, in the Western sense, became an element in Israel's defence ... Because Israel stood for Western values, her recent fight has provoked such a sympathetic response ...

Scalfari dissociated himself from these views in a column on the same page:

> For the first time we cannot agree with Arrigo Benedetti. Civilisation, my dear Benedetti, is never defeated nor ever triumphs in war; it triumphs in other contexts ... All we know is that every man should enjoy the same rights, and if he is technically backward, the greater responsibility

remains with those who could have helped him and failed to do so. This applies to the Negroes of Alabama and the Arabs in French Algeria and would still be applicable tomorrow should Israel become the Prussia of the Near East. We know, however, that it will not take this road and hope that Israel will win the peace as it has won the war. (*Espresso*, 18.6.67.)

Benedetti, in a final 'letter' to the *Espresso*, explained the sense in which he had spoken of a victory for civilisation. The communists joined in the argument and accused Benedetti of racism. Scalfari, for his part, spurned support from such quarters and wrote: 'Charges of racism against Arrigo Benedetti are not even worth discussing'.

In conclusion, it may be said that in Italy the Israeli conflict deepened the estrangement between the communists and the rest of the Left, from socialists to republicans. However, it did not aggravate foreign policy disagreements between the *Democrazia Cristiana* and the socialists, if only because the very speed of the Israeli victory rendered any incipient clash between the coalition partners impossible.

L'Humanité's Internal Contradictions

Roger Paret

In early May 1967 what is commonly called the Left in France had two major concerns in foreign politics: primarily the war in Vietnam, and secondarily the coup d'état which led to the establishment of a military dictatorship in Greece. In this respect, the leaders and militants of the left wing political groups and the chiefs of the French Communist Party took a view in no way differing, so far as is known, from the analyses of the world situation guiding Soviet diplomats: the spreading and prolonged war in South-East Asia remained the principal threat insofar as gradually worsening local incidents might provoke a direct clash between the two world powers. In a May Day speech at Lenin's tomb, Marshal Grechko, the Russian Minister of Defence, said: 'Imperialist aggression is a serious complication in the international situation, and this calls for unity among all the revolutionary and progressive forces of the world. If all the socialist countries, China included, would unite in action to come to the aid of our brothers in Vietnam the failure of the imperialist aggressors in Vietnam would come all the sooner.'

The struggle against the American military presence in Vietnam remained the main theme of the official Communist press. On 3 May thousands of demonstrators responded, in the Place du Châtelet and along the main boulevards, to the

191

call of the Communist Party and demanded the evacuation of the American forces and peace in South East Asia.

Nothing in the Communist press of that time, any more than in the other French papers, seemed to herald or even to hint at the imminence of a crisis in the Middle East. On 5 May, *Humanité* carried a short article about what it called 'Bonn's failure in the Arab countries', which summarized an *Al Ahram* report on the *Arab League* decision to break off negotiations regarding the re-establishment of diplomatic relations (severed in 1965) with the German Federal Republic. The Bonn mission of Abd el Khalek Hassouna, the Secretary General of the Arab League, had been cut short, observed *Humanité,* because 'the West German Minister of Foreign Affairs would not guarantee his country's neutrality in case of an Arab-Israeli conflict'. At the same time the Foreign Minister of the German Democratic Republic, Otto Winzer, was in Cairo at the head of an important delegation. For the reader it was ordinary diplomatic routine, a strengthening of the ties between the Socialist countries and the principal Arab State. The next day, an inset on page 3 stated that Herr Winzer's talks were causing anxiety to the Bonn Government, which threatened to consider recognition by Egypt of the Pankow Government as a 'hostile act'. But all this was of marginal importance; Vietnam, Greece, Bolivia (because of the Régis Debray affair) remained the main subjects of leading articles.

On 9 May, a short report in *Humanité,* based on despatches from agencies and correspondents published the night before in other Paris newspapers, summed up the extremely confused events (still confused today) which had provoked sudden tension in Syria.

> Workers and soldiers in arms are patrolling the commercial centre of the Syrian capital. Armed pickets have been stationed in front of certain mosques in the town and suburbs, notably in the Midan district, centre of the extremist organisation, the Moslem Brotherhood. Many of the inhabitants of the capital were yesterday unable to obtain bread or meat as a result of the plot instigated by the reactionary clergy and big business interests. Taking as

their pretext an article attacking religion, evidently with the aim of provoking popular feeling, reactionary forces led by Sheik Hassan Habanaki tried to disorganise the country's food supplies by calling the businessmen and their employees to strike. These disturbances were intended to open the way to intervention from Jordan by former officers who took part last September in a plot against the new regime in Syria. One of these officers, Tahran Zobi, recently returned from Amman, revealed the conspiracy on radio and television. Religious chiefs, leading businessmen and the author of the article were arrested.

The significance of this article, combining precise hints and unrealistic errors due to the use of a vocabulary unrelated to the realities of the Arab-Islam world (e.g. 'clergy', 'reactionary'), lies in the fact that on 9 May leading French Communists had established no immediate link between Israel and the menaces threatening the Baathist regime in Syria. Traditionally Husains's Jordan was presented as the principal Middle Eastern adversary of 'progressive' Syrians, the place where 'plots' and 'conspiracies' were hatched; the allusion to Colonels Hatoum and Joumaa, refugees in Jordan since the failure of their coup of 9 September 1966, emphasized the 'anti-Jordanian' aspect of the article. Significantly, Israel was not even mentioned.

On 10 May *Humanité*, reporting on Jacques Soustelle's official welcome in Tel Aviv and his talks with David Ben Gurion and Mrs. Golda Meir and with General Dayan, wrote:

> Soustelle will be present at the military parade organised for 15 May in Jerusalem. The representatives of the Great Powers have decided not to attend the military march-past since they think that it endangers the international status of Jerusalem as defined in the United Nations resolution of 1947.

In this very typical statement are found the associations of words, names and themes which for some years, especially since 1956, have been used to define the attitude of Communist Parties towards Israel; the memory of what Jacques

Soustelle, the former Governor General of Algeria, had come to represent for the Left in France contaminates not only the leaders of the *Rafi* Party whom he met, but also to some extent Israel itself. But this implication was also routine—accepted as expressing a connection between the 'colonialist' Soustelle and Israel, which was itself thereby convicted of 'colonialism'—it did not imply any immediate danger of a denunciation more vehement than usual.

Moreover, the leaders of the French Communist Party had other cares at this time. On 11 May the Political Bureau met to examine the results of the Conference of European Communist Parties at Karlovy Vary. It approved the articles that had been published; the declaration on the security of Europe, the call for an intensification of solidarity with North Vietnam and the condemnation of the military coup d'état in Greece. In all these documents there was not one word about the Middle East.

It was only on 18 May, the day after the French general strike, called to protest against the 'special powers' requested by the Pompidou Government, that *Humanité* announced 'State of alarm in Syria, Egypt and Iraq following Israeli troop build-ups on the Syrian border'. There was still no editorial, but an extract from *Pravda* headed 'Israel the focus of tension in the Middle East', which ran:

'Troop concentrations on the Israeli-Syrian frontier show that Israel is still the focus of tension in the Middle East. Israel has again organized anti-Syrian acts, and it is not by chance that its army has been hurriedly equipped with American war material including tanks . . .'

This was the first official intimation of what in the following days became and still is the official Soviet interpretation of the Middle East crisis, an interpretation also accepted by the leaders of the European Communist Parties. This approach—it must be stressed—coincided in all essentials with the arguments put forward at the time by the official representatives of the United Arab Republic and the Baathist regime of Syria in Western capitals. From the information at our disposal it is impossible to say whether the Russians were the first to work out this global strategy concept, or whether, on the contrary, it was the 'progressive' Arab governments and some of their Marxist or para-Marxist experts who thereby attempted to provide Soviet leaders with an ideological justification for intervention in the emerging conflict. Such information as we have seems to point to the second theory. Indeed, since the end of 1966 and especially in the early months of 1967, several responsible Syrians had with growing insistence been repeating—and above all encouraged others to repeat—that a new and serious conflict was imminent in the Near East, a conflict whose only cause, according to them, was 'the intention of American imperialism to use all means, internal or external, to break the popular power established in Syria by the revolution of spring 1966.' After the failure of Colonel Selim Hatoum's attempted coup d'état, the leaders of the radical group of the *Baath* and the trade unionists of the *Khalid* movement reiterated unceasingly —especially to the Russians—that the regime in Damascus was in danger, and that, having been unable to bring about its fall from within, the Americans were determined to destroy it 'from the outside' by encouraging the Israelis to attack Syria. In this way the struggle between the Arab states and Israel was taken out of its specific regional context and placed in the framework of a world-wide conflict between 'reactionary' and 'progressive' forces. According to the architects of this Baathist strategy there was no Israeli problem but simply, in Palestine, one example among others of the universal antagonism between popular liberation governments and the upholders of colonialism and imperialism. Interpreted within this ideological framework, the situation in the Middle East must appear almost Manichean in its reassuring simplicity: on one side Arab eagerness to 'liquidate the results of colonialism', and on the other, 'imperialism', of which the State of Israel is described and denounced as a mere tool. This comfortable formula allowed them to shift the conflict between the Arab states and Israel from its real basis in history and sociology to ideological grounds where it could be described as a new Vietnam. By such a prodigious piece of pseudo-dialectical juggling, the Israelis were then identified as 'imperialists' or even, retrospectively, as Nazis.

Accordingly, the Communist press could from then on present events from a point of view coinciding exactly with that of the Arab governments. On 19 May, *Humanité* had a

front page headline 'Reserves called up in Israel. Israeli
Mirage fighters attack UNO plane. UAR demands withdrawal of UN forces from its territory'. No taking of sides, but
an 'explanatory' article featuring extracts from agency dispatches, which all came from Arab capitals. This symbolic
procedure, also used throughout the crisis by the Russian
press, indicated that the Arab cause was just, and that only
Arab information was reliable; it also emphasized in the same
symbolic manner that the Communist Parties unreservedly
supported the Arabs. In this anonymous article, *Humanité*
said: 'Observers note that Tel Aviv is beginning to take the
precautionary measures adopted by Egypt in reply to attempted aggression against Syria seriously'. Much was also
made of the news from Damascus and Bagdad about the
mobilization of the People's Militia and the formation of
battalions of young volunteers. On 20 May, when the accent
was still on 'the struggle for peace in Vietnam'. *Humanité*
featured a paragraph at the bottom on the front page
asserting that 'three Israeli divisions are on their way to the
Egyptian border from which UN forces were yesterday
withdrawn'. The article, on page 3, was, in fact, a reprint
from *Al Ahram*. The paper also noted that:

> Units of the Palestine Liberation Army took up positions
> occupied for ten years by the UN troops. . . . All civilian
> traffic between the area around Gaza and the rest of
> Egyptian territory has now been halted. There are no
> trains, the roads are out of bounds and the aircraft that
> make the regular run to the small town of El Arish have
> been grounded'.

The article also quoted Marshal Abdel Hakim Amir:
'There should be no doubt either in the Arab East or outside
it that the United Arab Republic will strike back with all its
force at any attempt at aggression by Israel. It is time to put
an end to the political insolence and pretensions of that
country.'

On 22 May, *Humanité*, while announcing 'Five Israeli
divisions concentrated at the UAR border', also expressed
an official view in an article signed by Marcel Veyrier under
the headline 'The Middle East—who is stoking the fire?'

Restating the principle themes of Arab propaganda, Veyrier argued:

We must remember that threatening statements by Israeli leaders and Israeli troop concentrations on the Syrian border are the source of the new tension. Now statements and military movements of this kind cannot be taken lightly. The Tel-Aviv Government has a dangerous inclination to launch its aircraft and tanks against any Arab country. Without reviving the Suez affair of 1956, whose motives and aftermath are well known, we can no longer keep count of the brutal attacks of the last two years against Jordan (in November 1966), or more recently against Syria. . . . The measures taken by Egypt and other Arab States are caused by abundantly justified anxieties. Israel claims that its security is threatened by the repeated raids of Palestinian commandos. But these raids are difficult to assess. They reflect the complexity of an exceedingly delicate problem which can certainly not be solved by violence. . . . The plots against Syria are spear-headed by imperialist circles who have never given up the idea of imposing governments of their own choice in this part of the world. The present Government of Syria does not suit them. It is anti-imperialistic and commands a broad popular following, including trade unions and Communists. This is more than enough to worry those in London, Washington and even Paris who have always had the greatest stake in the Middle East, its riches and strategic nerve centres. And Tel Aviv has invariably supported the plans of these people. It is not by chance that the Israeli army is so well equipped with modern weapons.'

In the same issue, *Humanité* printed extracts from speeches made in Paris on Palestine Day by the Moroccan lawyer Abderrahman Yussufi; a member of the General Secretariat of the *National Union of the People's Forces*, the chief leftist opposition party in Morocco, Mr Yussufi declared that the struggle between the Arab states and Israel was neither 'racial nor religious' but that it was part of the 'battle waged between progressive forces and those of imperialism in the Middle East'. Thus everything conspired to reproduce for the Communist reader the traditional picture his ideological bias led him to expect; Arab countries 'in love with peace', anxious only to free their economies from the tutelage of the industrial West and menaced by the 'imperialist aggression' of which the Israeli Government could be shown to be the permanent instrument.

On 23 May, the anti-American theme was introduced into the Middle East crisis. Following the Syrian thesis, which the Egyptians also took over, the Communist press increasingly depicted Israel not as a state with its own policy, its own ambitions, problems and difficulties, but merely as a tool of American policy, as though it were the garrison of 'imperialism' in the Middle East. *Humanité* reprinted a report from a Lebanese paper to the effect that units of the Sixth Fleet had anchored off the coast of Gaza where the Egyptians had just taken up their positions. It recalled that several weeks earlier the Israeli Prime Minister, Levi Eshkol, had allegedly told a correspondent of the magazine *US News and World Report* that should war break out, Israel had been assured of support from the American fleet, and that this statement had never been denied, a fact which inspired *Humanité* to comment:

> The United States are directly implicated in the invasion threat brandished by the Israeli leaders in Syria's face. Damascus has recently opened negotiations with representatives of the oil company ARAMCO, whose black gold crosses Syria by pipeline (a few miles from the Israeli border), in order to obtain from them increased dues in line with those imposed on the Iraq Oil Company. ARAMCO is a purely American company, which partly explains the reasons for American intervention in this part of the world.

Humanité, in reporting the Egyptian decision to close the Straits of Tiran to shipping bound for Israel, quoted an Egyptian Foreign Ministry spokesman as saying: 'From the day of its creation we have been in a state of war with Israel. The Israelis have not passed through the Suez Canal and there is no reason why they should pass through the Straits of Tiran.'

On 24 May, Yves Moreau's first editorial, 'The Causes of

the Tension', appeared. It was the result of, and in some ways a commentary on, the official Russian warning of 23 May, which it often merely paraphrased. *Humanite* published it under a five column headline 'Aggression in the Middle East will be blocked by resolute resistance from the USSR and the united strength of the Arab countries'. In the text, all the themes already outlined were now presented with more brutal directness:

> After the armed attack on Syrian territory carried out by Israeli troops on 7 April, government circles in Israel have continued to build up the atmosphere of feverish militarism in the country. Most important of all, Foreign Minister Eban has hinted at vast 'punitive expeditions' against Syria, and called for a 'decisive blow' to be struck against it. By its decision of 9 May, the military commission of the Knesset (Parliament) has granted full powers to conduct military operations against Syria. The Israeli troops gathered on the Syrian border are in a state of full alert, and mobilization has been announced throughout the country. It is quite obvious that Israel would not have been able to act in this fashion without the direct and indirect encouragement of certain imperialists who hope to re-establish colonial oppression on Arab soil. In the present circumstances these people regard Israel as their main weapon against the Arab States, who are resisting imperialist pressure with a national and independent policy.

These contentions were echoed by Yves Moreau:

> The closing of the Gulf of Aquaba to Israeli shipping has no more caused the present disagreements than the legendary wave of the Bey's fan caused the conquest of Algeria in 1830. On Monday evening, President Nasser reiterated the reasons which had brought the Egyptian Government to the long series of decisions they have recently taken. . . . The President of the UAR explained that it was a question of preventing Israeli aggression against Syria. Egyptian disclosures on the subject of these preparations for aggression do no more than confirm and define what was already known. . . . The blow had long been prepared.

On 16 October of the previous year the Prime Minister of
Israel, Levi Eshkol, had passed a resolution through
Parliament which recommended military operations
against Syria on the grounds of self-defence. Nothing,
therefore, could be more false than the Western propaganda image of the poor innocent little State of Israel, exposed
to the hostility of the whole Arab world. Besides, behind
Israel stand the great imperialist powers. . . . The Egyptian
decisions have drawn the teeth of Israel's anti-Syrian plans.
In particular the withdrawal of the UN troops in response
to the request of the Cairo Government, has played an
appreciable part in hindering aggression. . . . As for the
closure of the Gulf of Aquaba to Israeli shipping, it is
misleading, to say the least, to describe it as a blockade
when it is only a return to the pre-Suez crisis situation.
Only the Israeli aggression of 1956 and the occupation of
Sinai by the aggressors opened for the Israelis a passage
formerly denied to them, since the Arabs regard the Gulf of
Aqaba as part of their territorial waters. Like so many
others, this question can only be resolved by peaceful
means, which implies particularly that Israel should at last
carry out the United Nations' resolutions on the rights of
the Palestinian Arabs. But, unfortunately, Israeli governments turn their backs on all peaceful measures.

And after wholesale denunciation of Soustelle, Dassault
and Baron Edmond de Rothschild, the editorial demanded
'complete solidarity with the Arab peoples in their fight
against imperialism and its agents in the Israeli Government'.
Although this article produced an undeniable sense of unease,
even in political circles very close to the Communist Party, it
was and remained an exceedingly clear exposition of the
official view supported by the leaders of Socialist countries
and the various Communist movements. Only the 'pro-
Chinese' faction championed, as usual, still greater verbal
intransigence.

On 25 May, the tone hardened. In the lead story, under the
heading 'Explosive situation in the Middle East. Threats of
American intervention', Yves Moreau wrote:

During the last twenty-four hours the crisis in the

Middle East has been further aggravated by London's and particularly Washington's behaviour. Harold Wilson, utterly contemptuous of Egyptian sovereignty, called yesterday in his Margate speech for the re-establishment of UN troops in the United Arab Republic. Must we remind him that these troops were only sent with the consent of the Egyptian Government, and that it had been clearly stipulated that they could only stay in Egypt as long as this consent was not withdrawn? Action such as Wilson suggests would transform the troops into an occupying force and their mission into a colonial expedition under United Nations auspices.

André Wurmser, in an attack on the journalist André Frossard, wrote on 26 May:

What I wish for the people of Israel, who are neither more nor less dear to me than any other people, is that they should live, and live in peace. This will be easier for them when they realise that not even the memory of Abraham and Jacob justifies the fact that 1,300,000 Arabs have been despoiled of their lands three thousand years later, and that the American subsidies, however indispensable they may be to Israel's budget, do not justify a policy which puts Israel in the same category as the anti-semites of South Africa.

André Wurmser is a brilliant, if sardonic, pamphleteer and he used his biting invective here to repeat precisely the terms used in the theoretical writing of the Arab and pro-Arab left. There is a tendency in these articles, either overt or implied, whether they come from members of the Communist Party or from independent intellectuals and scholars, to give the reader the impression, indeed conviction, that Israel is nothing but a particular manifestation of the general colonialist phenomenon. The anti-colonial left had fought French colonial capitalism in the politically and psychologically highly complex conditions of Indochina, Africa and, first and foremost, of Algeria—where the ambivalence was all the greater and more difficult to resolve because it was rooted not so much in people's minds as in the facts themselves—this anti-colonial left (not completely recovered from its miscalculations and its political and historical errors) felt to some extent called upon by the leaders of the radical wing of the Arab revolutionary movement to inject into its analysis of the Israeli problem those elements which it had already misjudged in Algeria. By an inexorable escalation, to which this type of argument lends itself, the denunciation of Tel Aviv's foreign policy inevitably ended in a condemnation of Israel itself as a permanent source of insecurity in the Middle East and a built-in device for aggression. That implications of such dialectics force the issue has never been lost on either the Baathist theorists and strategists or the *Arab Socialist Union,* Egypt's only political party, whose members were formerly the leaders of Communist groups or intellectuals of Marxist sympathies. For once Israel had somehow been identified with 'colonialism' its very nature was seen as having changed, and accordingly Marxist countries and parties had to make a radical change in their appraisal of it. Hence the methods of the Israeli government were no longer the subject of argument, which now called in question Israel itself and its existence as a State. This attitude of the radical Arab left differs only in its theoretical justifications from that of the most traditional Islamic elements, who believe that Israel in itself, through its structure and by its very existence, constitutes an act of aggression against the Arab peoples. It is difficult to avoid the argument's logical conclusions: since Israel is somehow an 'intrinsic' source of continual aggression against the Arab peoples and their fight for freedom, it must disappear, just as Europe's colonial influence disappeared from Egypt, Syria and Algeria and as American military influence disappeared from Vietnam.

At this point, the theoretical position of the French Communists, like that of the Soviet leaders becomes somewhat modified. However much Communist attitudes to Israel and the Arab countries may have evolved during the past two decades and particularly after Suez, the Government of the USSR has not abandoned all the positions it took up during the 1948 war between the new Jewish State and its Arab neighbours: positions which the French Communist Party have supported and defended point by point. At the

Vélodrome d'Hiver, then still the centre of the great emotional gatherings of the Parisian left, a mass rally organized by the French Communist Party (18 May 1948) welcomed the birth of the State of Israel. It is perhaps worth recalling what Florimond Bonte, Deputy for Paris and member of the Central Committee, said on this occasion.

> The new Jewish State has come into existence after the most agonising travail and through the heroic struggle of the best of the Children of Israel. I bring it the warm welcome of the French Communist Party, always an unflinching supporter of all fighters for freedom, democracy and independence.

According to *Humanité* (19 May 1948):

> Florimond Bonte, repeatedly interrupted by enthusiastic applause, bore witness to the support the Communist Party is giving to the Jewish struggle. Its Deputies were the first to sign the Jewish Union for Resistance and Mutual Aid's resolution in favour of the creation of Israel. Speaking of the Nazi persecution of the Jews, and of their fight against Fascism, Florimond Bonte emphasized that they had earned the right to safety.

Humanité took a still clearer stand in favour of Israel when it reprinted on 30 May and 1 June excerpts from two *Pravda* editorials; the first ran:

> It must be clearly stated that in making war on the young Jewish State the Arabs are not fighting for national interests or for their own independence, but against the right of the Jews to create an independent state of their own. In spite of their sympathy with the Arabs in their moves towards national freedom, the Soviets cannot but condemn the Arab States' aggression towards Israel.

The second article went even further:

> Arab armies attacked the State of Israel immediately after its establishment, in spite of the fact that this State was created on the basis of decisions taken by the United

Nations, of which various Arab States are members. Therefore the action the Arab States have taken constitutes an act of unprovoked aggression, an attack on the legal rights of the Jewish people and a violation of the basic principles of the United Nations Charter.

In 1967 the architects of Soviet policy could no longer be expected to reason in these terms, since 'progressive' governments, some of them professedly Socialist, had replaced the 'feudal' regimes in several of the most important Arab countries. In 1948 Israel was seen as an 'objectively progressive' country facing monarchies and emirates bound to the great colonial powers; nineteen years later the positions had been reversed. Israel had become the principal, almost the only, ally of the United States in the Near East, whilst Syria, Egypt, Algeria and even Iraq, in varying degrees, were now part of the 'Socialist camp'. All the same, neither the Soviet establishment nor the European Communist leaders have carried the ideological and political implication of their denunciation of Israel through to its logical conclusion. This ambiguity was undoubtedly one of the basic elements of the June crisis, and it is not impossible that in the future it will continue to be a source of considerable difficulty for the Russians in their relationship with the leaders of the radical group of the Arab revolutionary movement.

For the leaders of the USSR, Israel has become part of the imperialist coalition and must therefore be denounced and politically opposed; this does not mean, however, that they have arrived at the conclusions that the Arab revolutionaries draw from the same premises, conclusions to which they hope to convert the Russians, even against their will. Just before the outbreak of hostilities in 1967 and particularly during the fighting, this apparently only verbal difference in emphasis, had considerable influence on the Russian and on the Syrian and Algerian assessments of the situation. The theoretical viewpoint of the Arab revolutionaries was indisputably more consistent that that of the Russians, since the latter, together with the European Communists, refused to accept the full implications of their own statements.

This difficulty became particularly obvious when *Humanité*

dealt with theoretical aspects of the issue. On 26 May, 1967 the paper featured an Yves Moreau editorial entitled 'Aircraft-carrier diplomacy', in which the Party spokesman wrote:

> How can the United States dare to reproach Egypt for having exercised its sovereignty in territorial waters when they themselves try to dictate the law throughout the Mediterranean by maintaining there, more than twenty years after the Second World War and without any justification, a fleet of some fifty ships equipped with missiles and several hundred aircraft? It is a permanent danger to peace in the Near East, a threat of intervention in internal affairs to all the Mediterranenan countries, including the European ones, as we have just seen in Greece. The presence of this floating arsenal in the Mediterranean makes the provocations of the Israeli Government particularly dangerous.

The first part of this article conformed with the previous days' analyses, restating all the points emphasised by the Marxist Arabs; collusion between the United States and Israel, all responsibility resting with Washington, Israel being only one cog in the machine, and finally, through an effective process of gearing, identification of the Greek situation with that in the Middle East, producing an association in the reader's mind between the image of Israel and the hateful idea of 'Fascism'. But the contradictions in the Communist position appear when Yves Moreau added, without any transition,

> As for Israel, although the position of French Communists is quite clear, it has been misrepresented so often in certain commentaries that it may be useful to restate it. Firm supporters of the Arab national liberation movement, we do not intend to question here the existence of the State of Israel. We condemn the policy of its present leaders who act as tools of imperialism. Because of this policy Israel plays the same role in the Near East as West Germany plays in Europe.

This passage is highly significant; its internal contradictions highlight the Communist ambiguities. Israel is associated with the 'revenge-seekers of Bonn' and thus once more, as if by magic, identified with the bane of 'Fascism'. At the same time it is stated that a change of government could allow the Jewish State to stop being the 'tool of imperialism'. After this the conclusion seems inescapable that the aggression against the Arabs, whatever appearances may suggest, is not rooted in Israel's statehood, but only in the policy of a government allied to Washington. Although they use the same words as the Arab revolutionaries, European Communists apparently do not mean the same things.

These ambiguities and the misunderstandings they engender were to become increasingly pronounced. Between 26 May and 5 June the Communist press seemed to reflect the theories of the Arab left. The conflict was increasingly interpreted as a direct confrontation between 'Arab revolutionary countries' and the United States, a collision between Arab nationalism and the 'imperialist American' resolve to keep oil production under its control. But the more the Communist press intensified its attacks on American intervention, the louder Russian diplomats called for the withdrawal of American naval and air power from the Mediterranean, the more the 'Socialist camp' seemed to adopt the Arab view that Israel must cease to be 'the spearhead of imperialism in the Middle East', the more the actual divergencies began to show. They were manifest when, after the outbreak of war, the Russian Government followed a policy of peaceful co-existence and did not intervene directly in the field. All this was anticipated in Yves Moreau's editorial of 27 May—

What will be the next developments in the Middle East crisis? It would be easier to answer this question if we knew what President Johnson said to the Israeli Foreign Minister Eban who visited him yesterday at the White House. For Mr Eban has not concealed the aim of his trip, which was to obtain assurances that the United States was ready to use force against the UAR. Unfortunately, we have only too much reason to fear that Mr Eban received satisfaction rather than counsels of prudence. Indeed, the language of the American Ambassador in Cairo smacks strongly of 'ultimatum'. And in the Mediterranean, Admiral William Martin, Commmander of the Sixth Fleet, uses his air and naval forces for disquieting manoeuvres. If the United States has given, or is in the process of giving, the pledges asked by the Israeli Government, the consequences could be extremely serious. . . .

Responsibility for the crisis (Yves Moreau concluded) cannot be divided between the two sides. On one side there was preparation for war against Syria and the present outbreak of fighting with Egypt. On the other there were measures designed to prevent the Tel Aviv Government putting its plans into operation, and a determination to be ready for an eventual trial of strength, coupled however, with a desire for preservation of the peace.

On 30 May, after Mr Eban's return from Washington and the Security Council debate, in which the Soviet delegate Fedorenko demanded the unconditional withdrawal of the Sixth Fleet, *Humanité*'s editor-in-chief, René Andrieu, in an editorial called 'A clear look at the truth', believed that 'the trial of strength in the Middle East seems to have been adjourned for the moment, but the risk of full scale war is still present'. Elaborating the point, he went on:

It seems quite obvious to us that war is not a happy solution for either party and that some method of settling the problem must be found. But we must remember the position of the French Communist Party, which is that such a settlement must not bring into dispute [*ne doive pas mettre en cause*] the right of the Israeli people or their State to exist. This being clearly understood, let us add that passing pious resolutions is not enough—one must also have the courage to seek out the truth and to reveal it. And the truth, however bitter it may be to some who refuse to recognise it, and rack their brains to justify the unjustifiable, is that the Israeli Government with the shadow of American imperialism looming behind it, bears the main responsibility for having brought the Middle Eastern countries to the brink of war. . . . Israel, an artificially created State, has, in spite of the merits of its pioneers, only been able to survive thanks to the dollars it receives from

the United States, whether by public credit or private
funds. American imperialism could not miss the chance to
exploit this situation.

The next day, 31 May, René Andrieu repeated—

The Israeli Government and the Arab States seem to be
the protagonists in the drama currently being played out in
the Middle East, but it is American imperialism that
stands in the wings and bears the essential responsibility
for the dangerous situation on the main stage. The great
colonial powers are not resigned to seeing their domination
challenged by movements towards national liberation in
an area which they regarded as a private preserve. . . . Instead of coming to some arrangement with the Arab
countries, the leaders of Israel have chosen to impose their
views by force, counting on support from outside. They
found their support in imperialism, particularly American
imperialism, only too glad to have a weapon in its fight
against the Arab people's national liberation movement.
But if such an attitude is maintained for long it cannot fail
to have the gravest consequences for the Israelis themselves.

These two articles sum up the contradictions in the
Communist attitude to the Arab-Israeli war. They were
published after President Nasser's press conference of 28 May
and his contention that the fundamental and irreducible issue
was quite simply the existence of Israel as a State. The Arab
position was perfectly clear. Nevertheless editorials in the
Communist press seemed to suggest an identity between the
Arab and Russian viewpoints, as if they did not diverge on
the issue of Israel's existence. When Communist-inspired
statements took up all the arguments of the Arab revolutionaries, but hid their ultimate conclusions under a cloak of
silence, equivocation reached its peak.

In this way Yves Moreau (*Humanité*, 2 June) allowed
himself to interpret Syrian and Egyptian intentions in terms
that were the exact opposite of statements by President
Nasser, and by the Syrian Foreign Minister, Dr Ibrahim
Makos, to a representative of *Humanité*. 'On the Arab side

(maintained Yves Moreau) they are ready to sit down at the conference table'. On the same day the *Association of Islamic Students in France* published a statement highlighting the real divergencies:

Do not the rights of men, either individually or collectively, justify a fight to recover a country occupied illegally by an invader? Can someone who wants to go home be called an aggressor, and has anyone the right to reproach him for using force if this is the only means left to him? We believe that the French, who during 1914-1918 fought heroically against German imperialism to recover Alsace-Lorraine, will understand the Arabs and will be able to see who is the aggressor and who the victim. The Arab people are resolved to fight to the end to drive the invader from their province of Palestine, sure of their rights and of the support of all people who prize justice, for, unfortunately, in our times force alone can ensure the reign of justice.

The position of the Communist Party, like the attitude of the Soviet leaders was, until the opening of hostilities, contradictory. It was verbally consistent to the extent that, whatever the subject matter of the *Humanité* articles, they all gave the reader a picture of the Arab-Israeli conflict which related, at least in essentials, to a familiar ideological and political system ('Fascism', 'colonialism', 'imperialism', 'defence of the peace'). The serious inconsistencies were on the factual level. The 'resolutely anti-imperialist' declarations of solidarity were doubly deceptive, firstly because they did not correspond to the professed aims of the Arab revolutionaries, and secondly because there was considerable discrepancy between their verbal fervour and the lengths to which they were in fact prepared to go. In this respect the 'orthodox' communist attitude hardly differed from that of the various Chinese-inspired groups and movements. The latter professed an extreme 'leftist' position which, however, was purely verbal. In its issue published before the outbreak of fighting, *Humanité Nouvelle*, the weekly organ of the *French Communist (Marxist-Leninist) Movement*, upheld 'the just cause of the Palestinian people' even more resolutely (if this is possible) than the *CPF*. The article was a call to arms:

What is the real crux of the matter? To restore its land to a people, the Palestinians, for nineteen years the victims of an enforced Munich-style agreement. This was the means by which more than a million Palestinians were driven from their land when the State of Israel was formed. . . . They forged weapons for their liberation—the *Organisation for the Liberation of Palestine* and the *Palestine Liberation Army*. They know that only a people's war will restore their homes, will win them independence. They know that there can be no peaceful co-existence between imperialism, especially American imperialism, and a people engaged in a struggle such as theirs. Whether the imperialism works directly or through a third party, they know that conciliation in the spirit of Tashkent, extolled by the revisionists, serves the imperialist cause.

This obviously routine denunciation of the 'collusion' between the Kremlin and the White House may be able to provoke popular uprisings in China, but in France, even among the students, it was of negligible importance. Such leftist effusions do not appear to have unduly disturbed the leaders of the French Communist Party. Their real problem was to reconcile their 'unconditional' support of the Arab revolutionaries with their refusal to accept the destruction of the State of Israel. On this point European Communists were as embarrassed as the civil and military leaders of the USSR. In fact, in spite of their apparent firmness, they did not reply to the question put by the Communist journalist Jacques Coubard *(Humanité,* 26 May), a specialist in Middle East affairs:

What part does the Israeli Government play in the present confrontation between the movement for national liberation and the colonial powers, between the independent and progressive regimes and the policemen of America and Britain? Where exactly does the ruling group of Tel Aviv stand?

The official view has always been stated in very forceful terms: economically and financially Israel is completely controlled by American capitalists, Israel receives aid at one and the same time from the United States and from the 'revenge-seekers of Bonn', Israel is a veritable powder-keg. But the fact is, as experience has strikingly shown, that these peremptory declarations have been mere stylistic exercises or, more exactly, ritual repetitions of sacred formulae, which for half a century have referred to Marxist-Leninist tradition, but which no longer correspond to the practices of the Soviet Establishment, and even less to the practice of the European Communist parties. They all spoke of a 'people's war' while hoping that nobody would undertake it, and even resolving to do everything to make it impossible.

The Italian Communist Party and the Middle Eastern Conflict

Manfred Steinkühler

In current international debates, whether on the problems of East-West relations, European integration, the two Germanies, or the Middle Eastern conflict, there is always one voice which, though carrying neither the authority nor the responsibility of government, tries to make itself heard and command attention. It is that of the Italian Communist Party, a party which, despite its exceedingly critical attitude to the governments in power, has occupied within the context of Italian politics something akin to an official national opposition. This status not only gives the party its internal credibility, but also has provided it with a platform for extensive international activities. The *CPI* convincingly proved its independence and stature when it publicly dissociated itself from the occupation of Czechoslovakia by the Warsaw Pact countries. More recently it asserted that the first soundings of Chancellor Brandt's *Ostpolitik* had been taken in Rome, in short that the good offices of the *CPI* had helped to smooth the way for the new German-East Bloc rapprochement. The *CPI* also claims to be the first communist party—and in this respect ahead of those of the USSR and France—to have developed a positive approach to Europe, having worked out the theoretical foundations on which the vertical socio-political and the national horizontal structures would have to be based to enable the countries of the Eastern bloc to join the European Community. All these efforts and initiatives reflect the party's underlying and firmly-held belief in the possibility of closing the gap between the two power blocs; and it is within the context of such bridge-building aspirations that the *CPI* has formulated its approach to the Middle Eastern problem.

Soon after the outbreak of the Six Day War, the party's prescription for a settlement was 'immediate termination of all military activities and the observance of a general cease-fire, followed by negotiations which, based on the liberty, independence and national inviolability of the Arab countries and of Israel, would establish peace, enabling the Mediterranean nations, untrammelled by imperialistic designs and intrigues, to arrive at a better mutual understanding'.[1]

The day after this formula was published, Alberto Jacoviello, the well-known foreign affairs commentator of the *CPI*'s official daily *Unità*, praised the efficiency of the Israeli army.

'It must be acknowledged [he wrote] that this was a brilliantly conducted campaign which will rank among the classic examples of the strategy of the first strike.' At the same time he was at pains to stress the immutable realities, underlying the confrontation. 'All the skill and efficiency of the Israeli generals cannot alter the fact that no army operating under the conditions the Israelis have to face, can impose peace terms on an opposing side covering so vast an area as the Arabs.'[2]

In an official statement made a few days later (15 June) the *CPI* summed up what it regarded as the essential preconditions for the restoration of peace in the Middle East; a document in which for the first time special attention was drawn to the refugee problem.

> The conflict can only be resolved by peace negotiations which, while equally mindful of legitimate Arab rights and Israel's claim to national existence, at the same time deny any reward to aggression and tackle the dramatically aggravated refugee problem.[3]

This statement in certain respects anticipated the UN Resolution 242, on which, since its adoption, the Italian communists have based their attitude to the Middle Eastern conflict. But they have never interpreted the resolution as a weapon designed to reduce or weaken Israel. The party had continued to regard the peaceful co-existence of Israel and the Arab countries as an indispensable pre-requisite for any Middle Eastern settlement, insisting, however, that Israel should recognize the validity of refugee claims.

In the *CPI*'s view the two factors determining Israel's position in the Middle East are, externally, conflict with the Arab countries, and internally, the clash with the Palestinian refugees and their guerilla movement.

> Whereas Israel's expansionist and imperialist policies [wrote Romano Ledda] involved her in a number of collisions with Arab states which could be resolved either by war or through diplomatic channels, i.e. on the level of foreign relations, her confrontation with the Palestinians touches the very core of the State of Israel and calls in question both her spiritual aspirations and the manner of her emergence during the past twenty years. . . . The Israel problem concerns neither her boundaries nor her existence but rather the theocratic and racist nature of Zionism, still one of the main pillars of her domestic and foreign policies. In other words, it is rooted in her claim to a special kind of statehood, based not on well-known and clearly established historical events, but on ancient religious rights which serve to justify both her present boundaries and her expansionist expectations. Moreover, the fact that Israel represents a certain type of capitalist society containing seeds of imperialist ambitions easily adaptable to the wider designs of the West, is another feature of the image of the somewhat odd superstructure this country now presents.

Ledda doubted whether in her present form Israel could come to terms with the Arab world and therefore admonished the Israelis to rethink the foundations on which they have built their state.

> The people of Israel [he concludes] are called upon to consider their attitude and examine their consciences. They will have to decide whether the State of Israel's

Zionist mould and her essentially Hebrew character are conducive to the peaceful co-existence with Arab nations on which secure peace must ultimately depend.[4]

The Italian communists were, however, not convinced that Israel had subjected herself to this task of self-critical analysis, as a study by Kino Marzullo revealed.

Political conflict, the class struggle ·in particular, is unknown in Israel. Nor is there much hope of its revival until her international problems have been solved. Yet since a solution is hardly likely to emerge without the pressures provided by the class struggle, the situation remains suspended within a vicious circle of immobility.

Hence, in Marzullo's view the outlook for the future is distinctly bleak. Israel, he suggested, suffered not only from an absence of political controversy in general and the class struggle in particular, but concomitantly and possibly as a result of these shortcomings from the emergence of a new consumer orientated leadership which in turn encouraged the conformist trend.

These two ·tendencies [he concluded] are directly responsible for the third and perhaps the most disquieting trend. It is the indifference of the country's younger generation to all political issues, its retreat from the ideological positions of the past, and its eager surrender to the ideals of the consumer society.[5]

Their critical attitude towards Israel did not prevent the Italian communists from appraising the Egyptian position with equal candour. Commenting on the downfall of Ali Sabri and his friends, Alberto Jacoviello stated:

Recent events in Egypt have demonstrated beyond all doubt dissensions over domestic and foreign affairs within a leadership which has claimed and continues to claim the right to rule over a major country without any true participation of the masses.[6]

Nor did he hesitate to call the prominent and influential editor of the semi-official *Al Ahram*, H. Heikal, a liar because, before their ill-starred uprising, he had accused the Sudanese communists of making a bid for dictatorial power. 'To support and propagate Numeri's fabrications after the Khartoum executions can only be described as an act of consummate infamy.'[7]

To the Italian communists the Middle East conflict was quite obviously a manifestation of a wider struggle.

On the one hand [noted Gian Carlo Pajetta], it is part and parcel of the anti-imperialist confrontation in which the Soviet Union and the entire socialist camp opposes the leading imperialist power, the US, in one of the most explosive regions of the Middle East and the Mediterranean; on the other hand, it is a struggle by the national anti-imperialist forces among the Arab nations opting for a socialist solution, and under this aspect the conflict reflects the aspirations of a specific liberation movement within the colonial world.[8]

During Nixon's Rome visit (October 1970) Sergio Segre characterized America's Mediterranean policy as an effort 'to replace the absence of a political by a military presence'.[9] The signing of the Egyptian-Soviet treaty of alliance (May 1971) took the *CPI* by surprise and moved Alberto Jacoviello to consider the problem of Egypt's 'Sovietization', and to reassert the need for 'overcoming the dichotomy of the power blocs', one of the party's pet ideas.

The Cairo agreements [Jacoviello wrote] may possibly be used in a campaign designed to lend some credibility to the spectre of the Sovietization of Egypt. If so, such allegations would appear exceedingly stupid, particularly if they emanate from those who have contributed nothing to a solution of the Arab-Israeli conflict showing due consideration for the national right of the Palestinian people within a political framework that, in the interest of all Mediterranean countries, will get rid of alien influences. As far as we are concerned, it is hardly necessary to recall our past record or to remind readers that we have always encouraged policies aimed at reducing tensions created by the confrontation of the super powers.[10]

Given these views it is not surprising that the *CPI* continued to champion the cause of the Arab guerillas, even when their destruction by Hussein's army in September 1970 did not move the Soviet Union to abandon its stance of silent impassivity. 'The Palestine resistance has not been defeated [asserted Jacoviello], but has stood its ground against the royal troops, and continues to do so.' Ostensibly addressing himself to the Italian government, although his strictures may well have been meant for Moscow, he mused: 'How can the government in a moment like this justify its silence and indifference?'[11]

Nor for that matter did the party hesitate to support the official Egyptian line concerning the trial of Ali Sabri. Carlo Pajetta, notwithstanding the trial's distinctly nationalist and anti-communist undertones, declared: 'We shall continue to regard Egypt as the most important protagonist of the Arab revival.'[12] The dialectical strains to which Middle-Eastern events subjected the *CPI* become quite apparent if this quotation is compared with Jacoviello's assessment of the situation mentioned earlier in this article.

The party had also to face and rebut charges of antisemitism. Repudiating these accusations, it did not point to the many prominent Jews within the top leadership, people like Umberto Terracini, Gian Carlo Pajetta, Paolo Bufalini, Sergio Segre, among whom Pajetta and Segre have been particularly critical of Israel. Defending the party's record, Maurizio Ferrara declared:

> We recall the history of the recent past when Jews and communists faced the same Nazi execution squads. However, our consistent stand by our principles now compels us to speak out in support of the inalienable rights of the Arabs to live as a nation in their homeland; the same principled constancy impels us not only to proclaim our solidarity with the Arabs, but also to voice our criticism when the side we support takes what we regard as misguided actions.[13]

Such hankering after independence persuaded the Italian communists to plead—and in the event not unsuccessfully— for the Jews condemned in the Leningrad anti-Zionist trials, and for a relaxation of the emigration procedures. All this illustrates the inherent ambiguities in the posture of the Italian communists. Even so, two features have remained dominant; on the one hand, a certain eagerness to react to the problems of Central Europe and the Middle East independently and irrespective of the line favoured and followed by the Soviet Union, while, on the other hand, endorsing the developments brought about by Soviet pressure. This produces highly ambivalent and at times even contradictory responses. Thus the Italian communists have been quite prepared to recognize the legitimacy of the State of Israel while simultaneously jeopardising its very existence by questioning the validity of it Zionist origins. Romano Ledda in particular has seemed to stress these ambiguities. In doing so, he demonstrated the difficulties facing Israel whose enemies are anxious both to attain their own ends and to serve Soviet interests. The two objectives do not always coincide, and it is therefore difficult to visualize what Carlo Pajetta's 'socialist Mediterranean' would look like. How can the *CPI*'s demands for Arab and Israeli freedom, independence and inviolability be guaranteed? How does it imagine its hopes can be realised if, after the return of Yugoslavia to the Soviet fold, Russian power, reinforced by its Mediterranean bases, could span the gap between Europe and Africa? Does the *CPI* really believe it will be able to maintain its independence under such conditions? It may have its doubts on this score, and there may be an undertone of veiled relief in Jacoviello's recent statement: 'Nevertheless the armament industry is working full out on both sides, and at present it is quite impossible to foresee when this process can be arrested.

The non-communist world must realize that neither the Sixth Fleet, nor Israel, Italy or France, can singlehanded prevent a further expansion of Soviet power in the Mediterranean. Nor will mere military countermeasures stabilize a situation calling for a political programme guaranteeing the essential freedoms of all Mediterranean countries.

NOTES

1. *L'Unità*, 8 June 1967.
2. *L'Unità*, 8 June 1967.
3. *L'Unità*, 16 June 1967.
4. *L'Unitá*, 30 November 1968.
5. *L'Unità*, 4 February 1972.
6. *L'Unità*, 31 July 1971.
7. *L'Unità* 7 September 1971.
8. glan Carlo Pajetta, *Socialismo e Mondo arabo*, Roma 1970, pp.. 7-8.
9. *L'Unità*, 6 October 1970.
10. *L'Unità*, 29 May 1971.
11. *L'Unità*, 22 September 1970.
12. *L'Unità*, 8 September 1971.
13. *L'Unità*, 13 September 1970.
14. *L'Unità*, 16 February 1972.

American Radicals and Israel

Arnold Forster

The propaganda of political extremists in the United States—the far left, the far right, and the black separatists —has in recent years reflected a rare concurrence: a vehement opposition to Israel.

The parallel positions have each been based on the conspiracy theory of history that has long characterized all varieties of extremist thinking. The devil is 'Zionism', viewed by the New Left as the handmaiden of 'imperialism', by the Radical Right as that of world communism. To the racial separatists, the black nationalists, Israel represents an incursion in the 'Third World', with Jewish-Arab conflicts seen somewhat unaccountably as racial, the Jews being the alleged oppressors of 'black' Arabs.

A partially related phenomenon has been the emergence of anti-Semitic overtones in black extremist propaganda, particularly that of certain separatists. During the two-month New York teachers' strike late in 1968, a dispute in which so-called community control of black ghetto schools became a burning issue, feelings ran high between black pro-'community' leaders and the striking teachers (New York's teaching force is largely Jewish), and the controversy was marked by the appearance of a number of blatantly anti-Semitic tracts and handbills. Ultra-leftist and black militant publications, strongly opposing the teachers' union, tended in many instances to gloss over or even to excuse the bigotry—a few, such as the *African-American Teachers Forum*, published by black city teachers, added anti-Jewish slurs of their own. In the majority of such instances, the attacks on Jews were accompanied by references to Israel or were expressed in terms such as 'Zionist teachers'. *Zionist*, of course, has long been the cunning anti-Semite's code-word for *Jew*, but in the context of the extremists' present anti-Israel stance it provides a further conspiratorial insinuation.

The 'New' Left and the black separatists represent virtually a joint pro-Arab front in the United States. A key statement of the New Left view was the three-part series in *New Left Notes*, the publication of the radical white *Students for a Democratic Society*. The author, Susan Eanet, assailed Israel as 'racist' and 'expansionist', and declared:

> The metaphysical concepts of the 'homeland' and 'chosen people' grant the Zionists the right to expand and expand as long as they can win militarily. Therefore the position of the *Al Fatah* is that the Zionist must be defeated militarily before the Arab people can have national liberation.

Support for the Palestinian terrorists has been an essential part of the revolutionaries' stance. Handbills issued by *Youth Against War and Fascism*, a pro-Maoist group, called for 'All out support to the Arab Revolution!' A *YAWF* activist, Rita Freed, who also founded the radical leftist *Committee to Support Middle East Liberation*, called for an *Al Fatah* victory. She organized demonstrations at the United Nations protesting against 'US-Israeli aggression against the Arab people', and gave talks to raise funds for *Al Fatah*. Representatives of her committee disrupted a February 1969 panel discussion on the Middle East at a Milwaukee Jewish centre with shouts of 'Ho, Ho, Ho Chi Minh, *Al Fatah* will win!'

Students for a Democratic Society (SDS) published a pamphlet, the cover of which bore the symbol of *Al Fatah* and the notation: 'This symbol means 'Invaders! Get Out of Occupied Land!' The *SDS* also reprinted at least three pro-Arab articles originally published in *Tricontinental*, an arm of Fidel Castro's propaganda apparatus in Havana. Another *SDS* publication was entitled the *Manifesto of the Palestinian National Liberation Front (Al Fatah)*.

Israel, in the view of the far left, is a tool of Western imperialism. Consequently the Palestinian terrorists have been cast as 'liberators' in the mould of the Viet Cong or the original Castro army. But the actual challenge is to the very existence of Israel as a nation. In a letter published in *New Left Notes* an SDS member declared:

> The State of Israel must be abolished, its Zionist, racist government and its league with imperialism thoroughly exposed and fought, until the day that the land is again taken back by the Palestine refugees to whom it belongs—before it was stolen by the Israeli Jews. . . . Because of the huge support Israel has here in the United States, it is a great task for *SDS* to organize support for the Arab women and men freedom fighters and their organization *Al Fatah*. . . .

Organizations such as *SDS* and the *Young Socialist Alliance* (youth group of the *Trotskyist Socialist Workers Party*) have actively co-operated with the *Organization of Arab Students (OAS)*, which claims to represent all Arab students studying in the United States. The *OAS*, purportedly a 'cultural and education' organization, is in fact a major source of anti-Israel propaganda and agitation. Both on and off the campus, *OAS* chapters have concentrated on mobilizing support for *Al Fatah*.

The Arab cause in general, and Palestinian terrorism in particular, received extensive coverage in the official publications of the separatist *Black Panther Party* and the *Black Muslim* sect. The Muslims' *Muhammad Speaks* published an interview with Fatah leader Yasser Arafat, and on another occasion warm praise for Fatima Birnawi, a Palestinian Arab woman convicted of planting a bomb in an Israeli theatre. *The Black Panther* also published a number of articles in praise of the terrorists, including one in the issue of 4 January 1969 entitled, 'Palestine Guerrillas versus Israeli Pigs'. (An editor's note explained that this article had been 'submitted on behalf of the Palestine National Liberation Movement, *Al Fatah*. . . .')

Under the heading, 'Pronunciamento', *The Black Panther* (21 December 1968) reproduced a speech by Eldridge Cleaver, then *Black Panther Party's* Minister of Information in which he declared:

> We're going to call a spade a spade, a Jew a Jew, and a pig a pig. . . .Cleaver added: We're relating right now to the Third World. If the Jews like Judge Friedman (he presided at the murder trial of a Panther member) are going to be allowed to function, and come to their synagogues to pray on Saturdays, or do whatever they do down there, then we'll make a coalition with the Arabs, against the Jews, if that's the way you want it.'

Thus the *Panthers*, like some other black extremists, saw Israel and American Jewry as one, and their 'Third World' sympathies gave impetus to antisemitism on the domestic front.

Similarly, the sympathies of left-leaning black separatists were drawn to *Al Fatah* through its identification in the world revolutionary press with the so-called liberation movements in Cuba, Algeria and Vietnam. Wilfred Ussery, national chairman of *CORE* (the *Congress of Racial Equality*, which took an extremist turn since its early role in the integration struggles), told a radio interviewer in February 1969 that he supported the aims of *Al Fatah*, which he called 'the liberation forces', against the 'aggressive designs of the Zionists'.

When, early in 1969, the official student newspaper of Wayne State University (Michigan) was taken over (according to the *New York Times*) by black extremists, its editors called for a protest demonstration against a visit to Detroit by Israel's ambassador to the United States. On the night of the demonstration, sponsored by the student newspaper along with the *Young Socialist Alliance* (Trotskyist) and the *Organization of Arab Students*, a handbill was distributed in the name of these groups which denied the very right of 'existence of the Zionist racist Israel'. This very right of the State of Israel to live—not merely the responsibility for war or for refugees—is the question raised in much of the current propaganda from the radical left and the black separatists, and the answer is usually characterized by disturbing threats and predictions of violence that rival those of the Arab terrorists themselves.

The propagandists of America's radical right—as distinguished from the antisemitic hate fringe that hangs on the rightist edge—took longer to discover in their own kinds of conspiratorial thinking, the 'diabolical' Zionists and the 'beleaguered' Arabs. While the basic radical right group, the *John Birch Society*, tended toward some equivocation on the Middle East during most of the 1960s, remaining cool toward Israel while viewing Nasser's UAR as a 'Communist' satellite, there have been signs of a change in attitude—with the lurking ally of 'Israeli aggression' seen by the Left as 'imperialism', appearing to the Birchites as the familiar Red Menace.

In the February 1969 issue of the *Birch Society's* magazine, *American Opinion*, Tom Anderson, a member of the organization's National Council, wrote: 'On 15 May 1948 international Zionists established a State in Palestine and, with the help of the United Nations, proceeded to drive 1.5 million Arabs from their homes. Thousands of these unfortunate Moslems have been murdered, maimed and tortured.' In his weekly newspaper column Anderson wrote:

'The Jews massacred Arabs and stole their land, homes and personal possessions. Would wholly righteous people do that?'

Billy James Hargis, leader of the evangelistic far right-wing *Christian Crusade*, has assailed the commitment of 'liberals' as inconsistency: 'They justify Israel's crushing the Arab countries. You never hear a protest against Israel. . . .'

Attempts to pressure the American Congress into an anti-Israel position have continually been made by the Washington-based radical right group, *Liberty Lobby*, which believes that although liberals are usually 'pro-Communist' they somehow 'may want us to fight the Russians over Israel'. (The Board of Policy of *Liberty Lobby*, which has long been 'anti-Zionist', contains the names of a number of well known antisemites. The man behind its operations is Willis Carto, who has written that 'the defeat of Hitler was the defeat of America'.)

One of the Congressmen who has collaborated with *Liberty Lobby* in the past, Rep. John Rarick, a Louisiana Democrat, inserted in the *Congressional Record* of 13 February 1969 a four-part pro-Arab article by the right-wing Dallas pamphleteer, Dan Smoot. The article, appearing in *Dan Smoot Report* issues during January and February, had set the tone of the anti-Israel obsessions of the radical right. Smoot measured 'Zionist' success in the Middle East in such terms as 'wealth, power and influence of world Jewry', 'Jewish pressures' and 'the Jewish vote' in the United States. (In 1948, he wrote, Truman had 'needed the votes and powerful influence of the Jews'.) Smoot's analysis put Israel in a strange, suicidal conspiracy: Israel and the USSR, he wrote, were 'pursuing a common objective . . . . to isolate all Arab countries from the United States and drive them into the Soviet orbit'.

Smoot's Middle East solution: the creation of 'a new political state', a non-'theocratic' (non-Jewish) state 'with dominion over the entire area'. In short, Israel should be abolished.

It is this prescription in which an increasing number of America's political extremists and their organized propaganda mechanisms—whatever the direction of their extremism—appear to have found agreement. And the genuinely liberal establishment is adjusting its mind to the phenomenon of the radical right, the black extremists and parts of the New Left coming together in a common position about the Middle East.

Zionism and the New Left

Rudolf Krämer-Badoni

The points raised in this reply to the Anti-Zionist New Left were provoked by attempts of the SDS *(Sozialistischer Deutscher Studentenbund) to deny the Israeli Ambassador Ben Natan a hearing when, as a guest speaker in public debates organized by the* Jewish Students Association, *he tried to put the Israeli point of view. Members of the* SDS *then abused him as a 'Fascist' and, shouting such slogans as 'Zionists, clear out of Palestine', broke up the meetings. A plan to employ similar tactics in front of the Israeli stand at the Frankfurt Book Fair was finally abandoned. Both incidents moved the writer, in one instance to challenge the New Left to a public debate, and in another to publish an open letter in* Die Welt *touching on the issues which this article endeavours to analyse in greater detail.*

The orthodox Left, if uncritically inclined, can invoke the 25-year-old Marx, who, in his pamphlet *The Jewish Question,* castigated Jews as the very incarnation of bourgeois alienation. 'Their secular existence', he asserts, 'is based on profit, their secular culture on usury, while their secular God is money'.

Marx here referred to the Jewish milieu with which he was familiar, the milieu of the West European Jewries, who had for centuries been compelled to gain their livelihood as petty traders or moneylenders, and who still remained shackled to this tradition when he wrote his indictment. He regarded their condition as indicative of general economic developments rather than of their own unique existence as a dispersed nation. Traits which Marx described as representative both of the bourgeoisie and the Jews, are not, in fact, specifically Jewish and merely mirror his general view of bourgeois behaviour.

Marx understood the emancipation of the Jews as society's liberation from the Jews. In this way any specifically Jewish characteristics could be disregarded purely as religious superstitions. This view allowed Marx and, later, his disciples to assume that, since all the illusionary superstructures including religion were bound to disappear with the end of class exploitation, Jews would then inevitably become wholly integrated into society and concomitantly that antisemitism too would then disappear.

What Marx either did not know or was not particularly anxious to find out was that antisemitism was as old as Judaism. Moreover, what he could not then know (as we do now) is that, contrary to all Marx's predictions, antisemitism managed to survive in socialist societies, admittedly under new labels and with suitably adapted justification. Before starting their revolution, the bulk of the population and particularly the workers could be persuaded to await the propitious moment in an inexorable historical process, the coming of which could be speeded up by patient preparations and agitation. But to urge Jews, continually threatened by pogroms, to postpone all hope of salvation until after the revolution seems as fatuous as advising a drowning man to wait for his rescue until he has learnt to swim. Moreover, the story of the Jewish *Bund* tells its own tale about the fate of a Jewish Socialist organization during the Russian revolution.

The Left, in conformity with Lenin's teaching, concedes to colonial nations a national revolution as the first step in their revolutionary development. In this context, Zionism must surely be understood as the still uncompleted national revolution of an oppressed nation dispersed all over the world. This fact ought to be perfectly obvious to anybody who uses historical dialectics in analysing the phenomenon of 'the dispersed nation'. The prevailing Left-wing notion that

Zionism is a manifestation of colonialism is quite untenable, since Zionism represents an attempt by the Jews to overcome their colonial status.

This fact is in no way contradicted by the arguments which Chaim Weizmann used to induce the British to establish a Jewish national home. His statement, which the Left never tires of quoting, says: 'We are sure that if Palestine were to come under British rule and Britain would encourage Jewish immigration we can within a decade or two settle more than a million Jews who would develop and civilize the country and provide an effective defence for the Suez Canal.'

This, the argument runs, unmistakably reveals imperialist aspirations. But only to the unsophisticated; the dialectically trained student of politics would immediately ask how else could an imperialist power be persuaded to make political concessions. The critical observer knows how to distinguish between immutable objectives and the tactics employed to achieve them; none knows it better than the militant Left.

The correctness of this interpretation can be easily substantiated. For in 1907 Weizmann told the Hague Zionist Congress: 'If today governments grant us a charter, it is nothing but a piece of paper; once we are settled in Palestine it is totally different; then our title deeds will have been written with blood and sweat, and been insolubly cemented together. Our influence and our political credibility will grow in exact proportion to our strength and position in Palestine.' This has quite another ring. With regard to the ultimate end, Weizmann was quite uncompromising, which did not prevent him, when occasion offered, from presenting ruling governments with the kind of argument they understood.

The resettling within a historical environment, never totally abandoned by Jewish tradition, at first met with no resistance. When the 'Palestine Office' in Jaffa started to develop a Jewish housing estate (which later became Tel Aviv) to purchase land for settlements and to create organized communal institutions, no opposition was voiced. Terrorist Arab resistance began only when the Jewish desire for statehood became evident and practicable.

The Jewish return to the homeland was a revolutionary departure not only in the national but also in the social sense;

the Kibbutzim have been developed from models conceived by the Jewish social revolutionaries who, forced to flee from Russia after the abortive 1905 revolution, went to Palestine. The first Kibbutz was established in 1909 at the southern tip of Lake Tiberias, and within a year the settlers developed the institutional framework which provided the model for all later settlements.

The partly anarcho-syndicalist institutions which co-exist in Israel today with co-operative and state-socialist enterprises already represent a social development, which, in Leninist terms, is both the result of and a justification for the national revolution. If, moreover, a symbiosis between Jews and Arabs could have been effected and had given birth to a two-nation state, the course of history might have been profoundly altered. Whether for better or worse cannot be told; quite apart from the Arab Left, which applies to Zionism the Leninist formula of 'Imperialism as the highest State of Capitalism', there also exists an Islamic antisemitism. Believing all Jews to be members of a sinister conspiracy against mankind, this old-fashioned, but nonetheless virulent, anti-semitism, bases its assertions on quotations from the Book of Esther and that hoary Tsarist fraud, the *Protocols of the Elders of Zion*.

* * *

The existence of the State of Israel is, however, an established fact. Or is it? Not, apparently, in discussions with our Left-wing anti-Zionists; they tend to regard the Jewish state as a negligible quantity, as something not to be taken too seriously or which can be wished away. The Arabs, it seems, do not regard any solution other than Israel's total annihilation, her compllete de-Zionization and re-Palestinization, as acceptable. If *El Fatah*—unlike Shukeiri, the leader of the *Palestine Liberation Army*, who frankly admitted his intention to drive the Jews into the sea ('There won't be any survivors')—disclaims such intentions, it nevertheless overlooks a number of factors. *El Fatah* asserts that it merely desires to extirpate Zionism, contending that in their independent democratic Palestinian state all citizens, irrespective of their religion, would enjoy equal rights. But do they realize that even on that point they again reduce Judaism to the status of a religion? Furthermore, they seem to assume that the military destruction of the Jewish state and its entire administrative structure could not be achieved without slaughtering Jews in such vast numbers that the surviving remnant could easily be absorbed. *El Fatah's* scant regard for civilian life is amply demonstrated by the eagerness with which it accepts responsibility for most of the attacks on the residential areas in Israel. It cheerfully admits to the killing of innocent civilians, for, as one *El Fatah* member recently remarked. 'How do you expect people to act in a revolution?'

For our Left-wingers, the word revolution provides the key to the whole movement; revolution is what binds them in brotherhood with *El Fatah* and similar groups who look upon themselves as revolutionary opponents both of the Arab sheikdoms and of Nasserism. Moreover, all Arabs know and freely admit that the struggle against Zionism covers such a multitude of mutually contradictory objectives that it has, in fact, become a self-contained ideological system. It serves the Arab socialists as a means of bringing down feudal governments in their own countries. Meanwhile, these very governments use it to generate popular support without having to embark on meaningful socialist policies.

In this way, anti-Zionism in the Middle East tends to bridge conflicting class interests and national aspirations. For our German radical Left, anti-Zionism also threatens to become a self-contained system in which their authoritarian and anti-totalitarian factions are reconciled, and which one day may even produce—if only for tactical purposes—a disreputable and opportunistic alliance with Right-wing antisemites. Left-wingers fraternising with the militant anti-Zionists of the Middle East, where this sinister alliance has been a working proposition for many a long year, must in any event be prepared to meet Nazi extermination experts who managed to find sanctuary and employment in the Arab world.

*   *   *

Ideology, it should moreover be remembered, provides great powers with convenient excuses for pursuing solid, old-fashioned strategic advantages. The USSR, having lost two socialist naval bases in the Mediterranean, completely reorientated its Israel policy and gained Arab bases instead. Nor does the Soviet Union support only the progressive Arab regimes; on the contrary, the revolutionaries, who seriously began to threaten Nasser's role, are being destroyed by Soviet weapons. It is necessary to point out these ambiguities because, once fully realized, they should encourage our Left-wing radicals to have second thoughts about their unquestioning identification with *El Fatah* and similar groups. The Left-wing, one would think, should perhaps consider the inevitable fate of the Jewish masses should Arab plans materialize (not to mention what is happening already where Arabs are in control). This is a subject our Left-wing anti-Zionists studiously avoid in their speeches and pamphlets. But there cannot be the slightest doubt as to what de-Zionization of an established and well-functioning state would actually entail.

Other stock arguments of the radical Left are equally irrelevant to the realities of the situation, such as the vociferous denunciation of Israel as the tool of imperialist American oil interests. Israel, in point of fact, is an obstacle to these interests, and it is quite significant that in 1947 the oil lobby opposed the partition of what was then Palestine. The assertion that Israel acts, so to speak, as the spearhead of Jewish international finance (*i.e.* of the American-Zionist lobby) reaffirms well-known, baseless and disreputable exaggerations about the acutal power and cohesion of dispersed Jewish communities throughout the world. It is indeed deeply disquieting that our radical Marxists, who never tire of emphasizing the significance of the historical context in which each event occurs, entirely disregard the historical dimension when it comes to discussing the Israel-Zionist syndrome. This, they think, can be handled on a purely abstract, doctrinal level. However, all their dialectics will not resolve the dilemma, that in identifying themselves with the so-called 'people's war' of *El Fatah,* they also accept the physical destruction of the Israeli people.

Were the radical Left less obsessed by instant revolution, they could, without betraying their Marxist dogma, exercise some restraint and explain their attitude to their Arab friends by referring them to one of Georg Lukaçs' theories:

> The confrontation between capitalism and socialism remains the basic ideological issue of our era as a whole. It is nevertheless often misleading to explain every event and phenomenon of the day or even whole periods within an era in terms of this fundamental issue.

Our Left-wingers could therefore tell their Arab friends that the whole situation has not yet been clarified, that the ideological demarcation lines still remain fluid, that the possibility of further socialist developments in Israel have been too glibly disregarded, that the historical conditions have not been properly assessed, and they could therefore plead for more time to analyse the situation. In a general state of flux, they could offer their services as intermediaries. It is along these lines, however they may be modified, that a more subtle and sophisticated dialogue with the Arabs should develop, instead of the prevailing automatic response and the unthinking, utterly predictable reactions. Before the bar of history, the socialists of the latter decades of the twentieth century will make but a poor showing if they can offer only a simplistic, stereotyped approach to so complex a situation. No socialist worth his salt—unless he has the misfortune to live under the dictatorship of an omniscient Central Committee—need nowadays accept the part of a blinkered unreasoning zealot.

Lukaçs' bold formula does in fact describe precisely the Middle Eastern reality in which the basic class struggle interpretation is indeed irrelevant to the particular issue. The Left, if it could accept Lukaçs' view, need not expend so much dialectical energy on identifying 'reactionary nationalism' as the main justification of Israel's existence. However, even assuming that 'reactionary' would correctly describe the new state—although, as we have shown, it does not—since when has insufficient progressiveness become an offence punishable by genocide? The disqualifying epithet 'reactionary' is of particular importance to the German radical Left, for it permits it to question the *de facto* reality of the state of Israel, while the same Left never tires of insisting on the formal recognition of the Oder-Neisse line as an historical result of a *de facto* reality. How, one wonders, does the Oder-Neisse *de facto* reality differ from that of Israel?

Branding Israel as a tool of imperialism is another of those convenient stereotypes which, for all their dialectical ingenuity, hardly bear close examination. The charge is simply not borne out by the facts. One need only recall the Haganah's grim struggle against the British, or the American refusal to become involved in the 1967 Middle East crisis to appreciate how the attempt to forge a link between Nazism as the highest stage of capitalism and Zionism as the allegedly highest stage of imperialism forces the doctrinaire Left to perform the most bizarre of all its dialectical gyrations. Had the Left accepted the Lukaçs view, it could have spared itself these unbecoming and fraudulent intellectual exercises. To reduce Zionism to the socialist-versus-capitalist concept is a grave mistake, an unforgivable oversimplification and a deviation from Marxist thought by the Left itself.

Israel provides the New Left—not to mention the even more sterile old Left—with the greatest challenge to their critical, independent and unstereotyped thinking. Of all their arguments, the equating of Zionism with imperialism is perhaps the most dubious, and their opponents will be quick to expose and exploit this particular fallacy.

Most people are not predetermined supporters of Zionist views; they would probably prefer to see Jews fully integrated in their host societies. However, whether we like it or not, Herzl seems to have been right in saying that integration had failed, even though he did not live to see the most horrifying aspect of this failure. But be that as it may, neither the fact of the establishment of Israel as a revolutionary national state, nor that of Arab hostility to its existence can be denied. Although the rights and wrongs in this case may arguably not be all on one side, it is nevertheless impossible to condemn several million people to death in order to fit this conflict into a preconceived historical mould. Even our Left-wing radicals —without actually abandoning their socialism—can oppose this ultimate horror; for mankind, notwithstanding its secret resentments and brutal propensities, has never ceased to yearn for justice and the fulfilment of the socialist dream. Its ideals inspire all criticism, all social progress, and account for the continuing appeal of the socialist cause; mankind as a whole already condemns the sophistry of the Left-wing anti-Zionist and will increasingly do so in future. Israel exists; she wants peace, even though the anti-Zionists do their utmost to obscure her intentions. This the Left-wing anti-Zionists should realize before committing intellectual suicide rather than abandon a dishonest position dictated by an outdated and increasingly oppressive orthodoxy.

*   *   *

Since this article was written, a bomb has been planted in the *Gemeindehaus,* the communal hall of West Berlin's Jewish congregation. It was timed—but failed—to go off during the service commemorating the 'crystal night' pogroms of thirty-one years ago. Police investigating the case seized stacks of incriminating leaflets at the *Republican Club,* a popular meeting-place for members of the *APO* (Extra-Parliamentary Opposition). These proclaimed, under the banner headline 'Shalom + Napalm', their authors' intention 'to blow up the *Gemeindehaus* and to deface Jewish memorial stones with the "Shalom + Napalm" slogan'. Such action, the leaflet declared, was called for in view of:

the Left's continued paralysis in facing up to the theoretical implications of the Middle-East conflict, a paralysis for which German guilt feelings are responsible. We admittedly gassed Jews and, therefore, feel obliged to protect them from further threats of genocide. This kind of neurotic, backward-looking anti-Fascism, obsessed as it is by past history, totally disregards the non-justifiability of the State of Israel. True anti-Fascism consists in an explicit and unequivocal identification with the fighting *Fedayin.* Our solidarity with them will no longer be satisfied by purely verbal protests of the Vietnam variety, but will pitilessly combat the combination of Fascism and Israeli Zionism ... We shall, at the same time, broaden our struggle to

include all Fascists in democratic guise ... we shall build
up a revolutionary liberation movement in all the capitals ∴.. for all political power grows out of a barrel of a
gun.

The leaflet, according to the *Frankfurter Allgemeine Zeitung*
(13.11.69), was signed 'The Black Rats'.

The Meaning of
'A Democratic Palestinian State'

Yehoshafat Harkabi

The crux of the Arab conflict with Israel has been the problem of safeguarding the country's Arab character. Arab demands during the Mandate for the prohibition of the sale of land to Jews and curtailment of Jewish immigration served the same purpose: that of keeping the ownership of land and Palestine's ethnic character inviolate. The difficulties confronting the Arabs in their attempt to halt Judaization were aggravated with the end of the Mandate and the foundation of the State of Israel; from then on it was a question of turning back the wheel of history and erasing the Jewish state.

The problem of eliminating the Jewish state is heightened by the presence of a considerable Jewish population. For a Jewish state depends upon the existence of Jewish citizens and therefore elimination of the state requires in principle a 'reduction' in their number. Hence the frequency and dominance of the motif of killing the Jews and throwing them into the sea in Arab pronouncements. Their position, in so far as it was *political* (i.e. calling for annihilation of a state), was bound to have *genocidal* implications, even had the Arabs not been bent upon revenge.

When, after the Six Day War, the Arabs realized that their wild statements had irreparably harmed their international reputation, they moderated their shrill demands for the annihilation of Israel. Arab propagandists denied that they had ever advocated the slaughter of the Jewish population, asserting that, at most, 'Jewish provocations' had aroused their anger and wild statements which, they alleged, were not meant to be taken literally. Ahmed Shukeiry insisted that he never advocated throwing the Jews into the sea, that the whole thing was merely a Zionist libel. What he meant, he explained, was that the Jews would return to their countries of origin by way of the sea: 'They came by the sea and will return by the sea' (Palestine Documents for 1967, p. 1084).

After the Six Day War, Arab spokesmen put forward the concept of 'a Democratic Palestinian State in which Arabs and Jews will live in peace'. This slogan was well received and regarded by the world at large as evidence of a new Arab moderation. Many people overlooked the ambiguity of the pronouncement and disregarded the fact that it did not contradict basic Arab contentions: for the wording might well imply the reduction of Jews to an insignificant minority, which would then be permitted to live in peace. Once this line was adopted, its meaning was keenly discussed among the Palestinian Arabs.

An indication of the slogan's true significance, as understood by the Palestinian organizations, was circulated by the *Popular Democratic Front for the Liberation of Palestine*, reporting on the deliberations of the Sixth Congress of the Palestinian National Council. This *fedayeen* organization, headed by Na'if Hawatmeh, broke away from George Habash's *Popular Front for the Liberation of Palestine* (February 1969). A delegation of the *Popular Democratic Front* proposed to the Congress that the slogan 'Democratic State' should be given 'a progressive content'. The Congress rejected their resolution, suggesting that the main purpose of the 'Democratic State' concept was to improve the Arab image. Moreover, the inclusion of this slogan in the national programme would, it was stressed, impair the Arab character of Palestine. Nevertheless, since it had been well received abroad, the Congress considered it worth retaining.

The relevant passage in the *Popular Democratic Front's* report entitled 'Internal Circular concerning Debates and Results of the Sixth National Council' reads:

The slogan 'The Democratic Palestinian State' has been raised for some time within the Palestinian context. *Fatah* was the first to adopt it. Since it was raised, this slogan has met with remarkable world response. Our delegation presented Congress with a resolution designed to elucidate its meaning from a progressive aspect, opposing in principle the slogan of throwing the Jews into the sea, which has in the past seriously harmed the Arab position.

When the subject was first debated, it was thought that there was general agreement on it. But as the debate developed, considerable opposition showed itself. In the course of the discussion the following views came to light:

1. One which maintains that the slogan of 'The Democratic Palestinian State' is a tactical one which we propagate because it has been well received internationally.

2. Another suggests that we consider this slogan to be strategic rather than tactical, but that it should be retained even though it is not a basic principle. This position, but for a mere play on words, corresponds to the previous one.

3. The third view was more straightforward in rejecting the slogan and its progressive content as proposed by our delegation. The position of this faction was based on the assertion that the slogan contradicts the Arab character of Palestine and the principle of self-determination enshrined in the National Covenant of the [Palestine] Liberation Organization, and that it advocates a peaceful settlement with the Jews of Palestine.

This means that the Arab character which the country is to have after its 'liberation' would be undermined, if, taking the concept literally, a large group of Jews were permitted to remain. The Palestinian National Covenant stipulated that only the Palestinian Arabs had the right to self-determination, whereas the slogan of a 'Democratic State' makes the Jews partners. Moreover, such a slogan may imply reconciliation rather than a war *à outrance*.

Echoes of the debate in the Arab press also reveal something of the mood of the Congress. *Al-Hurriyya* (29.9.69), the *Popular Democratic Front* weekly, stated:

Even general slogans like 'Democratic State', which had

won support from the Palestinian Right, were rejected by the Sixth National Council. There appeared among the rightist ranks on the Council manifest racist tendencies in the solutions they proposed which were reminiscent of the well-known Shukeirian ones.

(The *Popular Democratic Front* calls itself 'The Left', and most other groups, especially *Fatah*, 'The Right'.) *Al-Muharrir* (9.9.69) reports:

After a long debate on this point ['Democratic State'] the need was expressed to reconcile the propaganda aspects of the issue with the necessary strategic aims. It was agreed that statements concerning the 'Democratic State' should be made only in the context of the general liberation of Palestine and annihilation of the Israeli entity, so that there can be no misunderstanding or comparisons between the waves of European Jewish immigrants into Palestine and the original sons of the country.

This means that the notion of a 'Democratic State' acknowledges the right of the Jewish settlers as well as those of the Palestinian Arabs, whereas in the official view only Palestinians have any right to the country.

The *Popular Democratic Front*, the most leftist of the *Fedayeen* organizations, claims to represent the Palestinian workers and peasants and cultivates a Marxist-Leninist class approach. It appears to be a growing force; its radicalism is a conspicuous trend in most Arab countries. The Egyptian weekly *Ruz al-Yusuf*, declared: 'One of the deepest and most palpable phenomena in the wake of defeat is the trend toward the Left in the Arab homeland' (8.12.69). The social content of the *Popular Democratic Front's* message is more likely to attract Palestinian youth than is *Fatah*, which postponed the proclamation of its social policy until after 'the end of the stage of liberation'. The *Popular Democratic Front* is very active in the West and maintains links with the New Left and is the most acceptable to the New Left among Palestinian organizations, including *Fatah*. Its conscientiously prepared papers for the Sixth Congress of the Palestinian National Council were collected in a 167-page book entitled *The*

Present Situation of the Palestinian Resistance Movement: A Critical Study (Beirut 1969). The proposed resolution concerning the Democratic State reads (p. 165):

The Palestinian National Council, in accordance with the Palestinian people's belief in democratic solutions for the Palestine question, resolves as follows:

1. To reject the chauvinist and reactionary Zionist-colonialist solutions advocating recognition of the State of Israel as one of the facts of the Middle East region, for these solutions contradict the right of the Palestinian people to self-determination in its country, and sanction the expansionist Zionist entity which is linked to colonialism, and hostile to the Palestinian and Arab national liberation movement and to all forces of liberation and socialism in the world.

2. To reject the Palestinian and Arab chauvinistic solutions advanced before and after June 1967, which advocate the slaughter of the Jews and throwing them into the sea, and also to reject reactionary solutions which support the consolidation of the State of Israel within secure and recognized boundaries as expressed in the ill-begotten resolution of the Security Council. These solutions are at the expense of the right of the Palestinian people to self-determination in their country, and introduce into the Middle East a racist-capitalist-expansionist state linked dialectically to international capitalism, which is hostile to the Palestinian-Arab and to world liberation movements as well as to all forces of socialism and progress in the world.

3. The struggle for a democratic popular solution to the Palestine and Israel question is based on the elimination of the Zionist entity in all institutions of the state (army, administration and police) and all chauvinist and Zionist political and co-operative bodies. It is based on the establishment of a Democratic Popular Palestinian State in which Arabs and Jews will live without discrimination, a state opposed to all forms of class and national suppression, conferring the right to both Arabs and Jews to develop their own national [*wataniyya*] culture.

4. By virtue of links which history and destiny have forged between Palestine and the Arab nation, the Democratic Popular State of Palestine will be an organic part of an Arab federal state of democratic content, hostile to colonialism, imperialism, Zionism and to Arab and Palestinian reaction.

In this way the 'democratic solution' is presented as a compromise between two chauvinistic alternatives—a Jewish state, and driving the Jews into the sea—as if these were comparable propositions. By this supposedly fair solution, the Arabs renounce the extermination of Jews, and the Jews renounce their state. Although the Palestinian state will become a popular democracy, its Arab character will be preserved by being part of a larger 'democratic' Arab federation. The final paragraph is meant to repudiate objections that a democratic Palestine would remain a stranger among the Arab nations and an obstruction to Arab unity.

The *Democratic Front's* pronouncement may be mistakenly interpreted as favouring a binational state: 'The Palestinian state will eliminate racial discrimination and national persecution and will be based on a democratic solution to the conflict brought about by the coexistence *(ta'ayush)* of the two people, Arabs and Jews' *(The Present Situation . . ., p. 136)*. The recognition of 'a Jewish people' is a significant innovation. Hitherto Arabs have mostly held that Jews constitute only a religion and do not therefore deserve a national state. However, this admission of a Jewish nationhood is qualified, for Jews as a people are not entitled to a state of their own but must settle for participation in a state of Palestinian nationality. Their nationhood, therefore, has only cultural and not national-political dimensions. Thus, Hawatmeh tells Luth al-Khuli, editor of *al-Tali'a:* 'We urged initiation of a dialogue with the Israeli socialist organization Matzpen, which advocates an Arab-Jewish binational state. But we have not been able to convince Matzpen to adopt a thoroughly progressive, democratic position on the Palestine question which would mean liquidation *(tasfiaya)* of the Zionist entity and establishment of a democratic Palestinian state opposed to all kinds of class and national suppression' *(al-Tali'a,*

November, 1969, p. 106). This means that the proposal for a binational state, as advocated by Matzpen, is not sufficiently progressive for Hawatmeh. In his view, Jewish nationhood implies only cultural autonomy for a religious community. But this is no innovation; Mr Shukeiry was prepared to grant the same.

One of the paradoxes of the *Democratic Front* is that, while the *Popular Front for the Liberation of Palestine,* from which—impelled by left-wing radicalism—it broke away, did not belong to the Palestine Liberation Organization, the *Democratic Front* does and is co-operating with Organizations much further to the right than the *Popular Front.* To be accepted in the Command of Armed Struggle, an arm of the *Palestine Liberation Organization,* the *Democratic Front* was required to declare itself 'loyal to everything written in the National Covenant as the minimal programme for the relations in the Command of Armed Struggle' (Abu Iyad in a conversation with al-Khuli, *al-Tali'a,* June, 1969). It is astonishing that the *Front's* 'democratic' proposals can be reconciled with the Palestine National Covenant (1968) and particularly with the status of Jews allowed to remain in the liberated state, as set out in Article 6.

Thus, despite all pretensions, the difference between the *Popular Democratic Front* and the other Palestinian organizations may relate merely to the size of the tolerated Jewish minority. A current notion among many Arab spokesman suggests that a considerable number of Israelis are in the country against their will and would leave if Zionism and the 'national coercion' it imposes were abolished. European Jews would not wish to live in a Palestinian Arab state, preferring to emigrate, while Jews from Eastern countries would 'rejoice' at the opportunity afforded them to return to their countries of origin. These are themes frequently touched on by the mass media. Contact with the Jewish community in Israel across the open bridges has not yet shaken these ideas. It seems that they play so vital a role in Arab thinking that it is difficult to change them. If a voluntary Jewish exodus after victory is a foregone conclusion, why spell out solutions involving violence? What do the Arabs lose if they declare that Palestinian citizenship will be given to all Israelis?

The *Popular Democratic Front*, by dissociating the annihilation of the State of Israel from the necessity of having 'to reduce' the number of her Jewish inhabitants, tries to humanize the Arab position. It should be noted, however, that its approach is basically neither moderate nor conciliatory. In the Arab-Israel conflict, the relevant political question is that of the attitude to Israel as a state and to her sovereignty. The *Popular Democratic Front* has unequivocally rejected Israel's right to statehood, as if it had to atone for its 'softness' towards individual Jews by a corresponding harshness against their state. In its view, Israel is not an independent country with individual, though odious, characteristics; she is rather part of everything sinister and inhuman in international life—imperialism, colonialism and capitalism—phenomena which must be fought to the bitter end. From the First World War onwards, Arabs insisted that Israel was set up and aided by colonialist powers and that only American imperialism assured her continuing survival. But leftists now regard the link between Israel and colonialism or imperialism as organic, and their opposition to her existence is thus intensified.

The *Popular Democratic Front* utterly rejects the Security Council resolution and indeed any possibility of a peaceful solution. Its stand on this issue is far more radical than that of most Arab states. Even the Khartoum Summit Conference resolutions are treason in its eyes: 'This conference offered the Arab peoples hollow promises, "no peace, no recognition, no negotiation with Israel", as though the question on the agenda were that of negotiation and peace and not of overcoming the aggression and annihilating its bases' *(The Present Situation . . ., p. 85)*. Acceptance of the Security Council resolution is treason even more infamous; for it implies recognition of Israel, even though Arab states excuse it as a tactical manoeuvre: 'The contention that acceptance of the Security Council resolution is a tactical manoeuvre aiming at the "elimination of the traces of aggression", in order to continue action for the liberation of Palestine, is a misleading, demagogic and fraudulent claim which arouses only loathing and nausea in the souls of Arab revolutionaries' *(ibid., p. 88)*. The solution offered by the *Democratic Front* to the National Council therefore emphasizes:

The national liberation movement will achieve a Democratic Popular Palestinian State only by armed struggle
and a people's war of liberation against Zionism, imperialism and reaction, by the destruction of the Israeli State
and liberation of the Jews from the Zionist movement
(*ibid.*, p. 167).

The radicalism against the State of Israel is matched by the
radical form given to their warfare. It is not accidental that
leftist *fedayeen* organizations like the *Popular Front* and the
Democratic Front see the struggle as world wide, and advocate
such tactics as attacking civilian planes, while an organization like *Fatah* dissociates itself, at least on paper, from these
activities.

The pronouncements of *Fatah* itself contain, though not
always explicitly, hints of genocide. *Fatah's* monthly, *The
Palestinian Revolution* (June 1968, p. 38), explains why a
conventional war does not suit the Palestinian goal: 'For the
aim of this war is not to impose our will on the enemy but to
destroy him in order to take his place (*ifnā'uhu lil-
hulūli mahallihi*). . . . In a conventional war there is no need to
continue the war if the enemy submits to our will . . . while in
a *people's war* there is no deterrent inhibition, for its aim is not
to defeat the enemy but to extirpate [*ifnā'*] him. A conventional war has limited aims which have to be observed, for
the enemy must be allowed to exist so that we can impose our
will on him, while in a *people's war* destruction [*ifnā'*] of the
enemy is the first and last duty.' The expression *ifnā'* used here
is extreme, its literal meaning being 'reduction to absolute
nothingness'. This does not mean the simple destruction of
army units but the total annihilation of the enemy as a whole.

Other *Fatah* spokesmen use more moderate language,
particularly in conjunction with the 'Democratic State'
concept. *Jeune Afrique* (3 March, 1970) reports a change in
Fatah attitudes reflected by articles in the *Fatah* press:

The [Palestinian] revolution rejects the proposition that
only Jews living in Israel before 1948 or before 1917 and
their descendants should be accepted. After all, Dayan and
Allon, both born in Palestine before 1948, are racist

Zionists who cannot aspire to Palestinian citizenship, whereas new immigrants may be anti-Zionist and contribute to the establishment of a new Palestine. One of the *Fatah* leaders, Abu Iyad, has announced in a press conference that not only progressive, anti-Zionist Jews but all Zionists ready to abandon their racist ideology will be received with open arms as Palestinian citizens. The Palestinian revolution is convinced that all Israeli Jews will change their attitude and subscribe to the new Palestine, especially after the destruction of the political, economic and military structures of the present oligarchy.

There is considerable confusion on this issue within *Fatah:* in fact, when the Kuwait newspaper *al-Siyāsa* reproduced this statement from *Jeune Afrique,* the spokesmen of *Fatah's* central propaganda office in Damascus (Middle East News Agency, 15 March, 1970) denied that the articles which *Jeune Afrique* had allegedly culled from *The Palestinian Revolution* were ever published there. However, there is reason to believe that such pronouncements were made, and that *Jeune Afrique* regarded them as authoritative, even though not officially sanctioned by the central organ of *Fatah.* For example, Abu Iyad, whose position in *Fatah* is second only to that of Arafat, made similar statements in an interview in *al-Tali'a* (June 1969). *Jeune Afrique* wished to attribute a moderate position to *Fatah* while policy decisions were still in a state of flux. However, it is likely that *Fatah* spokesmen will increasingly echo *Popular Democratic Front* formulations if only for tactical purposes. Changing a propaganda formula will probably not strike them as touching on questions of principle. *Fatah* in any case anticipates that terrorism will reduce the number of Jews. A public statement celebrating the fifth anniversary of the inauguration of *Fatah* activity (1 January 1970), predicted the spread of guerrilla actions to the heart of Israel's territory, until the Israeli

> will find himself isolated and defenceless against the Arab soldier in his house, on his land, on the road, in the cafe, in the cinema, in army camps and everywhere, far from the area controlled by the Israeli armed forces which assure him protection and safety. These acts will force him to

consider and compare the life of stability and repose he enjoyed in his former country and the life of confusion and anxiety he finds in the land of Palestine. This must necessarily impel him towards reverse immigration *(The Palestinian Revolution,* No. 22, January 1970, p. 8).

The Palestine's National Covenant's extreme line, restricting Jews to five per cent of the population (those who came before 1917 and their offspring), has become common knowledge and it is not unlikely that some Palestinians will now press for a change in the Covenant in order to give it a more moderate appearance.

The position combining annihilation of the state and the murder of its inhabitants (politicide and genocide) was in itself consistent. It provided a basis for the subsequent establishment of an Arab state. But the proposition advocating destruction of the Jewish state and turning it into an Arab one without doing away with its Jewish inhabitants is self-contradictory. The Arabs avoid this contradiction by clinging to the illusion that the Jews, anxious to emigrate, will reduce their own numbers. They also exaggerate the number of Palestinans. Even so, one wonders how they are to return to their former dwellings, unless the Jews are eliminated.

The Palestinians labour under another illusion concerning the effectiveness of 'the resistance', as they euphemistically call their guerilla warfare. Guerrilla warfare, on which the *Popular Democratic Front* and other Palestinian organizations rely, has a chance of success if it develops into a citizen's war. But *fedayeen* actions are essentially incursions from the outside and cannot be turned into war of Israeli citizens against their own government. Israel's control of areas with Arab populations does not fundamentally change the picture. The model of internal war is more appropriate to what may happen in Arab countries, wreaking havoc within them.

The declaratory recognition of partial rights for Israelis, expressed in the slogan of a 'Democratic State', although adding to the persuasiveness of propaganda and diplomacy, nevertheless represents a *retreat* from previous Arab positions. The contradictions inherent in the concept will, no doubt, provoke further seminars, heartsearchings, debates and inner struggles, and will provide another issue on which Arabs will divide. The Jewish community will continue to grow and hopes of absorbing it as a minority will become correspondingly more remote. Since the internal contradictions of their politicidal position will become increasingly obvious, it would appear that from an Arab point of view the whole 'Democratic State' concept tends to create more problems than it solves.

New Left Reappraisals

Ernest Hearst

The unscrupulous way in which the New Left has debased the coinage of language and distorts facts constitutes a bewildering and indeed astonishing phenomenon if only because unlike the Radical Right, it addresses itself predominantly to intellectuals. That, in a free society, a movement with intellectual pretentions can, without fear of exposure or ridicule, misinform its actual and potential supporters argues that the opium of unreasoning faith, irrespective of how it accords with known and ascertainable facts, is just as much in demand among the new Marxists as it was among the 'people' whose addiction they so eagerly castigated.

The London *Socialist Leader* (10 October 1970) in an article entitled 'Zionism—Religious Fascism' arrived at a strange redefinition of Zionism:

> The real crux of the present problem in the Middle East is actually to be found not so much in the creation of the State of Israel but in its peculiarly Zionist character which has been with it since its inception. For it is not only Christian 'fundamentalists' who believe in the literal fulfilment of biblical prophecy, at least as regards the Hebrew Bible (the Christian Old Testament). It was primarily in pursuance of, and for the eventual fulfilment of, such prophecies that Zionism was founded at the turn

of the century with the express purpose of restoring the
'Chosen Race' to Israel, to the 'Holy Land', Palestine, that
Jehovah the God of the Jews had given to their remote
ancestors but from which they had been expelled by
Roman pagan invaders in AD 70 exactly 19 centuries
ago. . . . Actually, the only claim that the Jews had to
return to Palestine was that their ancient tribal God
Jehovah gave it to them some 3,000 years ago; where, at
least if we are to believe the Bible, their ancestors treated
the original Canaanites very much as Hitler was later to
treat their own descendants. . . . The real paradox inherent
hitherto in the current State of Israel is that it was actually
founded for a different purpose from that which its present leaders advocate. Currently we have the still further
paradox of a Zionist racial state still claiming universal sympathy and support as a 'National Home' for the
Jews. . . .

German New Left anarchists—the true contemporary
representatives of a national tradition of ideologically justified inhumanity—went a step further. Kunzelmann, a
31-year-old *Kommunard* whose progress from Berlin student
politics to El Fatah terrorism was traced by *Encounter*
(November 1970) won national fame by telling his *SDS
(Sozialistischer Deutscher Studentenbund)* colleagues in a political
discussion: 'Enough of this *Scheiss-Geblabber!* What's really
important are my orgasm difficulties. . . . ' But by 1969, as
Encounter reported:

> On 10 November 1969, the anniversary of the *Kristallnacht*
> when the Nazis burned Jewish synagogues in Berlin (1938),
> a bomb was placed in the rebuilt Jewish Community
> House in the Fasanenstrasse. Kunzelmann's 'Sexual Poli-
> tics' were now taking on a grimmer note. Many Jewish
> memorials were paint-smeared with the words 'El Fatah'
> and 'Schalom and Napalm'. As his anarchist friends
> explained: 'These actions can no longer be defamed as
> some right-wing radical outburst—they are a decisive link
> in our international socialist solidarity. . . .' Their difficul-
> ties in making popular progress along these lines they
> attributed to something they called bourgeois Germany's

Judenkomplex. It was not so easy to get round the pro-Semitism which had grown up in post-war Germany after the Holocaust. Kunzelmann wrote from Amman: 'The struggle here makes everything simple. And we are lost if we don't take up this battle. . . . The left has not yet begun to understand this. Why? *Der Judenknax!'* (a 'thing' about the Jews). . . .

*   *   *

Nasser's obituary, published (October 1970) in the *Blätter für Deutsche und Internationale Politik,* a West German current affairs journal with academic pretensions, provides a startling example of the fact-management practised by the New Left. The 'reprogramming' *(umfunktionieren)* of widely-known facts must at first sight have seemed a forbidding task. It turned out to be a comparatively easy exercise in straightforward omission, although it is difficult to see how the naivety of the resulting stereotype can appeal to an informed and critical mind. But the need to make the facts fit a preconceived pattern of thought apparently proved too compelling to be resisted. The obituary runs:

> . . . Under Nasser's leadership land reform was first success-fully introduced. The new government also recognised that only the country's rapid industrialization could provide a stable basis for national independence and sovereignty. In order to produce the energy and food Egypt needed, the construction of the gigantic Aswan dam was contemplated. The US and other capitalist countries, the Federal German Republic prominent amongst them, were at first interested in financing the project, if only because they thus hoped to expand their economic and political influence in the UAR. But Nasser was not prepared to alter his policies or to surrender Egypt's hard-won national independence. He stood up to the blackmail attempts of the then US Secretary of State, Foster Dulles, who thereupon abruptly terminated the negotiations and stopped all further credits. Nasser then turned to the USSR.
>
> Hand in hand with the conviction that Western capitalists

neither were nor would be interested in the independent, healthy development of his country, Nasser realized the need to deny foreign capital the power to influence developments in the UAR. This was why the Suez Canal Company was nationalized in 1956. To prevent any fall in the company's profits British and French troops intervened, while, at the same time, Israel used the opportunity to bring her plans for expansion a step nearer to realization by occupying the Sinai peninsula right up to the Canal. World-wide protests compelled the occupying forces to withdraw. The Canal remained under Egyptian management and other foreign investments were nationalized. Nevertheless, because Egypt's bourgeoisie failed to support a balanced investment programme, the economy did not show the expected upturn. . . .

In February 1960, Nasser proclaimed the 'Second Revolution'. The key sectors of the economy, the Bank of Egypt together with other banks and insurance companies, followed by a large number of industrial enterprises, were nationalized. . . . In the course of policies designed to strengthen national independence, Nasser and his friends came to formulate new theories advocating a socialist approach to social and economic problems. This led to the founding of the Arab Socialist Union, a mass party, half of whose members must, according to its statutes, be of working-class or peasant origin. These developments show that the now emerging working class already represents a force to be reckoned with and that even amongst the peasantry there is an awakening desire to have a hand in the shaping of their future.

When, in June 1967, Israeli armies, in an attempt to turn back the clock in Syria and Egypt, and to overthrow Nasser, advanced even further into Arab territory than they had in 1948 and 1956, similarly motivated forces reared their head in the UAR. High-ranking officers and civil servants prepared a rebellion against the president and so actively supported the Israeli hawks and their US allies. The Commander-in-Chief, Marshal Amer, prevented a tactically sensible deployment of Egyptian anti-aircraft defences and so contributed no little to the military disaster of the Egyptian forces. At the same time he prepared a list of an alternative Cabinet. Faced with the planned *Putsch* of his immediate deputy, and the seemingly irresistible advance of the Israeli army, Nasser offered to resign on 9 June 1967. His internal and external enemies thought they had achieved their object. However, hundreds of thousands of Egyptians took to the streets of Cairo demonstrating in favour of their President, the continuation of his policies and his democratic reforms. Nasser withdrew his offer of resignation, and Amer was stripped of all his appointments. Two months later, after a further plot, legal proceedings were taken against the ring-leaders of the reactionary conspiracy. . . .

These developments [towards national independence and democratic progress—Ed.] were constantly over-shadowed by Israeli military activities, which an unrestricted flow of American armaments did nothing to discourage. After the 1967 war, hardly a day passed without Israeli troops probing beyond the cease-fire lines and penetrating deeper into Arab territory. While Syria, Jordan and the Lebanon had to suffer the intermittent attention of Israeli bombers, Egypt had to endure the brunt of their attack. The neo-colonialists in the United States and their ally Israel, aware of the threat posed by the democratic achievements of the broad masses in Egypt, were prepared to use every means in their power to wreck them. However, neither the bombing of Egyptian factories and schools, nor the systematic destruction of whole towns in the Suez area brought them any nearer to achieving their object. On the contrary, the people redoubled their efforts to defend their country against such attacks and to consolidate its social and cultural reconstruction. Recognizing the failure of these attempts at military blackmail, some American politicians still hoped to achieve partial success and drive a wedge between Nasser and the Arab people by producing a cease-fire plan. While they carried their point, they were not, of course, prepared to exert any pressure on the Israeli government to desist from bullying the Arab nations into making totally unacceptable concessions. These then were the considerations which gave rise to the so-called Rogers peace initiative of June 1970. . . .

Anti-Israel Extremism
in West Germany

Gerd Langguth

Radical left-wing activities among foreigners in the Federal Republic are chiefly based on the universities. At least fifteen organizations are known to exist; they include Arab, Greek, Ethiopian, Persian, Turkish, Vietnamese and Black American students. Their total membership is believed to exceed 3,000, spread among some 95 local associations, the most important being:

Generalunion Palästinensischer Studenten (GUPS)
Arabische Studentenvereinigung (ASV)
Conföderation iranischer Studenten-Nationalunion (CISNU)
Föderation iranischer Studenten in der Bundesrepublik and Westberlin (FIS)
Vereinigung irakischer Studenten (VIS)
Türkische Studentenföderation in Deutschland (ATöF)

Although *GUPS* itself is certainly not affiliated to *Al Fatah,* many of its members, despite their student status, belong to the latter. However, factional strife between the various Arab and Palestinian student groups in the Federal Republic has tended to diminish *Al Fatah* influence, while that of the more radical Maoist *Popular Front for the Liberation of Palestine (PFLP)* has gained ground. *GUPS* co-operates closely with the *General-union Palästinensischer Arbeiter (GUPA)* which like

GUPS has its headquarters in Cairo. *GUPA* was founded in 1969 and has, it asserts, since established 24 local branches in the Federal Republic.

Many students openly acknowledge their *Al Fatah* membership, and showed their allegiance by demonstrating in September 1970 in front of the Jordanian embassy. This demonstration, it will be remembered, was to have a more militant sequel. The headquarters of Middle East *Al Fatah* had ordered the occupation of the embassy, a plan which was foiled by the vigilance of the police, whose massive presence prevented any attempt to take over the building. Even though in this particular instance *Al Fatah* failed to attain its objective, it ought to be borne in mind that its members are bound by solemn oath to obey its orders implicitly.

Members of *GUPS* are lionized and militantly supported by a number of German radical left-wing student organizations, whose assistance they accept without, however, identifying themselves with any particular political creeds. They themselves seem to stand to the left of the German Communist Party *(DKP),* and its *Marxistischer Studentenbund Spartakus (MSB Spartakus).* GUPS propagates its views in a periodical, *The Palestine Revolution,* published in the Frankfurt *Resistentia-Schriften* series. Quoting Marx, Lenin and Mao Tse-Tung, the paper advocates 'revolution until victory is achieved' and armed struggle against 'Zionism'. It uses the current Marxist jargon in which 'the masses' it claims to represent play a dominant role.

The form the anti-colonialist war of liberation will take is an armed uprising of the organized masses. Many merely reformist movements, while anxious to gain the support of the masses, wish to carry on the struggle against the occupying power by way of strikes, demonstrations and passive resistance only. But this would merely inhibit the revolutionary élan of the masses and lead to apathy and resignation. . . .

Given the objective stage of development in the various countries, it can be asserted that an armed uprising is the only successful method of fighting the anti-colonialist battle. In short, a People's War of Liberation is the instrument of the destruction of Imperialism. *(Resistentia Schriften* Nr. 9 1969.)

Apart from the *GUPS*, the *Conföderation der Iranischen Studenten (CISNU)* founded in 1961, is perhaps the most dedicated and vociferous supporter of the Palestinian cause among the Federal Republic's foreign student organizations. Its membership consists of a variety of pro-Russian and pro-Chinese factions, precariously held together by a common identification with Arab aspirations. 'In the name of more than 70,000 Iranian students', a Munich pamphlet published in 1970 avowed solidarity 'with the just struggle of the Palestinian and of all Arab peoples against imperialism, Zionism and Arab traitors'. It also condemned 'the infamous conspiracy of American imperialism and Soviet counter-revolutionaries'. The appeal ended 'Long live the world revolution. People of the world unite, destroy American imperialism and its running dogs'. From an early stage, the radical German Left has maintained contact and cultivated relations with foreign student bodies, even when these did not fully accept their views and showed reluctance to become involved in German domestic politics. However, the German Left, ranging from the comparatively moderate *Sozialdemokratischer Hochschulbund (SHB)* to Maoist splinter groups do give their unqualified support in a number of leaflet campaigns to 'the armed liberation struggle of the Palestinian people'. *MSB-Spartakus, SHB, Liberaler Studentbund Deutschlands (LSD)*, together with some Arab organizations were signatories to a leaflet distributed in Cologne in 1970, which asserted:

> Our struggle for liberation is part and parcel of the independence movement of the third world and is of the same order as that in Indonesia, Latin America and Africa. We shall succeed in attaining our objective, the liberation from racialism, exploitation and discrimination. Long live the armed struggle against imperialism, colonialism, racialism . . .

Similar appeals were published under the aegis of such diverse groups as the representative German Students' Union *(ASTA)* (Aachen branch) and esoteric organizations like

Sozialistische Betriebsgruppe ML Aachen, Projektgruppe Internationalismus Bochum, Revolutionäre Kommunistische Jugend Köln, Haitianische Marxistisch-Leninistische Organisation Deutschland, etc.

Arab militants and German left-wing extremists co-operate in so-called 'Palestine Committees' set up to propagate the 'anti-Zionist struggle', particularly among students. The committee's Munich branch strongly sympathizes with the *DKP* and its student branch, the *MSB-Spartakus,* to whose inaugural congress in Bonn (May 1971) the Committee cabled the following message:

> At a time when imperialist intrigues in the Middle East gain ground—particularly the attempts to liquidate the Palestinian Resistance—the material and moral support extended by democratic and socialist students in the Federal Republic to the embattled Palestine people and other nations struggling against imperialism, Zionism and Arab reactionaries, is of supreme importance. Unification of the struggling masses in the deliberately neglected regions with the working clases in the imperialist countries—that is the basis of their ultimate and complete victory over the forces of imperialism . . .

In a similar vein, the *Munich Palestine Committee* attacked Axel Springer, the conservative, unashamedly nationalist though unwaveringly pro-Jewish West German press lord and *bête noir* of the entire left. One broad-sheet denounced 'this honorary citizen of a united Jerusalem' as an 'intimate crony of the Israeli arms dealer and part-time ambassador, Asher Ben Nathan'. In the same breath, Franz Joseph Strauss, the leader of the Bavarian branch of the *CDU,* the main opposition party, was reviled for his friendship with and offers of hospitality to 'the imperialist-Zionist wire-pullers'. His home was said to be the venue for shady arms deals 'between the most reactionary and aggressive of the West German monopolists and their Zionist accomplices'.

Palestine Committees have sprung up in many other university towns. The Bonn committee, which publishes *Al Thaura* (The Revolution), claims 'to have been founded by democratic and socialist students, from Germany and abroad, anxious to support the struggle of the Palestinian people for its national liberation (a) by such material assistance as the collection of medical supplies, financial donations, etc., and (b) by propagating and popularizing the objectives of the Palestinian liberation movement'. The Münster committee, probably leftward of the Communist party, attacks the USSR 'for posing as ·the friend of the oppressed nations while indulging in policies which inhibit the revolutionary élan of the liberation movements and so encouraging the forces of imperialism. Objectively, the USSR therefore oppresses the peoples of the third world just as much as US imperialism.'

Among the other organizations identifying themselves with the 'anti-Zionist struggle', *Trikaut,* specifically devoted to work among foreign students in the Federal Republic, and the *Verband Deutscher Studenten (VDS)* are perhaps the most active. At its general meeting (March 1971) the latter described the 'Zionist State of Israel' as 'a faithful lackey of US imperialism'. 'Supporting the efforts of the Palestine people to emancipate themselves from imperialism and Zionism under the leadership of the *PLO',* it has donated 7,000 DM towards this end. A plethora of other groups such as *Projektgruppe Internationalismus* in Bochum, Freiberg and Erlangen, *Internationalismusgruppe* in München Braunschweig, Giessen and Marburg, and *Proletarische Front Hamburg,* pursue similar aims.

Infatuation with violence and the language of hatred it inevitably engenders, tend to blur the dividing line between the New Left's anti-Zionism and plain antisemitism. A case in point is that of *internationale solidarität.* This group spontaneously sprang up to prevent the Vice-Chancellor of the Hebrew University from addressing a meeting at the University of Kiel. A leaflet distributed by *internationale solidaritat* culminated in the slogan, *Schlagt die Zionisten tot, macht den Nahen Osten rot* (Beat Zionists dead, make the Near East red). And, again, the broadsheet *agit 883* published by a group sympathizing with the anarchist Baader-Meinhof gang denounced the proprietor of a cafe patronized by the ·Left, who had nevertheless refused to display this particular news-sheet. 'Why are we made to pay swinishly extortionate entrance fees to get into the 'Park' to meet our friends? Why do we fork out 200,000 DM monthly for the benefit of this owner, this

Zionist pig? Do you know what the swine does with the money? He pays thousands of marks to Israel so that the war against the Palestinians and their colonization can continue.'

Predictably, the murder of the Israeli athletes during the Munich Olympics was widely condoned by the radical Left. Such criticism as it offered merely queried the effectiveness of an operation not welcomed or supported by the 'masses'. While terrorism as such was accepted, it was felt that this particular action was impolitic because it provided 'the so-called forces of law and order' with a convenient pretext for clamping down on political enemies. A leaflet circulated by the *Kommunistische Partei Deutschlands, Marxisten-Leninisten and Die Rote Garde,* spelt out the Left's attitude to terrorism. Describing the struggle of the Arab people as 'exemplary', it continued:

> Nor can we for our part dissociate ourselves from the struggle or from the use of revolutionary violence. Only by a people's war can we rid ourselves of our rulers and establish a genuine peace for the peoples of the world . . . We are no doves of peace building our nest among the smoking chimneys of armament factories. We are fighters for peace! And peace achieved neither by the ballot nor by the mollifying torchlight procession organized by the bosses of the *DGB* [German equivalent of the TUC—ed.]. Peace can only be attained by our relentless struggle against all imperialist warmongers. They must be forced to surrender their power. Reactionary power must be countered by revolutionary power. Only the dictatorship of the proletariat can bring peace!

In this spirit, the *Deutsch-Palästinensische Gesellschaft* regarded the murder of the Israeli athletes as a 'brave and resolute action of the Palestine revolutionaries'. Leaflets displayed on notice-boards at the University of Frankfurt praised the deed 'as a military operation in the Palestinian people's war of liberation demanded by tactical as well as political considerations'. The action, the leaflet asserted, must be recognized as 'a victory, though a costly one'. It went on to ridicule the 'official crocodile tears and condolence-cant', disseminated (among others) by the 'contemptible cohorts of journalists' who by their mendacity had also encouraged 'the guilty conscience demanding restitution for Jews'.

Similarly a representative of a social-democratic students' union was indignantly disowned by most other student organizations when he requested the Vice-Chancellor of Bonn University in an open letter to reconsider the credentials of two *Al Fatah* activists. Among those who publicly rebuked him was *ASTA*, the official German Students' Union. In their view,

> the events at the Olympic village merely served the bourgeois parties as a pretext to initiate a political campaign of repression and discrimination against progressive foreign organizations, Arab organizations now being singled out for special attention.

In the current climate of radicalization the ideologically uncommitted *Al Fatah* seems to be losing ground to the verbally more orthodox Marxist *PDFLP (Popular Democratic Front for the Liberation of Palestine)*. However, none of the Arab movements could function or influence the German scene without the co-operation and active support of the radical Left. This has proved and still proves invaluable in parrying the wide-spread demand for control of Arab subversives provoked by the Munich outrages and subsequent terrorist activities.

'Progressive' Auschwitz?

Bruno Frei

During the years which have elapsed since the Six Day War, the myth that the attacks made against Israel by the Arab armies and Palestine guerillas are anti-imperialist and hence 'progressive' has become absorbed into the philosophy of the 'New Left', giving the sympathies of student revolutionaries an inescapably biased approach. In their opinion Israel is a colonial fact, a 'spearhead' created in the back of the Arab peoples to prevent their emancipation from imperialism; she is expansionist by nature, her ideology (Zionism) is racist and her politics fascist. Hitler expelled the Jews, Dayan is driving out the Arabs. *Blitzkrieg* is *blitzkrieg,* occupation is occupation. The New Left, expressing solidarity with all peoples fighting to free themselves from the yoke of imperialism, aligns itself unreservedly with the Palestine guerrillas who aim at liberating Palestine from Zionism and imperialism (sometimes referred to as 'Zionist imperialism').

The growth of this myth is worth noting. The joint Soviet-Egyptian communiqué after Khrushchev's visit of 25 May 1964 stated that: 'The Soviet Union declares its full support for the Arab people's fight against the aggressive intentions of the imperialist powers, capable of using the Palestine problem as a *lever* to increase tension in the Middle East.' A year later, when Walter Ulbricht visited Nasser, the word 'lever' was replaced by 'spearhead', which has since become stereotype usage in Soviet political journalism.

This change of wording was not a question of semantics but of politics, Khruschev took care not to subscribe to the view that Israel had been created as a 'spearhead' against the Arab liberation movement, because that would only have all too flagrantly contradicted the critical Soviet role in passing the UN partition resolution of 27 November 1947. Walter Ulbricht, always a length ahead of the helmsman, and less inhibited by the UN minutes, adopted Nasser's formula repealing the legitimate existence of Israel, long before there was any talk about *blitzkrieg à* la Hitler.

According to pan-Arab philosophy, the creation of Israel in 1948 was 'an act of aggression', as was all Jewish immigration after the Balfour Declaration of 1917. Right from the beginning, the State of Israel had been planned as a base for the forces of imperialism in the Middle East. Palestine's liberation through armed conflict was therefore an act of defence.[1]

To the question: what is Israel? there are two diametrically opposed answers which form the basis of the argument concerning the 'act of aggression' and which naturally provide two diametrically opposed approaches; one leading towards a solution, the other towards the 'final solution'.

On the one side, we have the line of argument put forward by the Soviet Foreign Minister Gromyko in the UN General Assembly on 14 May and 26 November 1947. Whatever might have been the power-political or world revolutionary motives behind Soviet pressure to carve a Jewish state out of British mandated territory, the proposal 'to create, in place of one country, two states, one Arab and one Jewish' (Gromyko), was made against the background of the moral responsibilities confronting the Allies as a result of Auschwitz. Zionist expectations, hopes, or demands played a secondary role. Zionists had dreamt of Israel, it was the leading UN powers who created the State of Israel.

Homeless Jews, survivors of the massacre, were wandering through the cities of Europe in their thousands. 'The United Nations cannot and must not observe this situation without doing something about it, for that would not be in accordance with the principles laid down in the Charter' (Gromyko). In 1947 the homeless Jews were not asked whether they

were Zionists or anti-Zionists; the flood of concentration
camp survivors was channelled towards Palestine.

And this was the 'colonization'. The 'colonizing power' who
directed Jewish 'colonists' to the country and instigated the
establishment of the state, was the UNO. Responsibility for the
fact that in the first four years after the creation of the state one
million immigrants entered the country lies with the powers
who passed the partition resolution—in this instance with the
Soviet Union rather than with the USA. For the USA,
apprehensive that her Middle Eastern oil interests might suffer,
and in view of Arab resistance, had, on 16 April 1948, tried to
revoke the partition resolution and to set up a new trusteeship
instead. Again it was Gromyko who, together with the Jewish
Agency representative, prevented 'capitulation'.

The 'act of aggression', the birth of the State of Israel, so
strongly supported by the Soviet Union, was immediately
met with armed hostility from its Arab neighbours. The
confusion of ideas dates back to this moment. If the creation
of Israel was an act of aggression, then the Arab attack was an
act of defence. Without waiting for the theses of future
doctors of international law, the Israelis defended the UN
resolution—and their lives. Since then there has been continuous fighting and the question of who is the defender and
who the aggressor is becoming more and more obscured.

It was the wish of the comity of nations that the territory,
which had never, since the fall of Jerusalem in AD 70 (except
for 200 years under the Crusaders), been an independent
state, either Arab or Jewish, but always merely a dependency
of foreign powers, should be divided between the two peoples
living in Palestine so that the national aspirations of both
could be fulfilled. So much for the Israeli definition of Israel.

The other side presented a document so unequivocal that
the student of Middle Eastern affairs is saved the trouble of
relying on hypotheses or of drawing specific conclusions from
vague generalities. At the fourth Palestinian National Council meeting in Cairo (10-17 July 1968), the resolutions passed
by the first Palestinian Congress in 1964 were redefined and
made binding on all Palestinian resistance organizations. It
was noted that of the meeting's 100 participants, 37 belonged
to *Al Fatah*. This document lays down in 33 articles the

official programme of the Palestinian Liberation Front.[2]

The most important points are: the 1947 partition of Palestine is null and void, it contradicts the UN Charter which proclaims the peoples' right to self-determination (Article 19). The right to self-determination exists only for the Palestinian Arabs who exercise it as they wish and choose (Article 3). The Balfour Declaration is null and void, for Jewry is a religion; the Jews have no right to exist as an independent nation (Article 20). Zionism, inextricably linked to world imperialism, is the enemy of every liberation progressive movement. 'It is basically a racist and fanatic movement, aggressive, expansionist, colonialist in its aims, fascist and nazi in its methods'. Israel is a base for world imperialism, imperialism's spearhead and starting point (Article 22).

The platform goes on to proclaim that Palestine's liberation must come through armed conflict (Article 9) and to define 'liberation' as the conquest of the whole country and its exclusive occupation by Palestinian Arabs. Therefore (Articles 3 and 21) the 'liberation' is a war of defence, while the Israeli resistance is an act of aggression (Article 18). As a final solution for Israel's Jewish inhabitants, the platform suggests that those who were living in Palestine before 1917 can remain there as Palestinian citizens, the others must go (Article 6).

This solution is more radical than that proposed by the infamous Ehukeiri, envisaging victory, on the eve of the Six Day War. In a magnanimous gesture, he said that those Jews who were resident before 1947 should be allowed to stay. The same suggestion had been made in 1964. It was not until the 1968 meeting that the *Al Fatah* leader, Yasser Arafat, declared it the aim of the war of liberation to expel two and a half million Jews from 'liberated' Palestine, probably out of concern for the Arab majority in the future 'democratic' Palestine.

It follows quite naturally therefore that in *Al Fatah* literature the word 'cleansing' is used in preference to liberation. Stripped of its verbal wrappings, the aim of the Palestinian war of liberation is seen as a reality quite legitimately comparable with Auschwitz. We are faced with the paradox of a 'progressive' Auschwitz.

Al Fatah journalists are not always piously intent on declaring it their aim to restore an independent, democratic state of Palestine, where all races and religions can live peacefully together. Quite often they lay aside all pretence and express themselves plainly: 'The process of liberation involves not only the liquidation of the imperialist base, but the effacement of a society.'[3]

Y. Harkabi's paper *Fedayeen Action and Arab Strategy* (London Institute of Strategic Studies) shows the genocidal implications of current Arab 'liberation' policies.

This form of 'liberation' is nothing new, and in no way a consequence of Israel's refusal to give up the territory occupied after the Six Day War without an agreement on 'secure and recognized' borders. The words and their meaning are as old as the ashes of Auschwitz. One is reminded of the letter (20.1.40) in which Haj Amin El Husseini, Grand Mufti of Jerusalem, thanking the Führer for supporting the Arab liberation movement, pledged himself to win the support of the Mohammedans in the Middle East and in the Balkans for Hitler's war, and to recruit Mohammedans, especially Arabs, for the SS.[4] In return, the Führer was to help the Palestinian Arabs to rid themselves of the Jews along with the British.

The 'liberation of Palestine' formed an integral part of the 'Final Solution' and of Hitler's overall strategy. The Egyptian officer corps was also enthusiastic about this plan. One of the officers later explained: 'No-one—not even the greatest simpleton in the country—took the lie about 6 million murdered Jews seriously. . . . Our sympathies were on the side of the Germans in the second world war too.' Gamal Abdel Nasser, who made this frank declaration of sympathy for Hitler to the editor of the 'progressive' *Deutsche Nationalzeitung*, Dr Gerhard Frey (1.5.64), intimated during the same interview that in his opinion a peaceful solution to the Israeli problem was impossible.

Al Fatah, far from having a progressive or completely revolutionary concept of the 'people's war', continues in the tradition of the most obscure, the most reactionary, religious feudal upper classes of the days under the Mufti's administration. Then, too, terrorist attacks on Jewish settlements alternated with democratic promises of freedom of religion. Little though the aims and methods have changed, the brand-name has been altered radically. The Mufti called

upon Hitler as an ally in the fight against Zionism and
Bolshevism, Arafat is calling on Moscow and Peking to slay
Zionism and imperialism.

It is perhaps not surprising that the ultimate objective of
the Palestinian guerrillas does not differ from that of the old
reactionary feudal lords, although it certainly ought to come
as a surprise to progressive students. They should have
wondered why *Al Fatah* has no idea to what kind of society it
aspires once Israel lies in ruins. What sort of social structure
will emerge from the new Arab Palestine? Capitalist? Socialist? Feudalistic? Is every fighting movement in the Third
World *eo ipso* progressive? All revolutionary movements, the
FLN in Algeria, the Vietcong, the guerrillas in Latin America, joined and are joining battle against imperialism demanding specific economic, social and democratic rights. Is it not
in the very character of the fight against imperialism and for
national rights that the substance of what is termed 'progressive' lives? *Al Fatah* will not hear of it, but expressly demands
that all ideological differences within the national liberation
front be regarded as matters of 'secondary' importance. Does
Arafat not want to annoy the dollar-rich oil sheikhs and kings
who support him?

But the land stolen from the Arabs by acts of aggression is
now said not only to have served the purpose of settling the
homeless, but also of extending the aggression against the
Arab world inherent in Israel's existence. Israel, created as a
spearhead, also acts as a spearhead. This reproach, perhaps
true of the Sinai campaign of 1956, becomes absurd when one
comes to analyse the situation of 1967 and after.

Basically, the Arab states' active resistance against the
establishment of Israel in one part of Palestine, legitimate
under international law, is in itself a latent permanent act of
aggression, accentuated when Nasser, at his press conference
on 28 May 1967, opened the discussion on the military
concentration against Israel by reiterating the assertion that:
'The aggression lies in the mere existence of Israel.' This
contention tried to disguise the intended destruction of Israel
as a defence of Arab countries.

Guilt feelings had meanwhile repressed these threats against
Israel altogether or claimed they had been misinterpreted.

'The Arab people are unshakeable in their decision to wipe Israel from the face of the earth and to restore Arab honour in Palestine', boomed Radio Cairo on 25 May 1967. When Fedorenko branded Israel's blow struck in self-defence as 'an act of aggression' he flatly contradicted the Soviet definition of aggression, stubbornly defended by Moscow in dozens of UN resolutions and international agreements ever since the 1933 London Convention. Measured against what the Soviet Union understands and wants to be understood by aggression, Israel's Arab neighbours have been guilty of hundreds of individual acts of aggression since 1948. With the blockade of the streets of Tiran, the state of permanent aggression reached an unacceptable dimension. Even after the Six Day War there are still two interpretations of the word, which helps to promote the tragic masquerade which represents those who defend their lives, often ruthlessly, as 'aggressors', and those who plan the murder of a people as 'defenders'.

In the aims set out in the *Palestinian Liberation Front's* programme 'liberation' does not mean the removal of the forces of suppression, but the establishment of forces of oppression which in the given circumstances implies the physical liquidation of those who oppose the 'liberation'. Here also lies the root of a fatal misunderstanding that is beyond doubt quite intentionally nurtured. Should the Arabs agree to a political solution of the conflict,[5] provided that (a) Israeli troops completely evacuate the occupied territory and (b) a just solution is found to the Palestine question, in reality all this means is an 'Auschwitz in instalments'. If Nasser had been really striving for a lasting peaceful solution, he would not have fought against recognizing Israel, nor have clung to the Khartoum formula—'no negotiations, no agreement, no peace'. The pretence that Israel's existence is 'an act of aggression in itself', prevents recognition and qualifies each 'political solution' as a manoeuvre to win time for the next round, as well as showing the demand for the withdrawal of Israeli troops to the 1967 borders to be a cunning ruse within the framework of a war planned in two phases.

The desire to keep alive the urge to destroy can be seen most clearly in the use the Arab diplomats make of the expression 'just solution to the Palestine problem', guaranteed to act like a time-bomb. To the public, longing for peace, this means the refugee problem, a just solution to which certainly needs to be found urgently. There is no 'refugee problem' as far as the *Palestinian Liberation Front* is concerned. By demanding sovereignty over the whole of Palestine, they are creating the prospect of a new refugee problem, this time a Jewish one. For them, nothing less than complete sovereignty over Palestine is a 'just solution' to the Palestine problem. Neither the solution of the refugee problem nor the evacuation of the occupied territory is enough for liberation-minded Arabs. Thus the formula of a just solution to the Palestine problem, as used in the Arab press, is in reality a euphemistic term for the destruction of Israel.

Not one Arab government has dissociated itself from the Palestinian resistance organizations, their strategy and their programme. On the contrary, not only do they support them with money and arms, but their adherence to the cause of Arab unity has made them increasingly dependent on the terrorists who have become a powerful force.

The picture of David and Goliath has undergone strange changes. During the Six Day War, public opinion liked to look on Israel as David. Now it is usually the other way round, with Israel, strong and militant, represented as Goliath. But in reality the positions have not changed. The lives of three million Jews are threatened by one hundred million Arabs. The 'spearhead' is in fact the weapon of self-defence.

The use of the epithet 'progressive' to describe a movement whose political programme includes the destruction of three million people is no less obscene than the designation 'cleansing' was for the activity of the special SS detachments in Poland. If one points to the terrorist activities of the Palestinian guerrillas on the one hand, one must certainly not ignore Dayan's demolition of houses on the other. It cannot be denied that the influence of chauvinist, militarist, annexionist circles in Israel is considerable and may even become dominant. The sudden turn to the right at the most recent elections shows that the tide of chauvinism is rising. With the escalation of violence on both sides the prospects of a just solution to the conflict are receding. The vicious circle of violence, no longer confined to purely military considerations, has now affected politics to an alarming and increasing extent. Even Israel's friends are asking themselves whether the inflexible, indeed obstinate, attitude of the parliamentary majority and its government is serving the country's long-term interests. The establishment of Israeli settlements in the occupied territory, and the public statements of some ministers show that power is in the hands of the maximalists in Jerusalem. By lessening sympathy for Israel, this helps her enemies.

It is unquestionably true that the Israeli Government and economy maintain close links with the USA, but although Israel enjoys the support of American Jewry, it is in no way an ally of the USA, rather a thorn in the flesh of American oil magnates.

But supposing Israel were prepared, as a member of a US-dominated pact system, to put military bases at their disposal. Can one imagine that, to prevent Cyprus from becoming a NATO base, progressive students would incite the Turks in Cyprus to expel the Greeks? Has a progressive movement ever demanded the annihilation of a people who have opted for a reactionary regime? The battle to bring down the militarists and annexionists in Israel is a domestic one, and certainly not one to be fought by Palestinian guerrillas.

Hence the popular comparison to Vietnam, Algeria, Bolivia, etc., is quite inappropriate since the aim of a genuine liberation movement is to mobilize the people against outside exploitation; according to Yasser Arafat, his liberation movement's aim is to destroy a society, to expel a people, which in Israel's case means to exterminate them. Palestine is not occupied by Americans or Frenchmen, but settled by Jews, who have found or rediscovered a homestead there. 'Revolutionaries never threaten a whole people with destruction', Fidel Castro once said in an interview about the Israeli-Arab conflict[6] his anti-imperialist fervour notwithstanding.

It would be the task of the Left, the old and the new, to stop this descent into hell, to lift the confrontation off the national-chauvinist level on to the socio-political. There are reactionary and progressive forces in both camps. Instead of denouncing Israel as a whole, which is incompatible with the theory of class-warfare, the full weight of the European and American Left must be used to tip the scales, so that help and hope can be offered to the forces of the Left in Israel. The vicious circle of escalating violence exists precisely because the flood-tide of left-wing sympathy for the guerrillas lets the Israeli Right triumph. It would be the task of the non-Israeli Left to strengthen the Israeli Left in a future anti-imperialist, or at least bloc-free Israel, but this presupposes (a) a confrontation with the Right and (b) prospects of a secure peace.

In a face of a deadly threat, even when parading in the guise of socialist progress, the Israelis' natural instinct forces them to unite in a national front, which, cutting across the Left-Right dichotomy, looks for allies and arms wherever they can be found. If it is considered just that the Arabs are armed by the Soviet Union, why should it be unjust that Israel purchases arms in the USA, while they are still to be had? In the final analysis, the controversy over the supply of arms to the Middle East merely reflects the argument concerning the meaning of 'aggression' in connection with Israel's existence.

Just as, in Hitler's Germany, Zionism won many new supporters under the threat of persecution, so, in the face of similar Arab annihilation threats disguised as 'progressive thinking', Zionism continues to appeal even to those who still remain Marxists. In the face of the monstrous revival of antisemitism as 'anti-Zionism' and the unbelievable resuscitation of the *Protocols of the Elders of Zion* under the 'progressive' brand-label of a 'Zionist world conspiracy',[7] Zionism, as defined by the sixteenth Congress of the *Israeli Communist Party (Maki)* makes the essential Marxist point: 'Zionism is a national movement, which must be treated like any other national movement, e.g. its positive elements recognized and its reactionary elements rejected' (Point 40 of the resolution).[8] In its policy the *Israeli Communist Party* distinguishes between the bourgeois, pro-imperialist wing of the Zionist movement and the progressive workers' wing.

To justify her biased and unqualified support for the Arab encirclement of Israel, the Soviet Union advanced a theory according to which progress and retrogression are not to be defined in local, but in global terms. In the *Tass* statement, issued after Yasser Arafat's visit to Moscow,[9] an assurance was given 'that the people of the Soviet Union are definitely on the side of the Arab people, against the Israeli aggressors and their imperialist protectors; it supports the anti-imperialist national liberation struggle of the Palestinian Arabs'. Does this mean that the Soviet Government gives its sanction to the *Al Fatah* platform?

Israel may be annihilated; according to this theory that is a lesser evil—seen within the context of world events—and must remain subordinate to the overridding common good, the repression of American influence in the Middle East. Realist politics are not moral politics. Arguments such as these are used to justify the supply of arms to terrorists who plant bombs in warehouses and planes. It is hard to believe that this policy emanates from Marx and Lenin.

While admittedly an imperialist global strategy is at work, demanding an—unfortunately absent—anti-imperialist global strategy, the Israeli-Arab conflict ought to be isolated from the East-West confrontation. Its basic features make this a national and not an ideological conflict which has merely been used as a pawn in the contest between the two great world powers. The Middle East, alienated from its own peculiar problems, and having become a battleground between the great powers, is not to be pacified on the level of an ideological East-West argument. Such labels as progress and reaction, imperialism and anti-imperialism, render this a conflict only to be solved by world war. As with imperialism and anti-imperialism, there is progress and reaction on either side of the battle line. The desire to de-escalate the conflict was expressed, amongst others, by Herbert Marcuse. 'The ideal solution would be to set up a joint Arab-Israeli front against the forces of imperialism.'[10] To be sure, this 'ideal solution' will remain utopian as long as the myth persists and is encouraged that a socialist revolution in the Arab world presupposes Israel's destruction.

In order to come nearer to finding a solution that is not the 'final solution', the fighting in the Middle East must be recognized in its proper perspective, as a regional struggle between two nations sharing a narrow strip of land, both legitimately claiming their right to self-determination.

NOTES

1. Art. 18 of the Palestinian resistance organization's platform. Also Nasser at his press conference of 28 May 1967.
2. *Al-Hithaga Al Watussi al Filastini,* quoted here from the official English translation, 'The Palestinian National Covenant'.
3. 'Fatah-Pamphlet' No. 8, *The Liberation of the occupied Territory and the Means used in the Fight against direct Colonialism,* pp. 14-15. Also *Fatah Yearbook,* 1968, p. 39.
4. The Mufti is listed as a war criminal in Yugoslavia, because he recruited peasants for the SS in Bosnia.
5. Interview with *Le Monde,* 19 February 1970.
6. *Quaderno del Medio Oriente,* 3.
7. In 1968, 60,000 copies of the book *Jewry and Zionism* by Trofim Kornejewitsch Kitschko, a final year arts student, were published in Kiev by *Znanja* (Knowledge). This pamphlet revives the myth of the Elders of Zion in up-to-date form.
8. Information Bulletin, Communist Party of Israel Central Committee, Tel Aviv 1/1969.
9. *Le Monde,* 22-23 February 1970.
10. Herbert Marcuse's contribution to a discussion in July 1967, published in the paper 'Conditions and Prospects of Peace' in *The Middle East,* by Cercle Bernard Lazare—Paris.

Anti-Zionism in the USSR: from Lenin to the Soviet Black Hundreds

Robert S. Wistrich

The month of November 1917, which witnessed both the Balfour Declaration of the British Government and the Bolshevik Revolution in Russia, was a watershed in European, Jewish and World history. The sixty years which have passed since these dramatic events have seen no abatement of the historic antagonism between Communism and Zionism. Except for a brief period immediately preceding and following the creation of a Jewish State in 1948, considerations of ideology and *Realpolitik* have dictated a pro-Arab and anti-Zionist Soviet policy in the Middle East. Similarly, with the single exception of the Second World War when the Soviets were prepared to exploit Jewish world solidarity for their own purposes (to raise funds and win political support) they have sought to repress all spontaneous manifestations of Jewish nationalism within their own borders. Nevertheless, it would be mistaken to regard Communist attitudes to Zionism as constituting a monolithic, unbroken line of development which has undergone neither adaptation nor change. The historic situations of 1917, 1947 and the post-1967 period, to take only the most important turning-points, were strikingly different and not surprisingly they produced a very diverse pattern of Jewish challenge and Soviet response.

In the twenty years before 1917, a strong, well-organized Zionist movement had developed among the Russian and

Ukrainian Jewish communities. Opposition to this trend was most intense in the Jewish socialist Bund, thus giving to early anti-Zionism the character of an internal, Jewish family quarrel. Again, in the first decade of Soviet rule it was local, Jewish communist officials of the *Yevesktsiia* (a special section of the People's Commissariat for Nationality affairs) who were most active in harassing and denouncing the Zionist movement as 'counter-revolutionary', 'clerical' and 'nationalistic'.[1] Given the role of establishing the 'Dictatorship of the Proletariat in the Jewish street', these officials (many of them former militants of the Bund) far outstripped the Soviet government in their energetic, anti-Zionist zeal. The early Bolshevik leaders, ironically enough, showed proof of greater tolerance (or perhaps indifference) and did not decisively clamp down on Zionist organizations before 1924. In this respect it is interesting to recall that neither Lenin, Trotsky or Stalin had paid much attention to Zionism before 1917 though they unanimously repudiated the concept of a 'Jewish nationality' as unscientific and reactionary.[2] Lenin's writings on the Jewish problem before the First World War mainly revolved around his fierce critique of the Bund, its organizational concept, and its claim to exclusively represent the Jewish proletariat. Zionism was also barely mentioned in Stalin's theoretical writings of this period in contrast to the considerable attention he devoted to the Bund. This fact is conveniently distorted in contemporary Soviet literature on the subject which purports to follow Lenin and misleadingly equates Bundism with Zionism, as if they were identical nationalist 'heresies'.

Equally significant is the fact that after 1914, Lenin greatly modified his earlier 'Kautskyian' assimilationist perspective on both the national and the Jewish questions, favouring the free development of national minorities and ethnic groups on Russian territory and taking much greater account of movements for national liberation. Recognizing that the Russian Jewish masses were far from assimilated, he saw the need (partly perhaps in response to the Zionist challenge) for granting full civic *and* national rights to the Jews who were henceforth officially designated as a 'nationality'. In certain respects the Bolsheviks in the 1920s took over the former

Bundist policy of cultural-national autonomy while outlaw-
ing the Bund and other Jewish socialist (as well as bourgeois)
parties as obsolete remnants of the *ancien régime*.[3] One
temporary consequence of the Leninist policy was a flourishing socialist Jewish culture, mainly expressed in the Yiddish
language, with its own network of Jewish schools, scientific
institutes, publishing houses, newspapers and theatrical companies. But after 1930, the disbanding of the Yevsektsiia,
heralded the beginning of a sharp decline in this Yiddish
revival—a development which coincided with Stalin's drive
for industrialization, with his conversion of the Soviet Union
into a monolithic, totalitarian State and with the disintegration of the compact communities of the old Russian Jewish
shtetl.

It is important to realise that the anti-Zionism of the first,
post-revolutionary years was on the whole untainted with
antisemitism. The Resolution of the Soviet government 'On
the Uprooting of the Antisemitic Movement' (27 June 1918)
and Lenin's famous speech against the pogroms (recorded on
a phonograph in March 1919) with its ringing cry 'Shame on
those who sow enmity towards Jews, who sow hatred toward
other nations', had been unequivocal in tone.[4] Lenin's
emphasis on the progressive and internationalist role of the
Jewish intelligentsia[5] and on the class solidarity of Jewish
'toilers' with the proletariat of other nationalities was based
on warm sympathy as well as a shrewd analysis of the
objective situation. Moreover, he was genuinely outraged by
the anti-Jewish libels and persecutions of the Tsarist regime[6]
and by the pogroms of the White counter-revolutionaries,
with whom the Bolsheviks were engaged in a merciless
struggle. While he and other leading Bolsheviks did on
occasion reproach Zionism for preaching class-collaboration
instead of class-struggle, this also has to be seen in the
domestic context of 1917-20.[7] The impact of the Balfour
Declaration on Russian Jewry did arouse understandable
fears. There were pro-British articles in the Russian Jewish
press and pro-British demonstrations in Odessa and Petrograd which easily gave rise to the suspicion that Zionism
could become a dangerous anti-Bolshevik weapon in the hands
of the Entente.[8] Furthermore, the attraction of Palestine

as a rallying cry could have weakened the recruitment of the Jewish masses into the Red Army during the critical period of the Civil War. Finally, there was the irredentist threat posed by any movement of national separatism at a time when the new Soviet regime was fighting desperately for its very survival. Though Zionism was clearly far less dangerous than Ukrainian separatism it is not surprising that on the domestic front it could be viewed as a 'bourgeois' and potentially counter-revolutionary movement at that time.

Less significant in the early years, but of fundamental importance in the long run, was the Bolshevik assessment of the 'colonial question' in the Middle East. The British conquest of Palestine in 1917 and the Anglo-French partition of the entire region appeared to confirm Lenin's theory of the division of the globe among the imperialist powers. The Bolsheviks were fundamentally hostile to such 'annexationism' and one of the first acts of Leon Trotsky as Commissar for Foreign Affairs was to publish the secret Sykes-Picot treaty in order to embarrass the Entente and expose the hollowness of its 'democratic' promises to the Arabs.[9] The fact the Zionist leadership was then eagerly co-operating with the British government naturally encouraged the Bolsheviks to view it as a 'tool of imperialism'. This hostility was enhanced by the fact that in Bolshevik eyes, the British were indubitably the great colonial oppressors in the Middle East and the power considered the most intent on overthrowing the Soviet regime itself. Thus, it is not surprising that the Bolsheviks should seek to stir up revolutionary ferment among those backward populations that found themselves predominantly under British control, which included a substantial part of the Arab and Muslim 'toilers' of the East.[10] Given the global revolutionary and anti-colonial strategy of the Bolsheviks it was natural that in the aftermath of 1917 they would look to Palestinian Arab workers and peasants rather than to Zionist settlers as a spearhead of anti-British feeling in the area. Nevertheless, with the ebbing of their world revolutionary euphoria, relatively little attention was paid by the Soviets to the Middle East. The riots in Palestine in 1929 and the Arab revolt of 1936-39 did encourage a flurry of propaganda against 'Zionist imperialist oppression', but there was objectively no revolutionary situation in the region and the dogmatic, sectarian approach of the Comintern to colonial questions was unlikely to produce one.[11]

It should be evident from this historical context that while there was a tradition of communist opposition to Jewish nationalism on ideological grounds, which had pre-dated the First World War, this intensified because of a constellation of specific circumstances which only crystallized after 1917. The anti-Zionism of this period was indeed scarcely sharper in tone than Bolshevik condemnations of other forms of national separatism in Soviet Russia or movements such as Pan-Islamism and Pan-Arabism in the Middle East, which were seen as equally reactionary and anachronistic. Moreover, in contrast to the anti-Zionist crusade of the 1960s and 70s, Jewish nationalism was seen as peripheral to the main thrust of Bolshevik doctrine and its critique was largely left in the hands of the Yevsektsiia functionaries. In spite of their undeniable fanaticism in seeking to extirpate Jewish religious institutions, the Hebrew language and Zionist sentiments from Jewish life, the latter were probably sincere in their desire to improve the material conditions of Russian Jewry. Their struggle, however misguided and deplorable in its consequences, was ultimately conceived as being for the good of the Jews and not against them. Much the same can be said of the first generation of Bolshevik leaders, some of whom like Kalinin (the President of the Soviet Union in the 1920s) opposed the trend towards assimilation and even advocated a Soviet version of Zionism.[12] Kalinin believed that a dispersed national minority like Soviet Jewry could not become a nation without territorial concentration and extensive agricultural colonization. He hoped that Russian Jews would seize the opportunity to leave the big cities and settle as farmers in the Crimea, the Southern Ukraine, or some other territory in the USSR in order to prevent their erosion as a 'nationality'. The Birobidzhan experiment was precisely such an attempt to *normalize* the situation of Jews in the Soviet Union by creating the socio-economic pre-requisites for Jewish national existence.[13] In his speech in 1934, proclaiming Birobidzhan as a Jewish autonomous region, Kalinin made it clear that such a normalization along territorial lines was the only way to preserve a Jewish national culture.[14] Why then did this 'Siberian Palestine' prove such a fiasco, in spite of having the support of some other prestigious figures in Soviet public life including Chicherin, Maxim Litvinov and Leonid Krassin? Apart from the forbidding climatic conditions, notably the near-Arctic winters, wilderness and swamps, and the geographic isolation of the Far East, there was a much more fundamental defect. The whole project was bureaucratically inspired from *above* (it had the backing of the People's Commissariat of Agriculture and the Commissariat for Defence) conspicuously ignoring the cultural background, the social aspirations and spontaneous feelings of Russian Jewry.[15] Conceived in part for strategic reasons and as a counterweight to Palestinian Zionism, Birobidzhan had no roots in Jewish history or in Jewish national-religious sentiments—even though it sometimes imitated Zionist fundraising methods and contained residues of Zionist ideology and rhetoric. Needless to say, those enthusiasts (some of them former members of Poale Zion) who ecstatically praised Jewish territorial concentration and land colonization when it was practised in the Soviet Far East, considered this same policy a hopeless, petty-bourgeois deviation when successfully executed in Palestine. By the end of the 1930s with the consolidation of Stalin's totalitarian absolutism, not only were the last vestiges of organized Zionism in the USSR eradicated[16] but the leaders of the Yevsektsiia and the organizers of the Birobidzhan project had themselves been exiled, imprisoned or purged.

It was the Nazi attack on the Soviet Union which for the first time induced a temporary change in official attitudes to Jewish nationalism. Although this was a period when Great Russian nationalism was itself on the upswing and antisemitism had greatly increased (as Nazi racial propaganda penetrated the Soviet Union) the authorities were obliged to encourage national and religious feelings among different ethnic groups in order to strengthen resistance to the German invaders. The Jewish Anti-Fascist Committee set up in April 1942 had precisely this purpose—to win support among Jews at home and abroad for the Red Army.[17] Stalin apparently considered the sympathy of world Jewry important enough during the war to outweigh the fundamental Soviet dogma that Russian Jews could have no feelings of solidarity for Jews outside the USSR. Even the so-called 'myth' of a world Jewish people (so relentlessly attacked in Soviet anti-Zionist propaganda) was allowed open public expression in order to win the political goodwill and the assistance of British and American Jewry. For the first time in August 1941 a voice could be heard over Radio Moscow, that of the famous Yiddish poet Perets Markish, addressing his 'Brother Jews' all over the world as one people and one army. It was also at this time that the Red Army Colonel, Itzik Feffer, could write his stirring poem 'I am a Jew', with its heroic Maccabean and quasi-Zionist strains;[18] similarly, the head of the Jewish Anti-Fascist Committee (JAC), the celebrated actor Solomon Mikhoels, could speak of a 'community of fate' binding all Jews together and even describe Zionism as a 'great idea' during his war-time visit to London, though it was not, (he emphasized), applicable to Soviet Jewry. More significant still, the secretary of the Jewish Anti-Fascist Committee, Shachna Epstein, wrote in November 1944 in *Aynikayt*, 'Unity', (the organ of the JAC) that the Jews have a 'right to political independence in Palestine'.[19] None of this could have been done, of course, without Stalin's blessing and clearly seems to presage the turn in post-war Soviet policy towards support for a Jewish State. But this poses a number of problems of interpretation with regard to the inter connection between official communist dogma on Zionism, the Middle Eastern and global policies of the USSR and the long-standing antisemitic traditions of 'Mother Russia', renovated in their modernized Soviet version.

Stalinist Russia of the immediate post-war years appears to have exactly inverted the Bolshevik position of 1917. Whereas Lenin and many of his closest followers were genuine internationalists, ideologically anti-Zionist, but also either sympathetic or indifferent on the internal Jewish problem, Stalin and his entourage between 1945 and 1953 were Great Russian cultural imperialists, mildly pro-Israel in foreign policy and both anti-Zionist and strongly antisemitic at home. How can one explain this apparently schizoid Stalinist policy? Why should the brief Soviet-Israeli honeymoon which suddenly reversed thirty years of Communist opposition to the Yishuv as a counter-revolutionary tool of British imperialism, have coincided with the 'Black Years' of Soviet Jewry? Before attempting to understand the reasons for Moscow's volte-face on the issue of a Jewish State in Palestine, it is important to realize that the Soviet antisemitic campaign had *preceded* the arrival of Golda Meyerson (Meir) in the Soviet Union as ambassador of Israel, and her celebrated appearance at Moscow's Grand Synagogue during the Yom Kippur festival of 16 October 1948.[20] Moreover, Stalin's campaign which began in 1946 and continued until 1953 had two faces—it was directed against both 'Jewish nationalism' and 'cosmopolitanism'—but there was one target, namely the destruction of the intellectual élite of Russian Jewry.[21] The attack on 'Jewish nationalism' (which was part of a broader onslaught against 'bourgeois nationalism' in general) was initiated by *Aynikayt* which along with its publishing house *Emes* ('Truth') and with the sponsoring Jewish Anti-Fascist Committee, was closed down in 1948. This campaign which declared Jewish nationalism and Zionist sentiments to be absolutely incompatible with Soviet patriotism was in fact designed to justify in advance the destruction of Soviet Jewish culture. This had been virtually accomplished by the end of 1949. Already with Mikhoels' assassination at the beginning of 1948, it was clear that Stalin had no further use for the Jewish Anti-Fascist Committee since he no longer needed the support of world Jewry or of the nationally minded Jewish Communist intelligentsia, which he physically liquidated in 1952. Though the so-called 'rootless cosmopolitans' in literature and the arts did not suffer such a brutal fate they were also sharply denounced as 'alien' to communist ideology and as enemies of Soviet culture. This onslaught against the anti-national character of 'cosmopolitanism' and its so-called defamation of the great Russian nation and of Russian man, was directed primarily at the *assimilated* Jewish intelligentsia and reached its peak in 1949.[22] In both cases, though from opposite poles, it was the alleged lack of Soviet patriotism and the potential disloyalty of Russian Jewry which was under assault. However, it must be emphasized that not until

1952-53 were the accusations of 'Jewish nationalism' and 'cosmopolitanism' fused by means of an explicit Zionist conspiracy theory, which linked Israel and Western imperialism to the so-called 'Doctors' Plot' against the lives of Soviet leaders. Thus before 1952, Stalin had not yet organically related his 'anti-Zionism' to visceral antisemitism and it took another four years before his successors completed the triangle by adopting a systematic anti-Israelism. This final consummation was accelerated by Khrushchev's switch to an aggressive pro-Arab policy in the Middle East.

What then caused the pro-Israel turn in Stalin's foreign policy during 1947/48, which it must never be forgotten had coincided with the suppression of Jewish nationalism and Zionism at home? What if anything, was the relationship between domestic and foreign policy? Was there any connection at all between the intermittently friendly and indifferent inter-state relations of Moscow and Jerusalem and the Jewish problem in the USSR? A clue to this paradox is suggested by Ilya Ehrenburg's well-known article published in *Pravda* on 21 September 1948 which clearly reflected the official standpoint and was intended as a warning to Soviet Jewry not to become emotionally involved in the dramatic revival of the Jewish State. Ehrenburg made it plain that while the Soviet Union sympathized with the aspirations for Jewish statehood in Palestine, it was highly critical of Israel's 'bourgeois' leaders who already then were branded as tools of Anglo-American imperialism. It was the duty of the Israeli working-class to repulse not only the Arab invaders but to fight against their own 'bourgeois' government which exploited them. Moreover, Ehrenburg denied that there was any such thing as a Jewish 'people' or even any affinity between Jews in different countries; this he claimed, was the invention of Zionist 'mystics' and Jewish nationalists whom he sharply condemned.

Ehrenburg's views were undoubtedly close to those of Stalin, who had always believed that the Jews would disappear through assimilation and denied that they were a nation, since they lacked a common language, territory, economic life or culture.[23] In Palestine, however, these same pre-requisites would make the emergence of a new 'Israeli' nation compatible with the classic Stalinist definition; but it was stressed in Soviet publications that this had nothing to do with Russian Jews, whose aims and future were indissolubly linked to the building to communism. At the time, there were some left-wing Israelis prepared to accept this, since they looked upon the USSR not only as an ally, but as a model society which was the true fatherland of socialism. They failed to understand that Soviet support for Israel was not motivated by common ideology or sentiment and could also co-exist with the intense repression of Jewish culture at home. Mistakenly believing that Stalin backed Israel because it was a 'progressive', democratic state, they ignored the international factors that determined Moscow's policy with regard to both Jews and Arabs in Palestine in the post-1945 situation.

Stalin's patronage of Israel in 1948 was not a momentary aberration but a perfectly rational decision in terms of Soviet *raison d'état*.[24] At that time the Russians had no allies in the Middle East and they were confronted with a Jewish movement for national independence in Palestine which was not only anti-British but in 'objective' Marxist-Leninist terms, stood in the forefront of the anti-colonial struggle. For a variety of reasons it had suddenly become important for Soviet Russia to enter the Middle East; her southern flank (Iran, Turkey) was exposed at a time of rapidly growing East-West tension; she feared that the Persian Gulf and Middle East oil might fall completely under Anglo-American domination; above all she wished to weaken or if possible even to split the Western alliance, and the Middle East was the likeliest area to inflame Anglo-American rivalry. The Palestine question seemed a perfect opportunity to isolate the British from the Americans and prevent the consolidation of their Cold War partnership against the Soviet Union. The acrimony caused between President Truman and the Attlee government over the issue of Jewish immigration from Europe to Palestine had already sown seeds of Anglo-American discord. The tacit toleration by the Soviet Union of the *Brichah* (illegal emigration to Palestine) from Eastern Europe was therefore no accident.[25] The issue of displaced persons was intensely emotional in the aftermath of the Holocaust and it was a reasonable assumption that world public opinion would strongly condemn Britain for closing the gates of Palestine to the survivors of the concentration camps. The Soviets had every interest, therefore, in embarrassing Britain by temporarily encouraging this movement of Jewish refugees to Palestine. Anglo-American contradictions might be reinforced at a critical time when Britain was already over-extended in India, Pakistan, Ceylon, Greece and Turkey, and badly needed American support if it was to avoid a debacle in Palestine.

Moreover, the Soviet Union could simultaneously appear in the guise of a compassionate great power concerned to make amends to the Jewish people for the terrible sufferings they had endured at the hands of the Nazi barbarians. The post-war *prise de conscience* about the Holocaust made it possible for the Soviets to present their sympathy for the Jewish claim to a homeland in Palestine as a moral decision rather than an exercise in opportunism and power politics. This was one case where Soviet *Realpolitik* happened to coincide with the world conscience. Andrei Gromyko's so-called 'Zionist' speech of 14 May 1947 which evoked the 'unparalleled torture and torments' of the Jewish people during the Second World War, could in fact be described as Stalin's Balfour Declaration in reverse, intended to throw the British out of Palestine. 'No nation in Western Europe' Gromyko told the United Nations, 'was able to extend the required help to the Jewish people in defending its rights and physical survival against the violent deeds of the Hitlerites and their allies. This explains the aspiration of the Jews to their own State. It will be unjust if we ignore this aspiration and deny the Jewish people the right to realise it.'[26]

It is significant that neither in this speech nor elsewhere, did Gromyko or any other Soviet leader refer to the Zionist movement as the inspiration of the Jewish struggle in Palestine. This was consistent with Stalin's transient pro-Israel and permanent anti-Zionist attitudes and with the whole tradition of Marxist-Leninist theory which had always branded the Jewish national movement as 'moribund' and 'reactionary'. The Holocaust theme in Gromyko's speech was probably used for propagandist purposes and contained an explicit reproach against the passivity of the Western powers in the face of the 'Final Solution'. This argument suppressed the fact that the Soviet government had always (for internal reasons) denationalized the Jewish victims of Nazi atrocities on its own soil. The number of Jewish casualties in Russian lands occupied by the Germans had in reality been proportionately greater than anywhere, except for Poland. Furthermore, collaboration with the Nazi genocide (e.g. by Ukranians, White Russians and Lithuanians) had been very extensive. In other words, the Soviet Union had proved no more capable than the Allies of defending the lives of defenceless Jewish citizens. Had this been admitted, of course, then Gromyko's argument could equally have been used to justify Jewish emigration from the Soviet Union to Palestine.

The Soviet desire to weaken the West and undermine British interests in the Middle East at a time of mounting Cold War confrontation was clearly paramount in Stalin's calculations. But did he actually believe that in return for Russian diplomatic and military support, the new Jewish State could transformed into a Soviet-style 'people's democracy' and a future communist base in the Middle East? The idea that a Zionist Israel could eventually have become an agent of Russian Communist expansionism seems highly improbable, even from the perspective of 1947/48. True, the founding-fathers of Israel were nearly all Russian Jews, many of them inbued with Russian culture and the fin-de-siècle Marxist outlook. There were too, Zionist leaders like Moshe Sneh, chief of the Haganah from 1940-46, who genuinely believed that the Yishuv should orientate itself to the Soviet Union for the sake of the anti-British struggle. This was also the conviction of Hashomer Hatzair and its successor, Mapam (The United Workers' Party) founded in late 1947, which tried hard to reconcile Zionism with Marxist-Leninist doctrine. Furthermore, left-wing Zionist circles in the Palmach (the élite force of the Haganah) were not unsympathetic to the Soviet Union and it is just possible that Stalin miscalculated in believing that they might soon reach prominent positions in the Jewish State, swinging it to a pro-Soviet course.[27] But none of these individuals or groups had a really broad mass base in Israel though they counted for considerably more than the Israeli Communist Party, ultimately the only reliable vehicle of Soviet interests—which in the first National Elections of 1949 polled a modest 3.44% of the votes.

If the Soviets genuinely underestimated the basic Western-orientation of the dominant Zionist leadership (and this is doubtful) they still had little to lose by supporting the Jewish movement for independence from British rule. But why did they prefer the Jews to the Arabs as allies in this anti-British struggle? The simplest explanation is that between 1945 and 1948 it was the Palestinian Jews who were actually engaged in armed struggle and sometimes even in terrorism designed to terminate the British occupation. From the standpoint of communist theory and Soviet interests, the Jewish revolt was striking a blow against Anglo-American domination of the Middle East and therefore it was depicted as a 'progressive' war of liberation. Arab nationalism, on the other hand, (whose anti-Western character was definitely underestimated by the Soviet leadership at that time) had been tainted with Nazi and fascist associations during the 1930s and 40s, and was militantly anti-communist. One need only mention that the Palestinian Arab leader, Haj Amin el Husseini had actively served the Axis Powers in Berlin during World War II. Other Arab leaders in Iraq, Egypt and Syria had been strongly attracted by fascist ideology and the example of Hitler's Germany. In 1945 the Arab world still appeared to be largely controlled by reactionary monarchs, effendis and feudal cliques, mostly tied by treaties and alliances to British interests. In this context, it is no surprise that Stalin did not take seriously the embryonic movements for independence in the Arab world. When Arab armies under the orders of the Egyptian potentate King Farouk, Nuri Said Pasha of Iraq and King Abdullah of Transjordan attacked Israel in 1948, apparently with British connivance and backing, it was predictable that the Soviets would condemn this 'reactionary war conducted by the chieftains of the Arab League under British control'.[28] Stalin had no intention of allowing Great Britain to regain control of Palestine through the back door, opened up by advancing Arab armies.

Support for Jewish independence in Palestine was the only means by which the USSR could initially penetrate the

Middle East, but once Israel ceased to be a possible source of Soviet influence in the region it was clearly expendable. If there was no open hostility towards the Jewish State between 1948 and 1952 this was largely because the Arab world was still considered to be lacking in revolutionary potential. Hence the Soviet Government preferred to adopt a neutral policy of non-intervention in Middle Eastern affairs during this period.[29] The crisis in Soviet-Israeli relations which first occurred in January-February 1953 was unrelated to the Middle East and was a direct result of Stalin's increasingly paranoid antisemitism. The six Jewish physicians accused in the notorious 'Doctors' Plot' on 13 January 1953 were charged with being 'Zionist spies' linked with the 'Joint Distribution Committee' as well as agents of the British and American secret services. When the USSR broke off diplomatic relations with Israel in February 1953, (they were restored in July) antisemitic, anti-Zionist and anti-Israel motifs had for the first time coalesced.

This unholy trinity of Soviet propaganda remained in force under Nikita S. Khrushchev, in spite of his bold de-Stalinization policy. The main difference after 1955 was the increasing primacy of the anti-Israel theme which was largely dictated by Khrushchev's aggressively pro-Arab strategy in the Middle East.[20] The Arab alliance was perhaps inevitable once the Soviet fleet expanded and the Kremlin rulers embarked on the old Russian imperial dream of expansion towards the warmer waters of the Mediterranean and the South. But one should be wary of explaining Soviet behaviour in terms of immutable categories derived from the past or geo-political determinism. Under Khrushchev, a fundamental re-orientation had taken place with regard to movements of national liberation in the Third World.[31] In contrast to Stalin who was highly sceptical as to the revolutionary potential of non-aligned and non-communist nationalist leaders,[32] Khrushchev believed that 'radical' anti-imperialist regimes in the Third World were the natural allies of the USSR. The new Soviet interest in the developing countries coincided with the rising tide of national liberation symbolised by the Afro-Asian Conference at Bandung in 1955. In the same year Khrushchev decided to grant military assistance to Nasser's Egypt. The Sinai campaign of 1956 in which Israel was identified with Anglo-French aggression against Egypt greatly reinforced the anti-Israeli motif in Soviet foreign policy. The tone of the note sent by the Soviet Prime Minister to the Israeli government on 5 November 1956 was extremely menacing and claimed that the 'very existence of Israel as a state' was in jeopardy.[33] Henceforth, until 1967, the Jewish State was invariably characterized in the Soviet press as a 'puppet' of Western imperialism, ready to launch unprovoked attacks on its neighbours.[34]

In contrast, leaders like Nasser, Kassem and Ben Bella in the Arab world, were extravagantly hailed as 'progressive', even when they had savagely repressed the communist parties in their own countries. The Soviet Union now regarded itself as the patron-saint of the national liberation movements in the Third World and was prepared to overlook hostility to communist activities by local nationalist leaders, provided it served their foreign policy interests. Both Ben Bella and Nasser were awarded the title 'Hero of the Soviet Union' in 1964 and praised as 'revolutionary democrats', already on the road to socialism.[35] Increasing competition with the Chinese Communists for influence in the developing world no doubt contributed to this radical trend in Soviet global strategy. Although with the fall of Khrushchev, a more cautious policy emerged, which recognised the economic and political backwardness of the Third World, this had no apparent effect on Soviet assessments of the Arab-Israel conflict.[36]

With regard to Zionism and the internal Jewish problem, Soviet policy under Khrushchev continued its repressive techniques against all manifestations of Jewish nationalism. In spite of de-Stalinization, the Soviet leadership kept silent about the liquidation of the Jewish intelligentsia between 1948 and 1952, nor did it permit any references to Stalin's antisemitism. Zionism was organically linked with Judaism as a reactionary trend rooted in the idea of the 'exclusiveness of the Jewish people'.[37] Popular broadcasts, magazines and pamphlets invariably found a 'Zionist hand' at work in any attempt to assert Jewish identity, let alone to express sympathy for Israel or the Jews of the Western world. It was under Khrushchev that Kichko's notorious *Judaism without Embellishment* was published by the Ukrainian Academy of Sciences in October 1963. Apart from the crudely antisemitic illustrations, the text, which openly identified Judaism with the greed and usury of Jewish bankers, with Zionism, Israel and Western capitalism in a universal conspiracy, was exceptionally virulent by then prevailing standards. It was eventually withdrawn from circulation as a result of world-wide protests, with which the radical intelligentsia and western communist parties were prominently associated. However, in the course of Khrushchev's general onslaught against religion, the Soviet media continued to vilify Judaism as a subversive, parasitical and repulsive faith. In the early 1960s, antisemitism also appeared in a more covert form in the USSR with the campaign against 'economic crimes' in which the Jewish origins of those sentenced and executed were frequently underlined in the press. This together with the various quota devices discriminating against Jews in employment, belied Khrushchev's claim that Western charges of antisemitism were a 'vicious slander on the Soviet people'.[38] Nevertheless, it is true to say that the pre-1967 patterns of anti-Jewish prejudice in the USSR were relatively unsystematic in comparison with the organized defamation which has been practised in the Soviet media since the Six-Day War. The constant escalation and sheer intensity of these campaigns, waged under the banner of anti-Zionism, indicate that this motif has now become an integral part of official Soviet state ideology. Its starting-point was initially, no doubt, an attempt to explain away the Arab debacle of June 1967; secondly, to politically isolate Israel by denouncing its 'treacherous aggression' and to force it to give up occupied territories by exposing its 'barbaric crimes' and so-called 'genocide' against the Palestine people.[39] But the methods and tactics employed by the Soviet media, which within days of the Israeli victory, branded Dayan as a 'pupil of Hitler' and world Zionism as a racialist, criminal conspiracy no longer had even a tenuous connection with Marxism-Leninism.

Zionism which had not been considered significant enough to warrant a single article by Lenin or the early Bolshevik revolutionaries has today been elevated to a central role in Soviet demonology. Not even Stalin's paranoid, antisemitic delusions of 1952-53 can compare in their scope and range with the thousands of articles, lectures, broadcasts and films which daily vilify Judaism, Zionism and Israel in the USSR. The only comparable analogy would be the monstrous and terrifying spectre of *Das Weltjudentum* in Nazi propaganda of the 1930s and 40s—this time with the roles reversed.[40] In place of the Nazi myth about 'Jewish Bolshevism', the Russian communists have fabricated the even more mendacious thesis of 'Jewish Nazism'. According to Yevgeny Yevseyev, author of *Fascism under the Blue Star*, one of the leading examples of this licensed state pornography, the octopus-like tentacles of world Zionism are more far-reaching and dangerous than those of all other varieties of fascism put together.[41] The villainy of the Jewish bourgeoisie is in fact unequalled anywhere in the world. According to this and other recent Soviet publications, Zionism is the great invisible power whose influence extends into every sphere of politics, finance, religion and the communications media in the capitalist countries. This international Mafia, which is controlled by big Jewish bankers and capitalists, also has a vast intelligence network and unlimited financial resources at its disposal. As early as 4 October 1967, *Komsomolskaya Pravda* was able to make the fantastic claim, with the aid of utterly bogus statistics, that 'the adherents of Zionism in the USA number from 20 to 25 million people . . . Jews and non-Jews'. According to this paper, Zionists allegedly owned 80% of local and international news agencies, comprised 70% of American lawyers, 60% of the physicists and 43% of the industrialists in the United States. In other words, the United States itself was a 'Zionist colony', a tool of Jewish financial power and manipulation. Little wonder, then, that Yury Ivanov in his *Beware! Zionism!* published in Moscow (1969) and hailed as the first 'scientific' work on the subject, could define Zionism as 'the ideology, the ramified system of organization and the political practice of the big Jewish bourgeoisie that has merged with the monopolistic circles of the USA and of other imperialist powers. Its basic content is militant chauvinism and anti-communism . . .'[42]

The new breed of Soviet pseudo-Marxists are forced to rewrite history in order to explain to innocent readers the origins and goals of this 'fascist, criminal conspiracy'. A clear illustration of methods employed by such propaganda hacks is the book by Vladimir Begun, *Creeping Counter-Revolution* (1974). In his introduction to this work, A. M. Malashko pointed out that in the past, Soviet historians had accepted an unjustifiably benign view of the role of Zionism, which regarded antisemitism as its basic cause. Begun's study corrects this error by presenting Tsarist antisemitism as 'the spontaneous reaction of the oppressed strata of the toiling population to their barbarous exploitation by the Jewish bourgeoisie'.[43] We learn that Polish, Ukrainian and Byelorussian peasants 'reduced to despair by merciless exploitation . . . avenged themselves on their oppressors, making no exceptions whatsoever on grounds of nationality'. The Khmelnitsky massacres and later anti-Jewish pogroms were primarily directed against economic exploitation, 'the personification of which were the rapacious Jewish tenant-farmers, money-lenders and publicans.'[44] Dmitri Zhukov, reviewing Begun's book in the mass circulation periodical *Ogonyok* agreed fully with this line of argument, claiming that the antisemitism of the Russian masses was indeed a justifiable form of class-struggle.[45] Thus, the *pogromchiks* mobilized by the Tsar and the ultra-reactionary Black Hundred organizations in defence of the old order, have been elevated by the Beguns and Zhukovs into precursors of a new and better socialist world. The difference between this and the decree of the Council of People's Commissars (27 July 1918) which pointed out that 'the anti-semitic movement and anti-Jewish pogroms are fatal to the cause of the workers' and peasants' revolution', need hardly be stressed. But standard texts against antisemitism written by men of the calibre of Lenin and Gorky do not suit the Black Hundred psychology of the present-day rulers of the Kremlin. Hence, it is no surprise to find that in 1972 the journal of the Soviet embassy in Paris, *URSS*, reproduced almost word for word extracts from a pamphlet published in 1906 by the antisemitic 'Alliance of the Russian People'.[46] The only significant divergence in the modernized Soviet version was the substitution of the code-word 'Zionist' for

'Jew'. This article consisted of fabricated quotations purportedly from Jewish religious writings, designed to prove that Judaism was a man-hating religion which claimed divine sanction to massacre gentiles. On 24 April 1973 a Paris Court found the French publisher of *URSS* guilty of incitement to discrimination, hatred and racial violence.[47]

But identical propaganda goes unpunished in the Soviet Union today. It has become virtually obligatory in so-called 'academic' publications, ostensibly about Zionism, to present Judaism as a creed that calls for genocide and the enslavement of non-Jews. Already the rehabilitated Kichko in his *Judaism and Zionism* (Kiev 1968) had claimed that the Jewish faith in toto was based on the doctrine of a 'superior race' and the 'the chauvinistic idea of the god-chosenness of the Jewish people, the propaganda of messianism and the idea of ruling over the peoples of the world'. Zionists had consciously built on this foundation to educate Jews 'in the spirit of contempt and hatred towards other peoples . . .' in order to justify the 'extermination' of the Palestinian Arabs. According to Kichko: 'Judaism teaches that Jews should force the subjugated people in the invaded lands to work for them as a people of priests.' In the writings of Kichko, Ivanov, Yevseyev, Begun and other 'specialists' it is the cruel, vindictive Yahweh and the dogma of the 'God-chosen nation' which lies at the source of Zionist 'criminality'—an antisemitic theory utterly remote from any Leninist analysis. Thus Vladimir Begun writes in his *Creeping Counter-Revolution* that 'Zionist gangsterism . . . has its ideological roots in the scrolls of the "holy" Torah and the precepts of the Talmud'.[48] The sources of Zionist 'racism' and Israeli 'aggression' in the Middle East therefore lie in the utterly reactionary and corrupt character of Judaism as a faith and code of conduct.

Similar notions can be found in Zhukov's review article of 12 October 1974, 'The Ideology and Practice of Violence' which in the style of medieval Jew-baiting evokes the 'cruel approach of the Talmud that taught the religious Jews to hate the non-believers, the "goyim", to cheat them by all means, and if possible to destroy them'.[49] This standard refrain of Christian antisemites throughout the ages, is used by Zhukov to justify his equally typical allegation that

'Zionist hooligans in Israel erase whole villages, rape little girls and force defenceless Arabs to crawl for hours on their knees.'[50] As Yair Tsaban, Secretary of the Central Committee of Maki (the Israeli Communist Party, no longer recognized by Moscow) put it: 'Not just fifty years divide Lenin from Zhukov, but an ethical and philosophical abyss divides them, and no use of any Marxist vocabulary and no adornment with Lenin-quotations will manage to bridge the gap.'[51]

More recent articles in Soviet publications have continued the antisemitic trend. Vladimir Kiselev writing in March 1975 summarized the theoretical base of Zionism as 'anti-Marxism, national chauvinism and mysticism . . . bellicose anticommunism, adventurism and terrorism'.[52] The theory of a 'world Jewish nation' and the myth of the 'chosen people' were fabricated to 'substantiate an attitude toward other people as "inferior", as representatives of a "lower race", and to provoke hostility against these "gentiles" as inevitable antisemites'.[53] In common with other Soviet publicists, Kiselev claimed that the Zionists had established 'direct contacts with the fascist regimes in Italy and Germany' because they were objective allies. Naturally, he did not mention the far more extensive collaboration of Stalin with Hitler before 1941, nor the ties between Arab nationalists and the fascist regimes. Another omission characteristic of contemporary Soviet literature is the blanket of total silence now surrounding Communist support for Israel in 1948. History has been rewritten to show that 'the policy of aggression and expansion was adopted by Israel's Zionist leaders from the very start'.[54]

The variations of these and other important themes such as the 'Zionist' role in subverting socialist Czechoslovakia in 1968-69[55] and acting as a 'Trojan Horse' for Western Imperialism in Asia and Africa are seemingly endless and to catalogue them all would fill several libraries. The essence of this literature is always to portray 'World Zionism' as an all-pervasive, menacing and perfidious force which threatens not only the existence of the socialist countries, newly independent states and various movements of national liberation, but of all mankind. Two very recent examples of the genre will suffice to recapitulate some of the basic themes of contemporary Soviet anti-Zionism. On 22 July 1977 a Tass commentary announced the publication by the prestigious Academy of Sciences of a 176 page book entitled *International Zionism: History and Politics*. In this so-called 'scientific' work which can fairly be described as a Soviet version of the *Protocols of Zion*, the international banking-system, the military-industrial complex and the key industries of the capitalist world are described as having been taken over by the Jewish bourgeoisie which allegedly uses Zionism as a cover for its activities.[56] According to this book, the stealthy penetration by 'Zionists' of key strategic positions in the economy is designed to establish a Jewish-controlled 'super-government' consistent with Jewish 'messianism', which aspires to 'mastery over all mankind'. Behind the pseudo-Marxist phraseology it is not difficult to detect the familiar strains of the 'Jewish world-conspiracy' which supposedly seeks to enslave all non-Jews through its secret and occult financial power.[57]

At the same time in a remarkable example of what a psychologist would describe as 'projection', two very recent articles in *Soviet Weekly* by Ruvim Groyer explain why Zionism is indeed a 'racist' doctrine and how the Zionist leaders 'collaborated' with the Nazis in the liquidation of Polish Jewry. Concluding his first article of 1 October 1977, the author brazenly asserted: 'There is no doubt that top-echelon Zionists and Hitlerites were drawn together by their common social nature.'[58] (This absurd claim, repeated ad nauseam, has now become part of the staple diet of all Soviet literature dealing with Zionism.) In his second piece on 10 October, the author after describing so-called 'racism' in Israel towards Palestinians and Oriental Jews, concludes that the Israelis are 'a worthy heir to Hitler's National-Socialism'. The severity of this campaign which totally identifies Zionism with Nazism and lays such heavy stress on the 'bestial hatred' of other peoples supposedly inculcated by Judaism, cannot be accidental.[59] It has little in common with Marxist theory or even with traditional Communist attitudes towards Palestine and the Arab-Israeli conflict. Moreover, this propaganda which has full official backing and sanction and all the immense resources of a totalitarian State appara-tus at its disposal, cannot be dismissed as the work of a lunatic fringe. It raises a serious question as to whether the present Soviet leadership does not seek to physically destroy Israel and 'liquidate' the Jewish problem in the USSR in drastic fashion. The second intention, it has been said, would have been put into practice by Stalin had he lived longer.[60] In a slightly milder form it was carried out by the Polish Communist party in 1968 when by means of mass expulsions it made Poland virtually *judenrein* in a few months. But this would appear impractical in Soviet Russia which has a population of over two million Jews, and whose present rulers have no apparent desire to return to the terror and intimidation of the Stalin era, which might place their own positions in jeopardy.

Why then have the heirs of Marx and Lenin consciously adopted antisemitism as an instrument of domestic and foreign policy, on a scale equalling if not surpassing that of their Tsarist precursors?[61] Why has Zionism replaced fascism and Nazism as the blackest force of 'world reaction' and 'counter-revolution' in current Soviet terminology? Why have the language of the *Protocols* and *Stuermer*-like caricatures[62] been allowed free rein in the Soviet media, thereby sowing the ugly seeds of hate, fear and anxiety?[73] Why, in short, has the Kremlin deliberately chosen to superimpose the pogrom tradition of the autocratic Russian State over the class-struggle doctrines of Marxism-Leninism, just sixty years after the Bolshevik Revolution? In so far as any rational analysis of this disturbing phenomenon is possible, there are two different levels of explanation which might account for this development.

The first interpretation, which seems to me more plausible, is that there is a hard-line policy towards Jews at home and abroad which is a function of internal tensions and may even be a product of the crisis of the Soviet system as a whole. In this order of explanation, the antisemitism of the Soviet authorities must be viewed as primary, having the character of an obsessive fixation for which anti-Zionism is essentially a convenient mask. If this is the case, then the continuing Middle East crisis and the role of Israel as an obstacle to Soviet foreign policy objectives is largely extraneous and offers no more than a pretext. The deeper motivation is to

prevent by coercive methods and intimidatory propaganda
the emergence of any non-conformist, dissident or nationalist
trends within the Soviet empire which could be a source of
disaffection or even disintegration. In this context, it is
probably significant that the Soviet authorities have at times
presented dissidence as a 'Jewish' interest and tried to
identify the Zionist and the dissident as one and the same
person. Since the 'Zionist' can more easily be portrayed as a
visible, concrete, *internal* enemy with foreign associations, this
helps to discredit the dissident phenomenon as a whole.[64]
Xenophobic, anti-intellectual and antisemitic feelings which
are solidly anchored in the population of the Soviet Union
can be manipulated to this end. The emphasis on World
Zionism as a vast centre for subversion and anti-communist
propaganda, for espionage and slander of the Soviet system
serves the same purpose. 'Zionist' intrigues against Czechoslovakia and other socialist countries infected by liberalism
and 'revisionism' are heavily stressed as a warning by the
rulers to any would-be opponents of the system. Since Jews
have indeed played a prominent role in dissident movements
both in Russia and eastern Europe, hard-liners in the
Kremlin may see in anti-Zionism a very valuable weapon to
discourage non-Jews from any association with these dangerous 'instruments of imperialism'.

Even more important, the pressure for Jewish emigration,
dramatized so effectively by Israeli and world opinion in
recent years, poses a very serious problem for the Soviet
leadership.[65] The Zionist revival within the USSR and the
bold, defiant methods of the Jewish activists, with their
stream of petitions and appeals, was not something that could
be openly admitted in the Soviet mass media. On the
ideological level it has challenged the whole Communist
claim to have 'solved' the Jewish question in the Soviet
Union. In foreign policy, it arouses the strong objections of
the Arab States and the Palestinians who not surprisingly
protest that the USSR is reinforcing the economic, scientific
and military potential of Israel at their expense. Still more
serious, it raises the old Bolshevik spectre of national separatism and threatens to reopen the whole Pandora's box of
unresolved national grievances within the Soviet Empire. The

Jewish emigration movement and the resurgence of Jewish
nationalism have exposed the Leninist nationalities' policy
for what it has really become in the 1970s—a façade behind
which stands the cultural imperialism of Great Russian
chauvinists. Not only has this nationality policy been a
disaster for the Jews, but it has also been a failure for the
Ukrainians, the Georgians, the Armenians, the Volga Germans, the Crimean Tartars and the Baltic peoples. There is a
great danger to the Soviet regime in the fact that mass Jewish
emigration might spark off similar demands from other
non-Russian nationalities. Hence, the demonization of 'Zionism' and the exposure of its organic links with 'imperialism'
may serve the very important function of keeping other forms
of 'bourgeois nationalism' in check. This is particularly
striking in the Ukraine where the anti-Zionist campaign has
been especially virulent and strives to link Jewish with
Ukrainian 'bourgeois nationalism' as tools of 'White' counter-
revolution. Soviet policy in the Ukraine has followed the
classic imperial strategy of 'divide and rule', constantly
emphasizing the historic enmity of Jews and Ukrainians.[66]
The anti-Zionist crusade, by reinforcing traditional Ukrainian antisemitism and Jewish suspicions of their neighbours
(heightened by memories of the Ukrainian collaboration
during the Holocaust) intensifies existing tensions and thereby serves a valuable diversionary purpose.

Finally, the anti-Zionist campaign has the more immediate
aim of intimidating the activists in the Jewish community
who are harassed, persecuted, exiled, threatened with punitive trials and imprisoned in order to discourage them and
others from making demands for emigration. At the same
time the vilification of their cause serves to isolate them from
other nationalities and from any potential allies in the
Russian intelligentsia who might be inclined to press for more
liberal domestic policies. By depicting Zionists as the willing
accomplices of the Nazis and as architects of a criminal
conspiracy against the Soviet motherland, the regime clearly
hopes to destroy any residue of sympathy for their lack of
national rights, in the Soviet population as a whole. The
mobilization of assimilated Soviet Jews in the anti-Zionist
campaign helps the general credibility of the whole operation

and it is probably intended to divide the Jewish community against itself. It is, unfortunately, a fact that among the most prominent crusaders against Zionism there are several individuals of Jewish origin.[67]

While these internal factors, which may also be related to a power-struggle within the Soviet elite,[68] provide reason enough to understand the motivations of contemporary Soviet anti-Zionism, a second order of explanation must be considered. It is conceivable that the intense hostility to Zionism of the Soviet leadership arises more from foreign policy considerations than domestic pressures. If this is the case, then it is not so much a camouflage for deliberate antisemitism as a response to the fluctuating Middle East crisis and a reflection of fundamental strategic attitudes to the Arab-Israeli conflict. Thus one could argue that the Soviet drive for predominance in the Middle East spearheaded by the military caucus, has encountered in Israel a dangerous proxy for American interests in a crucial area of super-power confrontation. Anything that weakens Israel will also undermine the Western world as a whole.[69] The depiction of Israel as a dangerously aggressive, expansionist State and the attacks on its 'racist' and 'fascist' character are therefore designed to isolate it in world opinion and to remove a vital obstacle to Russian strategic interests in the area. Once the Soviets had decided in 1955 that a pro-Arab strategy was the key to their expansion in an important region of the globe, there was no compelling reason that they should not try to undermine the Jewish State. Their anti-Zionism, which already had a long ideological history of its own, could only be further reinforced by the need to support the positions of clients who were intent on the destruction of Israel at any price. Hence, in order to win Arab favour, the tone of Soviet anti-Israelism inevitably became more violent and aggressively hostile. Soviet foreign-policy-makers might also see the value of intensifying ideological attacks on Zionism in order to mobilize domestic public opinion for a pro-Arab policy that was not necessarily popular among tax-payers.[70]

If the current anti-Zionist crusade were really a derivative of Soviet foreign policy then its future course would largely depend on Russian global strategy and its underlying objectives in the Arab-Israel conflict. This is a controversial topic and different interpretations are clearly possible. It might be argued that Moscow has gained relatively little from its commitment to the Arabs who have remained intransigently hostile to communism and intensely suspicious of Russian expansionism. Since the death of Nasser and the expulsion of Soviet advisers from Egypt in 1972 the Kremlin has clearly lost considerable influence in the Middle East. Its efforts to court the Ba'athist regimes in Iraq and Syria have, for example, been only a partial success. Moreover, before the October war of 1973, its cautious posture and reluctance to risk a direct military confrontation with the United States in the Middle East angered the Egyptians and the radical groups in the PLO. Hence, it was not difficult for the Chinese Communists to accuse Moscow of collusion with the United States in restraining the Arab liberation movement. The crisis in Soviet-Egyptian relations, for example, was directly related to Moscow's refusal to deliver new offensive weapons systems to Sadat.[71] Nevertheless, Kremlin leaders accepted their political defeat in Egypt with surprising equanimity. Their experiences with other Arab nationlist leaders have been equally disillusioning and must have led some Kremlin strategists to wonder whether the Arabs were not expensive, unreliable and even dangerous allies. The inability of the USSR to influence the behaviour of Arab political elites against their will, has in fact been a striking feature of recent Middle East history, which was highlighted by Sadat's decision to go to war in 1973 against Soviet advice.[72] During the war, the Soviet goal of Arab unity against Israel and the United States on an 'anti-imperialist basis' was briefly attained, only to collapse in its aftermath. Instead, American influence in the Middle East was greatly strengthened and the Soviet Union could do nothing to prevent Egyptian and Syrian disengagement agreements with Israel under Kissinger's auspices. Thus the October War singularly failed to establish the USSR as a dominant power in the region and closer ties with Libya, Iraq and the PLO have provided no real compensation for this erosion of the Russian position.

Whether the Soviets support or oppose the long-term Arab goal of destroying Israel is another matter. Officially, the

USSR has tended to favour a political rather than a military solution to the Arab-Israeli conflict. Its immediate aim after 1967 was to isolate Israel economically and diplomatically, and weaken Western support for it. Before 1973, however, it did not see the Palestinian problem as central, often criticizing the 'nationalist' and extremist tendencies within the PLO and particularly its over-emphasis on 'armed struggle'.[73] In discussions with Arab communists (recorded in 1971/72) the Soviets apparently took the view that the Arab slogan of *eliminating* Israel was tactically unsound and could not on principle win the support of the USSR, of the international communist movement or of world opinion. On the other hand, they argued that the political struggle against the 'racialism of the State of Israel, its reactionary qualities, its colonialist character' was necessary and legitimate. The Soviets continued to distinguish between Zionism as an 'imperalist movement of the Jewish bourgeoisie' and the 'people of Israel' who were entitled to their national self-determination. Hence, their opposition to the nationalist formula of the 'liberation of Palestine', interpreted by the PLO in the sense of denying the existence of Israel as a national State and seeking its annihilation.[74] This extremist view was condemned by the Soviets as 'unrealistic', contrary to proletarian internationalism and as entailing the unacceptable risk of a Third World War to achieve its realization. The objective of the Palestinian resistance should instead be to collaborate with the Arab States and the USSR in 'eliminating the consequences of the Israeli aggression' of 1967 and in securing the right of return of the Palestinian Arabs. They should therefore mobilize their forces against the Israeli occupation of the conquered territories and seek alliances with leftist and 'democratic' elements inside Israel. The ultimate object of such alliances would be to eliminate the 'Zionist tendencies' of the Israeli state.

This was the official Soviet position designed for Arab and foreign consumption before 1973. But in the light of internal anti-Zionist propaganda in the Soviet Union (which never mentions points of disagreement with the PLO) and of Soviet behaviour during and after the October War, it has largely been overtaken by events. There is for example, evidence that

Boris Ponomarev, the Secretary of the Central Committee of the CPSU told Yasser Arafat in December 1973 that the Arabs had received enough military support to get to Tel Aviv and back three times over. As to the destruction of Israel, Ponomarev reportedly said: 'If you can do it, that's your business, not ours.'[75] Since the war, Soviet-Palestinian relations have steadily improved and are now on a level with those existing between the USSR and the radical Arab States. Not only is the PLO recognized by the Soviets as the sole representative of the Palestinians but the USSR has strongly backed Palestinian national self-determination and the creation of a Palestinian state on the West Bank and the Gaza Strip. The Kremlin now talks solemnly of the 'inalienable rights' of the Palestinians to their own independent statehood without specifying its attitude to the long-term goals of the PLO.[76] Undoubtedly, the Soviets see the PLO as their most important trump-card in sabotaging any Pax Americana in the Middle East at their expense and as a counterweight to Egypt's pro-American policy. The importance of the PLO has grown still further as a result of Soviet difficulties with Syria during the Lebanese Civil War. The Syrian intervention in Lebanon against left-wing Muslim and Palestinian forces supported by the USSR was perceived by Moscow as inimical to its own interests.

Do these developments signify that the Soviet Union is now irrevocably committed to Palestinian statehood and even in the long run, to undermining Israel's right to independent existence? Certainly, Moscow has become ambiguous about Israel's borders, sometimes supporting the 1949 armistice agreements and sometimes even referring to the 1947 partition lines.[77] Publicly, it is in favour of a Palestinian mini state and plays down PLO declarations about the 'democratic, secular State'. (Neither the Soviet Government or press ever mention the fact, for example, that the PLO still does not recognise Israel.) No doubt, however, tensions in the Moscow-PLO relationship also persist, and the Kremlin will prefer to keep its options open.[78] It may well be that this relationship is subordinate to more long-term interests of the Soviet Union —whether towards a settlement in the Middle East or in the direction of a more aggressive strategy in the region as a whole.[79] It is impossible to say with any certainty whether Moscow is genuinely interested at the present time in resolving the Arab-Israeli conflict or in allowing it to fester. What seems probable is that given Israeli military strength and a continuing American commitment to its defence, the Soviets do not contemplate the disappearance of the Jewish State in the forseeable future.

If this analysis is correct, then it suggests that Soviet foreign policy has been a contingent but not a determining factor in the militant, anti-Zionist campaign of recent years. Hence, as in the twilight of the Stalinist era, it is even conceivable to envisage a future improvement in Soviet-Israeli relations, without any corresponding change in the treatment of Soviet Jewry. In other words, there is no necessary correlation between the antisemitic, anti-Zionist and anti-Israeli themes in Soviet domestic and foreign policy. In certain circumstances these elements may coalesce and at other times they may become disentangled. What is profoundly disturbing about the present situation is the great expansion in Soviet worldwide power (especially its naval strength) which has coincided with an intensely nationalist and antisemitic phase in its domestic policies. The current anti-Zionist crusade, it would appear, owes more to the revival of the pogramist Black-Hundred ideology and programme in the USSR than to any Leninist tradition. The implications for Israel, for Soviet Jewry and for the Western world as a whole of this Russian imperial expansionism and mounting Judeophobia are not encouraging.

NOTES

1. On the role of the *Yevsektsiia*, see the comprehensive study by Zvi Y. Gitelman, *Jewish Nationality and Soviet Politics. The Jewish Sections of the CPSU, 1917-1930* (Princeton, 1972).
2. This was in tune with the general view of Marxists in Western and Central Europe before the First World War. See 'Marxism and Jewish Nationalism: The Theoretical Roots of Confrontation,' in this book.
3. M. Rafes, 'Evreii i Oktiabr'skaia Revolutsia', *Zhizn Natsionalnostei* No. 1 (January 1923), p. 237.

4. See N. Lenin, *O Evreiskom Voprose v Rosii* (Moscow, 1924). Introduction by S. Dimanshtein, p. 6.

5. Ibid, p. 17.

6. V.I. Lenin, *On the Jewish Question* (New York, 1934), p. 3 '. . . only entirely uneducated and completely oppressed people can believe the lies and slanders which are being spread about Jews . . .'.

7. Ran Marom, 'The Bolsheviks and the Balfour Declaration, 1917-1920' in this book.

8. Joseph Ariel 'The Good Tidings of the Balfour Declaration in Odessa' (Hebrew), *Heawar* Vol. XV (May 1968), p. 120. See Marom, ibid.

9. Chimen Abramsky, *War, Revolution and the Jewish Dilemma.* An Inaugural Lecture delivered at University College London (1975), p. 21.

10. Stalin's article 'Don't forget the East' *Zhizn Natsionalnostei,* 24 November 1918 (included in *Sochinenia,* Vol. IV, Moscow 1949, pp. 171-3) indicates the hopes which the Bolsheviks attached to a rising of Muslim 'toilers' in the East.

11. Jane Degras, *The Communist International 1919-1943, Documents,* Vol. I (Cass, London, 1956) pp. 143-8. Also Paul Novick, *Palestine: The Communist Position, the Colonial Question* (New York, 1936).

12. Kalinin was exceptionally philosemitic, though from Russian peasant stock. See Jack Miller, 'Kalinin and the Jews: A Possible Explanation', *Soviet Jewish Affairs,* (1974) Vol. 4 No. 1, pp. 61-5.

13. Henry Bulawko, *Mise Au Point. Les Communistes et la Question Juive* (Paris 1971) pp. 85-8 for statements by Kalinin on the Jewish Question and Birobidzhan.

14. Zvi Gitelman, op. cit., pp. 416-18.

15. C. Abramsky, 'The Biro-Bidzhan Project, 1927-1959', in Lionel Kochan (ed.) *The Jews in Soviet Russia since 1917* (London, 1970), pp. 62-75.

16. On the harassment and persecution of Zionists in the USSR, see Avieh Leib Tsentsiper, *Eser Sh'not R'difot* (Tel Aviv, 1930), and Guido Goldman, *Zionism under Soviet Rule: 1917-1928* (New York, 1960).

17. Leonard Schapiro, 'The Jewish Anti-Fascist Committee and Phases of Soviet Anti-Semitic Policy During and After World War II', in: Bela Vago/George L. Mosse (eds.), *Jews and non-Jews in Eastern Europe 1918-1945* (Jerusalem, 1974), pp. 283-300.

18. Itzik Feffer, 'I am a Jew' (translated from the Yiddish by Joseph Leftwich) in: *Calling all Jews to Action* (London, 1943), p. 9.

19. Quoted in J.B. Schechtman, 'The USSR, Zionism and Israel', Kochan (ed.) *The Jews in Soviet Russia,* op. cit. p. 114.

20. On the mood among Russian Jewry at this time, see Yehoshua A. Gilboa, 'The 1948 Zionist Wave in Moscow', *Soviet Jewish Affairs* Vol. I (1971) no. 2, pp. 35-9.

21. Yehoshua A. Gilboa, *The Black Years of Soviet Jewry* (Boston, 1971) and the important article by Benjamin Pinkus, 'Soviet Campaigns Against "Jewish Nationalism" and "Cosmopolitanism", 1946-1953', *Soviet Jewish Affairs* (1974) Vol. 4, No. 2, pp. 53-72.

22.   Ibid.

23   J.V. Stalin, 'Marksizm i Natsionalni Vopros', *Sochinenia*, Vol. II
      (Moscow, 1949) p. 300.

24.   For this period, see Arnold Krammer, 'Soviet Motives in the
      Partition of Palestine, 1947-48', *Journal of Palestine Studies* Vol. II, No.
      2 (Winter 1973), pp. 102-19 and Yaacov Ro'i, 'Soviet-Israeli Rela-
      tions, 1947-1954', in: M. Confino/Shimon Shamir (eds.) *The USSR
      and the Middle East* (Jerusalem 1973), pp. 123-46.

25.   For Russian attitudes to this problem even before 1945, see 'The
      Soviet Union and the Jews during World War II'; Documents
      introduced by Lukasz Hirszowicz, *Soviet Jewish Affairs* Vol. 4 (1974)
      no. I, pp. 73 ff.

26.   Yaacov Ro'i, *From Encroachment to Involvement. A Documentary Study of
      Soviet Policy in the Middle East 1945-1973* (Jerusalem, 1974) p. 39.

27.   See Arnold Krammer, *The Forgotten Friendship: Israel and the Soviet Bloc
      1947-53* (Urbana, Illinois, 1974).

28.   *Daily Worker*, 29 June 1948 quoted in: Robert S. Wistrich, *The Myth
      of Zionist Racism* (London, 1976), p. 23.

29.   Yaacov Ro'i, *From Encroachment to Involvement.* op. cit., p. 115.

30.   Walter Laqueur, *The Struggle for the Middle East, The Soviet Union and
      the Middle East 1958-1968* (London, 1972).

31.   Uri Ra'anan, 'Moscow and the "Third World" ', *Problems of Commun-
      ism* XIV (January-February, 1965).

32.   On Stalin's Cold War ideology which excluded the possibility of a
      'third force' or non-alignment in the struggle between capitalism and
      Socialism, see Robert C. Tucker, *The Soviet Political Mind*, (London,
      1972), pp. 229-31.

33.   For the text of Bulganin's note, Ro'i, op. cit. pp. 190 ff.

34.   See, for example, K. Ivanov/Z. Sheinis, *The State of Israel. Its Position
      and Policies* (Moscow, 1958).

35.   Morton Schwartz, 'The USSR and the Leftist Regimes in Less-
      Developed Countries', *Survey* (Spring 1973) Vol. 19, no. 2 (87) p. 217.

36.   David P. Forsyth, 'The Soviets and the Arab-Israeli Conflict', *World
      Affairs* Vol. 134 (Autumn 1971) pp. 132-42.

37.   Schechtman, 'The USSR, Zionism and Israel', op. cit, pp. 119-20.

38.   The publication of Yevtushenko's celebrated poem 'Babi Yar', in *Lit-
      eraturnaya* (21 September 1961) aroused Krushchev's ire because it
      explicitly acknowledged the persistence of Russian antisemitism.

39.   On 6 July 1967, *Pravda* quoted a statement by Brezhnev to military
      academy graduates. 'The Israeli aggressors are behaving like the
      worst of bandits. In their atrocities against the Arab population it
      seems they want to copy the crimes of the Hitler invaders.'

40.   For a suggestive analysis which focuses on the indigenous tradition
      of Russian racism, see Mikhail Agursky, 'Russian Neo-Nazism—
      A Growing Threat', *Midstream* (February 1976) pp. 35-42.

41.   Yevgeny Yevseyev, *Fascism under the Blue Star* (Moscow 1971) and
      'Zionism in the System of Anti-Communism', *Nautchny Kommunizm*
      (1974) no. 1.

42. Y. Ivanov, *Ostrozhno! Sionizm!* (Moscow, 1969). For fuller extracts see the *Bulletin on Soviet and East European Jewish Affairs* (London) No. 3, January 1969.

43. Vladimir Begun, *Polzuchaya Kontrrevolyutsiya* (Minsk, 1974), p. 79 Extracts from this work have been published by the Institute of Jewish Affairs (London, 1975) with a translation by Howard Spier.

44. V. Begun, *Creeping Counter-Revolution,* ibid. p. 29 (Spier translation).

45. Dmitri Zhukov, 'The Ideology and Practice of Violence', *Ogonyok,* 12 October 1974. For the parallel text in Russian and English of this review, see *Israel At Peace* (organ of the Communist Party of Israel (MAKI)) January 1975, No. 1.

46. The article first put out by the semi-official Novosty Press on 22 September 1972 gave rise to legal proceedings because it had appeared in a French-language journal.

47. See Emmanuel Litvinoff, *Soviet Antisemitism: The Paris Trial* (London, 1974) for the full story.

48. V. Begun, op.cit., p. 151.

49. Zhukov, op. cit.

50. Ibid.

51. For Tsaban's sharp protest, *Israel at Peace,* op. cit Zhukov's article also prompted the American Communist organ, *Daily World* 10 May 1975 to reluctantly comment that it 'clearly propagates anti-Semitic stereotypes and it violates the precepts of Soviet socialism and Leninist principles. It is unquestionably deserving of the severest criticism'.

52. Vladimir Kiselev, 'Zionism. Weapon of Anti-Communism', *Soviet Weekly* 15 March 1975.

53. 'Zionism. The Link with Imperialism', *Soviet Weekly* 22 March 1975.

54. Vladimir Kiselev, 'Zionism—Imperialism's Trojan Horse', *Soviet Weekly* 5 April 1975. c/f. *Bolshaya Sovetskaya Entsiklopediya* (Moscow 1972) Vol. 10, p. 325 which now claims that the Arab-Israeli war of 1948 was caused by Anglo-American imperialism and the intrigues of international Zionist circles.

55. In connection with Czechoslovakia, there has been particular emphasis on the Zionist role in the mass media and its espionage techniques, e.g. V. Bolshakov 'Anti-sovetizm-profesiya sionistov', *Pravda* 19 February 1971.

56. William Korey, 'Protocols Revived', *Jewish Chronicle,* London, 23 September 1977.

57. For further examples, see Shmuel Ettinger, 'Anti-Zionism and Anti-Semitism', *Insight* Vol. 2. No. 5 (May 1976).

58. Ruvim Groyer, 'Why We Condemn Zionism?', *Soviet Weekly* 1 October 1977.

59. For a particularly hysterical example of this genre, see 'Zionist Heirs of the Gestapo', *Za Rubezhom* 3 October 1973.

60. Isaac Deutscher, *Stalin* (New York, 1967) 2nd ed., p. 627.

61. For the full documentation of this fact, see William Korey, *The Soviet Cage. Antisemitism in Russia* (New York, 1973).

62.　On the visual manifestations of this propaganda, see Judith Vogt, 'Old Images in Soviet anti-Zionist cartoons', *Soviet Jewish Affairs* (1975) Vol. 5. No. 1 pp. 20-38.

63.　Shmuel Ettinger, *Insight* (May 1976) op. cit. points out that 'no other subject has been given so voluminous attention by the mass media of the Communist bloc'. In this context, the hour-long documentary about Zionism, entitled 'Traders of Souls' shown on national television in the USSR on 22 January 1977 is particularly disturbing. See William Korey, 'The smell of pogrom', *Jewish Chronicle* 18 March 1977. The best-selling antisemitic novels by the former naval officer Shevtsov, *Love and Hatred* and *In the Name of the Father and the Son* (1970) are also symptomatic.

64.　See Emmanuel Litvinoff (ed.) 'Jews, Dissent and the Future', *Insight* Vol. 2, No. 4 (April, 1976). Also the personal testimony of Roman Rutman, 'Jews and Dissenters: Connections and Divergences', *Soviet Jewish Affairs* (1973) Vol. 3 No. 2 pp. 26-37.

65.　Jonathan Frankel, 'The Anti-Zionist Press Campaigns', *Soviet Jewish Affairs* No. 3 (May 1972). pp. 1-26 makes a strong case that this was a decisive factor in the anti-Zionism of the 1969-1971 period.

66.　Israel Klejner, 'The Soviet Ukranian Press on Zionism and Israel' *Soviet Jewish Affairs* (1974) Vol. 4, No. 2, pp. 46-53.

67.　'Soviet Anti-Jewish Jews', *Insight* Vol. 3, No. 7 (July 1977).

68.　Victor Zorza, 'Soviet Anti-Semitism and the Crisis in the Kremlin', *Herald Tribune,* 3 August 1977.

69.　Boris Guriel, 'The Soviet-Jewish War', *New Middle East* No. 19 (April 1970), pp. 46-8.

70.　See Nadav Safran 'The Soviet scene: A personal view', ibid, p. 45 who suggested seven years ago that the Soviet public was 'sullenly resentful of the diversion of scarce Soviet resources for further commitments in the Middle East in the form of additional military aid to the Arab countries and perhaps even use of Soviet personnel . . .'

71.　See the declarations of Sadat as reported in the *New York Times* 25 July 1972.

72.　On the background to the October war, see Galia Golan, *Yom Kippur and After. The Soviet Union and the Middle East Crisis* (London 1977).

73.　On the early period, see Lawrence L. Whetton, 'Changing Soviet Attitudes towards Arab Radical Movements', *New Middle East* (March, 1970), pp. 20-28 and for the Soviet critique of Palestinian 'adventurism', Moshe Ma'oz, *Soviet and Chinese Relations with the Palestininan Guerilla Organizations* (Jerusalem, 1974).

74.　These discussions are documented in 'The Soviet Attitude to the Palestine Problem' (From the Records of the Syrian Communist Party, 1971-72), *Journal of Palestine Studies* Vol. II, no. 1 (Autumn 1972).

75.　*The Observer* (London) 30 December 1973. See also J. Kimche, 'Brezhnev's Geneva Priority', *Midstream* (February 1974) pp. 14 ff.

76.　The formula that any Middle East settlement must satisfy 'the legitimate national demands of the Arab people of Palestine, including their inalienable right to establish their own state' has become standard in Soviet statements. See *New Times* (May 1976), Vol. 19, pp. 4-5.

77. Since 1973 a number of Soviet publications have come very close to Palestinian demands on this question. E.g. V.P. Ladeykin, *Istochnik Opasnago Krizisa. Rol Sionizma V Rasshigani Konflikta Na Blizhnem Vostoke* (Moscow, 1973). See the comments of Lukasz Hirszowicz, 'A Soviet Exposition of Extremist Views', *Soviet Jewish Affairs* (1974) Vol. 4, No. I, pp. 110-14 and the recent article by E. Primakov, 'Zionism and Israel Against the Arab People of Palestine', in *Asia and Africa Today* (March/April 1977). The contents are summarized in *Insight* Vol. 3, No. 7 (July 1977).

78. 'Moscow "keeping options open" ', *Jersulem Post* 13 April 1976, p. 8.

79. See Robert O. Freedman, *Soviet Policy Toward the Middle East since 1970* (New York 1975) and Galia Golan 'The Soviet Union and the Arab-Israeli Conflict', *The Jerusalem Quarterly* (Fall 1976) I, pp. 8-17. Also her article 'Soviet Policy in the Middle East: Growing Difficulties and Changing Interest', *The World Today* (September 1977). Dr Golan optimistically believes that the USSR now wants a settlement because it recognizes that its real control over the Arabs is limited and that the conflict with Israel has not aided its penetration of the region.

Documents

ATTITUDES OF THE LEFT

Excerpt from an article 'Violence and Aggression are the Guiding Principles of Israel's Official Policy' published by *Neues Deutschland* (9.10.1973), the mouthpiece of the GDR's ruling Socialist Unity Party *(SED)*.

In the Middle East—for years, thanks to imperialistic and aggressive Israeli policies, the turbulent centre of tension and military confrontations—war has again broken out. Tel Aviv's military clique, cynically turning the facts of the situation upside down, insinuated that it 'had been treacherously attacked on a religious holiday of fasting and prayer'. Actually, the aggressor state had repeatedly and for months provoked dangerous crisis situations. Brutal commando raids by the Israeli secret service alternated with military provocations directed against Egypt, Syria and the Lebanon. The Golda Meir-Moshe Dayan gang stopped at nothing to demonstrate before all the world Israel's determination to pursue her policies of territorial expansion, murder and violence.

Large scale call-ups of reservists, unmistakable statements of intent by leading politicians, and troop concentrations along the armistice lines in Syria and Egypt have now been followed up by Israel's military action. The unleashing of the conflict—rehearsed for years by Tel Aviv in 'partial mobilizations'—was, so to speak, merely the logical consequence of preparations deliberately pursued over a long period of time.

The confrontation in the Middle East is the immediate result of Israel's continuing policy of aggression against the peoples and countries of Arabia. It burst into open warfare when the tensions which Israel, supported by the forces of imperialism, had so assiduously built up, passed the flash-point she had all along sought to attain.

The *Presse Informationen* (12 October 1973) of the *Committee of the Anti-Fascist Resistance Fighters of the German Democratic Republic* published the following protest resolution:—

'Against the Criminal Machinations of Israel's Military Clique.'

Once again Israel's military clique has attacked Egypt and Syria and kindled the torch of naked war. It is the fault of the Israeli government that all efforts to find a peaceful solution to the problems of the Middle East have failed and that this region has become one of the world's danger points. Their criminal machinations also aim at sabotaging endeavours towards a global detente.

Unrestrained imperialistic greed, acquisitiveness and in-humanity are the motives behind the new aggressions of the Meir government. The indiscriminate bombing of towns and villages, the cowardly slaughter of innocent women, children and helpless old people, demonstrate the mentality of these enemies of peace.

The *Committee of the Anti-Fascist Resistance Fighters of the GDR* identifies itself with the world-wide declarations of solidarity with the Arab peoples engaged in a just struggle of national liberation and independence. The scrupulous adherence to the United Nations' Security Council and General Assembly resolutions must form the basis for an immediate and complete Israeli withdrawal from all occupied Arab territories and for the acceptance of the Palestinian people's legitimate claims.

The *Committee* wholeheartedly supports the demand for the immediate evacuation of all territories occupied by the Israeli aggressors, and in this grave and fateful hour assures the Arab nations of its sympathy and solidarity.

The toilers of the GDR and with them the *Anti-Fascist Resistance Fighters* also entertain fraternal feelings for the progressive, peaceful, anti-fascist forces in Israel who are fighting a courageous and forlorn battle against reactionaries, imperialists and warmongers.

We wholeheartedly welcome the initiatives by the Soviet Union, the GDR and other nations to secure the immediate cessation of this bloody and costly conflict, and their endeavours to safeguard the peace of the Middle East.

The Central Committee of *MAKI*, the Israeli Communist Party, passed a resolution (17 November 1973) outlining plans for an Israeli-Arab peace, which among others, stressed the following points.

The fact that the Egyptian-Syrian aggression that reached dimensions and force mainly as a result of Soviet support was repelled by Israeli defence forces, helped to undermine the delusion prevalent in the Arab world as if it were possible to force Israel upon her knees by the sword, especially if this effort is accompanied by extensive political activities (precipitating the oil crisis, exerting pressure on the African states to sever their relations with Israel, etc.).

The fact that the war was waged and that it ended in this manner, helped to undermine the delusion that prevailed among the Israeli public and in important government circles, as if it were possible to hold indefinitely the territorial status quo, or as if this in itself could guarantee Israel's peace and security.

The results of the war, the collapse of various delusions on both sides and international pressure—all these are now apt to create more appropriate conditions for Israel-Arab negotiations in general and for Israel-Egyptian negotiations in particular. The fact that, in the wake of the Egyptian-Syrian failure in this war, Arab factors, and above all Egypt, have agreed to the principle of negotiations with Israel for establishing a just, lasting peace in our region, as Resolution No. 338 says, is also enhancing the chances of peace.

Published by *Israel at Peace,* organ of the Communist Party of Israel, November 1973.

THE JEWS AND THE REVOLUTION

. . . The hatred of tsarism was directed particularly against the Jews. On the one hand, the Jews provided a particularly high percentage (compared with the total of. the Jewish population) of leaders of the revolutionary movement. In passing, it should be said to their credit that to-day the Jews provide a relatively high percentage of representatives of internationalism compared with other nations. On the other hand, tsarism knew perfectly well how to play up to the most despicable prejudices of the most ignorant strata of the population against the Jews, in order to organize, if not to lead directly, the pogroms—those atrocious massacres of peaceful Jews, their wives and children, which have roused such disgust throughout the whole civilized world. Of course I have in mind the disgust of the truly democratic elements of the civilized world, and those are *exclusively* the Socialist workers, the proletarians . . .

The bourgeoisie, even in the freest republican countries of Western Europe, know only too well how to combine their hypocritical phrases about 'Russian atrocities' with the most shameful financial transactions, particularly with financial support of tsarism, and with imperialist exploitation of Russia through the export of capital, etc.

From a Lecture on the 1905 Revolution, delivered in Zurich by Lenin.